THE DE

COMMUl

ZINACANTAN

FRANK CANCIAN

THE DECLINE OF COMMUNITY IN ZINACANTAN

Economy, Public Life, and

Social Stratification, 1960-1987

STANFORD UNIVERSITY PRESS

STANFORD, CALIFORNIA

Stanford University Press
Stanford, California
© 1992 by the Board of Trustees of the
Leland Stanford Junior University
Printed in the United States of America

Original printing 1992
Last figure below indicates year of this printing:
03   02   01   00   99   98   97   96   95   94

CIP data are at the end of the book

Stanford University Press publications are distributed
exclusively by Stanford University Press within the
United States, Canada, and Mexico; they are distributed
exclusively by Cambridge University Press throughout
the rest of the world.

PREFACE

This is a study of Zinacantán, a municipio (township) of Tzotzil-speaking Maya in the highlands of the Mexican state of Chiapas. In the 1980's roughly 15,000 people lived within the boundaries of the municipio, but, of course, those boundaries did not isolate the people of Zinacantán from the world, nor did they homogenize internal relations. On one side, the regional, national, and international economies in which Zinacantán was set are crucial to the story told below—for from them came many of the forces that transformed Zinacantán between the early 1960's and the late 1980's. On the other side those same forces in combination with some internal ones led the hamlets within Zinacantán to replace the municipio as the principal arena for much of public life. Thus, by the 1980's, units both bigger than and smaller than the municipio were important in the everyday experience of Zinacantecos; their worlds had become smaller as well as larger. I have tried to shift across these system levels or units of analysis (call them what you like) without much fuss—in part I suppose because it is not always obvious why the analysis should go in one direction rather than another.

My work in Zinacantán is embedded in the Harvard Chiapas Project. Since the project's fieldwork in Zinacantán began in 1957, its director, Evon Z. Vogt, and his students and research colleagues have produced dozens of monographs and articles (see Vogt 1978; Bricker and Gossen 1989). Vogt's genius for nurturing scholars includes his ability to promote independent work; and many (like me) who began as students continued to work in Zinacantán years, even decades, later. Thus, there is an extraordinary intensity and continuity in the record since the late 1950's. The works of George Collier, Jane Collier, John Haviland, Robert Laughlin, Professor Vogt, and Robert

Wasserstrom have been particularly useful in orienting this study.

My personal history in Zinacantán began in 1960, when I went there to do fieldwork for my dissertation (Cancian 1965), and continued in the late 1960's with a study of corn farming (Cancian 1972). By the summer of 1971, when I returned to finish a photo essay (Cancian 1974b), I had worked in Zinacantán for more than 30 months. In the summer of 1980, after an absence of almost ten years while my children were growing, I visited again. The fear of being forgotten and unwelcome gave way to the excitement of finding that I had old friends, and sometimes relations with their children and grandchildren, who had now grown. Field research for this project, which began in 1981 and stretched over six years, is described in Appendix A.

Much of my recent fieldwork was done in Nachig, one of the older and larger hamlets. I gathered information about every one of its more than 300 households, recorded life histories of several men, and attended public and some private events there. Since I will sometimes take the people of Nachig to be representative of the people of Zinacantán, I will say more about Nachig's special characteristics as the story develops.

Chapter 1 is devoted to the theoretical issues most directly important to the study, but there are two other issues, history and gender, about which something needs to be said—for they have been central to much recent anthropological thinking. This study became historical for a variety of reasons, including the intellectual climate in anthropology. Despite emphasis on the 1960's and the early 1980's, the two periods of my most intense fieldwork, this is in no sense a restudy. The intervening period is documented in various ways, and the 1970's are crucial to the analysis. Recent emphasis on gender is not reflected in what follows. This is a study of men—in large part because of my long-term personal investment in the study of the extra-household economy and public life, which were dominated by men in Zinacantán (at least through the first several layers of analysis). The limitations associated with this personal investment made continuing my old focus more productive for me than more extensive documentation of female perspectives on these topics during these years. I hope someone will add them soon.

After I adjusted my wants to discoveries made along the way and to the realities of fieldwork, I was able to collect most of the data that I wanted. Thus, the "data" at once served an independently determined plan of analysis and determined that plan of analysis. Besides general information and case materials that shape the context at every level of analysis, the data include national and state government economic and demographic statistics, censuses of the hamlet of Nachig, autobiographical statements, Zinacanteco tax and public service records, and accounts of public meetings. Some of the data are from published public records, and references are given to the sources; some are from interview notes that include information given in confidence and are by convention not public. In addition there are the data from the censuses of Nachig I made in 1967 and 1983, and updated in 1987 (Appendix C), and the data from cargo waiting lists (Appendix D). These, when coded for quantitative analysis, provide almost complete anonymity to individuals, so I have prepared computer files in a format that will make the data easy to use for various purposes, including alternatives to the analysis made below. The files (the Nachig Data Set and the Lists Data Set) contain all the variables used here and others that I have not used in my analysis. They may be obtained (identified as the Zinacantán Data Sets) from the Interuniversity Consortium for Political and Social Research (P.O. Box 1248, Ann Arbor, Michigan 48106-1248), or from me (Department of Anthropology, University of California, Irvine, California 92717). Because these data will be available, I give less detailed breakdowns in the text and appendixes.

The identities of the people mentioned in this study are not disguised. Most people are identified by shortened hispanicized names (Vogt 1969: 144–45). Personal statements are used with the permission of those who made them, and most events involving named individuals were public. In a very few cases I have omitted descriptions of relevant illegal activity, or altered details to prevent the identification of individuals.

The meaning of informed consent, or permission to use information provided to an anthropologist, is at best ambiguous in a place like Zinacantán, where many people cannot read. Most people helped me because of trust built up over many years, or because they trusted a person who trusted me. Some of the men who worked with me for the first time knew that others had worked with me and seemed to want to see what it was all about. Zinacantecos who were formally interviewed were first shown my publications in English (Cancian 1965, 1972) and Spanish (Cancian 1976), and sometimes a book of photographs (Cancian 1974b). They were told that my current work concerned changes, especially changes in work since my visits to Zinacantán in the 1960's, and that what they said would be part of the new project. Thus, they were in a position to censor their remarks to fit the situation. Nonetheless, most spoke very openly. I have tried to be discrete with their confidences, both here and in the field when I was talking with other Zinacantecos.

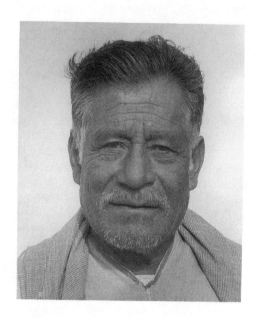

Guillermo Pérez

Pablo Ramírez

Mariano Martínez

ACKNOWLEDGMENTS

Many people and institutions have been generous in their attention to my project. In Zinacantán, Guillermo (Yermo) Pérez, an elder statesman of the hamlet of Nachig, was my mentor. He oriented me, took initiative to improve my knowledge, and facilitated my contact with others who could help me. Mariano Martínez, the senior official in Zinacantán's religious hierarchy in 1983, and Pablo Ramírez of San Cristóbal de las Casas, for many years a government and PRI (Partido Revolucionario Institucional) party official concerned with Indian municipios in the area, also gave in many ways from their extensive knowledge and personal resources. All three made my work a rewarding personal experience.

Many others in Zinacantán contributed both knowledge and practical help. I am especially grateful to Domingo Pérez and Juan Vázquez of Navenchauc, Juan de la Torre, Antonio de la Torre, and Mariano Anselmo Pérez of Hteklum, and José Hernández of Apaz. The 11 Nachig men whose stories are told in Chapter 4 gave interviews, as did Mariano Pérez and José Sánchez of Hteklum, Lorenzo López and Mariano Pérez of Paste, José Gonzales of Tierra Blanca, and Marcos Pérez and Manuel Hernández of Vochojvo.

Padre José Luis Argüello, Patricia Armendáriz, María Elena Fernández Galán, and Mario Toledo, all residents of San Cristóbal de las Casas at the time of the research, helped in various ways, as did two anthropologists, Robert Laughlin and Robert Wasserstrom. The staff of the Centro de Investigaciones Ecológicas del Sureste library in San Cristóbal was frequently helpful.

Funding for research trips from 1981 to 1983 came from the Wenner-Gren Foundation, and from the Mexico/Chicano Program, the Faculty Research Committee, and the School of Social Sciences at the University of California, Irvine. A grant from the National Science Foundation (BNS-8310676) supported extended fieldwork in 1984 and various research expenses before and after that, and a related NSF Research Experience for Undergraduates grant supported a research assistant for a year.

For research help in the field and in libraries in Mexico City and San Cristóbal in 1984, I am indebted to María Ester Enríquez and Héctor Hugo Hernández, students at different campuses of the Universidad Autónoma Metropolitana in Mexico City, and to their respective mentors, David Barkin and Claudio Lomnitz. I was lucky to have Mimi Wan, Daniel Coble, and David Frossard as research assistants at UCI after the main fieldwork was done.

Among the many people who helped prepare the manuscript I am especially grateful to Ziggy Bates, the late Wilma Laws, and Helen Wildman for skillful word processing done in the midst of technological change, and to Chase Langford and Cheryl Larsson for the maps. Thanks for varied, often very timely, contributions are owed to Kathy Alberti, Pete Brown, Debora Dunkle, Lauren Greenfield, Shelby Haberman, Anita Iannucci, Cecilia Ramos, Kim Romney, Raimundo Sánchez, Socorro Sarmiento, and Jesús Villatoro.

Finally, my special thanks go to Peggy Barlett, Carole Browner, Steven Cancian, George Collier, Stuart Plattner, Art Rubel, and Evon Vogt, who usually managed to be simultaneously kind, perceptive, and frank in their responses to a preliminary draft of this book, and to Francesca Cancian, who did all that and much more.

CONTENTS

APPENDIXES

TABLES, MAPS, AND FIGURES

MAPS

FIGURES

*Nineteen photographs accompany
the text*

ACRONYMS AND ABBREVIATIONS

ANDSA	Almacenes Nacionales de Depósito, S.A.
CFE	Comisión Federal de Electricidad
CIES	Centro de Investigaciones Ecológicas del Sureste
CNC	Confederación Nacional de Campesinos
CNEP	Campaña Nacional Erradicación del Paludismo
CONASUPO	Compania Nacional de Subsistencias Populares
CODECOA	Convenio de Confianza Agraria
CODECOM	Convenio de Confianza Municipal
COPLAMAR	Coordinación General del Plan Nacional de Zonas Deprimidas y Grupos Marginados
COPRODE	Comité Promotor de Desarrollo del Estado
CUC	Convenio Unico de Coordinación
IMSS	Instituto Mexicano del Seguro Social
INFONAVIT	Instituto Nacional del Fondo para la Vivienda de los Trabajadores
INI	Instituto Nacional Indigenista
ISSSTE	Instituto de Seguridad y Servicios Sociales de los Trabajadores del Estado
PAN	Partido de Acción Nacional
PEMEX	(also Pemex) Petróleos Mexicanos
PIDER	Programa Integral de Desarrollo Rural (in some sources: Programa de Inversiones para el Desarollo Rural)
PRI	Partido Revolucionario Institucional
PRODESCH	Programa de Desarrollo Socioeconómico de los Altos de Chiapas
SAHOP	Secretaría de Asentamientos Humanos y Obras Públicas

SAI	Secretaría de Asuntos Indígenas
SARH	Secretaría de Agricultura y Recursos Hidráulicos
SCT	Secretaría de Comunicaciones y Trasportes
SDE	Secretaría de Desarrollo Económico
SDR	Secretaría de Desarrollo Rural
SDUOP	Secretaría de Desarrollo Urbano y Obras Públicas
SOP	Secretaría de Obras Públicas
SPP	Secretaría de Programación y Presupuesto
SUB-SAI	Sub-Secretaría de Asuntos Indígenas
SUB-SDR	Sub-Secretaría de Desarrollo Rural
UNICEF	United Nations (International) Children's (Emergency) Fund

A NOTE ON CONVENTIONS

The following Spanish terms are used as English in the text: "cargo," "ejido," "Ladinos," "Zinacantecos," "municipio," and "almud." "Cargo" refers to the religious positions described in Chapter 6, "ejido" to land granted under the national land-reform program (see Chapters 2 and 6), "Ladinos" to non-Indian Spanish speakers, and "Zinacantecos" to the people of Zinacantán. "Municipio" refers to the territorial, governmental unit (township or county) which coincides with the Zinacanteco ethnic group. The almud is a measure of volume equivalent to 15 liters. "Cacique," meaning political boss, and "milpa," meaning cornfield, are listed in *Webster's Ninth New Collegiate*.

Names of religious and some civil positions are also rendered in Spanish. Other roles and institutions are given descriptive English names, for example, "Scribe," "Head of the Church Committee." "Hamlet" has been used for the subunit of the municipio called "paraje" in Spanish; "Elders" (capitalized) has been used for the six cargoholders, the Alcaldes Viejos and Regidores, known as the "moletik" in Tzotzil.

Chapter 4 presents accounts of the working lives of 11 Nachig men. When one of these cases is relevant in other chapters, the man's first name and double capital letters that facilitate finding the case in Chapter 4 appear in the text, for example, "Mariano EE." The men's full names appear along with the code letters in Chapter 4.

The dollar sign ($) indicates Mexican pesos, and amounts are listed in current pesos. In references to periods after 1976, when inflation began to alter exchange rates, daily wages for construction workers are usually listed to help calibrate the amounts. The exchange rate for Mexican pesos to one U.S. dollar (data from IMF

1989 and before, and monthly reports) was 12.5 from 1955 to August 1976. Annual averages (rounded to the nearest peso) were 15 in 1976, 23 from 1977 to 1980, and 25 in 1981. In 1982 the rate was 27 in January, 48 in June, and 96 in December. Annual averages for 1982 to 1987 were 56, 120, 168, 257, 612, and 1,378. In December 1987 the rate was 2,200, and it remained fairly steady at this level through 1988.

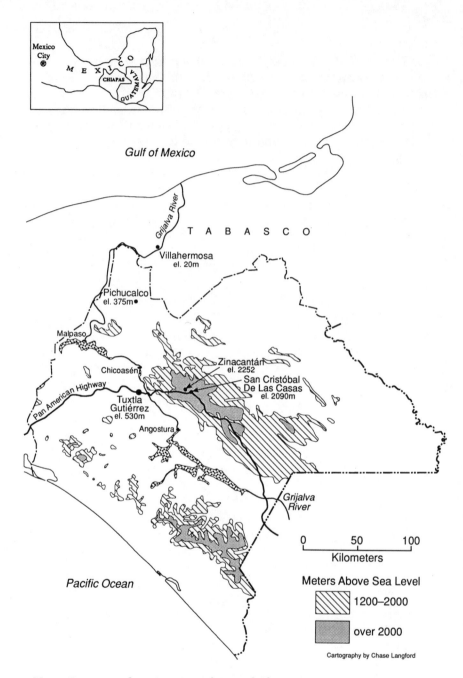

Map 1. Important locations in and around Chiapas, 1983.

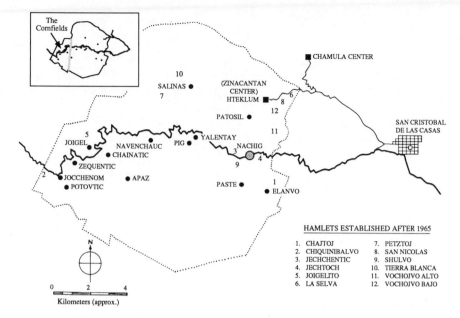

Map 2. Hamlets of Zinacantán, 1983. (After Vogt [1969: viii, 156; with additions], by permission of Harvard University Press)

HAMLETS ESTABLISHED AFTER 1965

1. CHAJTOJ	7. PETZTOJ
2. CHIQUINIBALVO	8. SAN NICOLAS
3. JECHCHENTIC	9. SHULVO
4. JECHTOCH	10. TIERRA BLANCA
5. JOIGELITO	11. VOCHOJVO ALTO
6. LA SELVA	12. VOCHOJVO BAJO

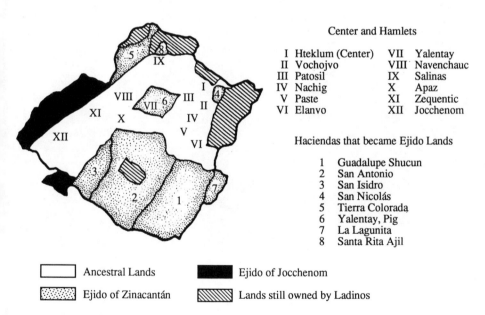

Center and Hamlets

I	Hteklum (Center)	VII	Yalentay
II	Vochojvo	VIII	Navenchauc
III	Patosil	IX	Salinas
IV	Nachig	X	Apaz
V	Paste	XI	Zequentic
VI	Elanvo	XII	Jocchenom

Haciendas that became Ejido Lands

1	Guadalupe Shucun
2	San Antonio
3	San Isidro
4	San Nicolás
5	Tierra Colorada
6	Yalentay, Pig
7	La Lagunita
8	Santa Rita Ajil

Ancestral Lands

Ejido of Zinacantán

Ejido of Jocchenom

Lands still owned by Ladinos

Map 3. Ejidos in Zinacantán, 1962. (After Vogt [1969: 28], by permission of Harvard University Press; originally from Edel [1966])

THE DECLINE OF
COMMUNITY IN
ZINACANTAN

1 /   INTRODUCTION

When I first went to Zinacantán in 1960, I found a tight-knit community of peasant corn farmers. Zinacanteco men dressed in a distinctive costume that set them apart from their neighbors, and almost all of them were dedicated to the ceremonial life that defined the boundaries of their community. For the most part, they shut out the world around them and concentrated on each other. About a decade later the national government built roads, sought to develop the region's agriculture, and began to exploit its vast hydroelectric and petroleum resources. By the early 1980's, many of the men had stopped farming; they frequently dressed in European clothes, battled each other in political parties, and differed in their dedication to local ceremonial life. The tight-knit community of the 1960's was on the wane.

In 1960 anthropologists studied communities—with as much regularity as Zinacantecos wore their costumes. They sought to understand the workings of small, somewhat separate, local populations, and usually paid little attention to the larger political and economic systems in which they were set.[1] But this changed too; by the mid-1970's the study of peasants had been transformed by ideas about capitalist relations of production, the penetration of the state, and the place of peasants in the larger political economy. If I may be allowed a few broad strokes, a summary is simple: "world-system" replaced "community" in the halls of academe and, to a lesser extent, in Zinacantán as well.

This book is about both these changes. The changes in Zinacantán are the explicit focus of the description and analysis that follow, but of course what I chose to look at in Zinacantán and in the larger political economy was shaped by academic debates about how to study the hundreds of millions of people who are peasants or their immediate descendants. The debates themselves will be discussed only briefly—in this chapter, at the ends of the three parts, and finally in Chapter 12, when the details of the intervening chapters will be available to constrain and concretize the generalizations and abstractions. By the end of this chapter it will be apparent that I am a localist—one who believes that local systems have their own logic and that generalizations about local life that are derived from principles of global political economy replace the limitations of earlier community studies with a different kind of oversimplification.[2]

The ideas used to orient this study are simple and widely known. While they sometimes lead to different, even contradictory, interpretations of familiar trends in the lives of peasants and their communities, they all provide insight.[3] They all help with my effort to understand Zinacantecos and other people who are in similar situations in today's world. As that effort proceeds, a minor parallel metatheoretical struggle to understand the relation of these ideas (theories) to the process of understanding life in Zinacantán goes on. Always in the background, it becomes more explicit in later chapters.

Ideas About Peasant Communities

Here I will briefly sketch the ideas that most influenced my selection of questions to investigate and data to gather: first those concerning community boundaries, then those about change, and finally, in a separate section, those that distinguish economic, political, and social aspects of life.

Eric Wolf's (1955, 1957, 1986) characterization of a closed corporate peasant community is central to my thinking about peasant communities and their boundaries. In an oft-cited paragraph Wolf generalizes about peasant communities in Mesoamerica and Central Java:

[They] maintain a body of rights to possessions such as land . . . put pressures on members to redistribute surpluses at their command, preferably in the operation of a religious system, and induce them to content themselves with the rewards of "shared poverty" . . . strive to prevent outsiders from becoming members of the community . . . [place] limits on the ability of members to communicate with the larger society . . . are corporate organizations, maintaining a perpetuity of rights and membership . . . and are closed corporations, because they limit these privileges to insiders, and discourage close participation of members in the social relations of the larger society. (1957: 2)

Wolf's ideal type emphasized the bounded nature of the peasant community, its inward-looking, socially intense, egalitarian social life, and the important role of the religious system in the social control of wealth.

In 1960 Wolf's type fit Zinacantán quite well. Participation in the religious ceremonial system, the cargo system, sharply marked the boundaries of the community; i.e., it separated members from non-members. While Zinacantán had many economic and some political connections with the larger system, the cultural system—the patterns of behavior and norms of interaction among Zinacantecos and between Zinacantecos and the supernatural—was limited to Zinacantán (Cancian 1965).

Ideas about change in peasant communities like Zinacantán are of two basic types. Broadly speaking, one of them conceives the dense, closed, egalitarian, peasant community as a primordial human form that contrasts with modern urban society. It takes the community as part of the received human condition, emphasizes the conservation of tradition, and sees change as dissipation of the peasant quality and acquisition of the urban quality. In its logic it is close to classic linear evolutionary thinking. The other type sees the same peasant community as the product of interaction with an environment that the community does not control. It explains change by reference to change in the environment. Its logic is historical, and closer to cyclical than to evolutionary thinking.

Lenin's vision of the differentiation of the peasantry stated in *The Development of Capitalism in Russia* is currently the most important scheme that uses linear evolutionary logic. Lenin saw a process in which peasants differentiate into two classes. He said:

Undoubtedly, the emergence of property inequality is the starting-point of the whole process, but the process is not at all confined to property "differentiation." The old peasantry is not only "differentiating," it is being completely dissolved, it is ceasing to exist, it is being ousted by absolutely new types of rural inhabitants—types that are the basis of a society in which commodity economy and capitalist production prevail. These types are the rural bourgeoisie (chiefly petty bourgeoisie) and the rural proletariat—a class of commodity producers in agriculture and a class of agricultural wage-workers. (Lenin 1899: 176–77)

This approach, like its contemporary Marxist descendants,[4] fits many changes that occurred in Zinacantán after the 1960's—especially the very substantial shift from farming to wage work, and the political conflicts between groups said to be organized around economic differences.

Modernization theorists also use a primordialist approach to change in peasant societies. Of course, in their scheme, center stage is taken by transformation of the individual, not by transformation of the relations of production. Peasants, isolated and defiant, become farmers, connected and compliant. But the logic is the same, and the movement is in the same direction. They (the peasants) stop being them, and become more like us. This too happened in Zinacantán after the 1960's.[5]

Eric Wolf and G. William Skinner provide the second, more historical, vision of change. As they see it, peasant communities open when the larger society is peaceful and safe, and offers opportunities to peasants who leave their communities; they close when the larger society is dangerous and uninviting. Wolf says:

When [Mexican] society is politically secure and opens its windows on the world in economic expansion and widening trade, the Indian communities retreat [i.e., open] and often disintegrate in retreating. . . . When, however, the larger society disintegrates into an arena of gladiatorial combat and people abandon their exposed positions in industry and commerce to seek security in the rural area, then the Indian communities again wax strong. (1960: 3)

In the paper just quoted, Wolf noted three such cycles since the seventeenth century, the last closing during the chaos of the revolution in the early part of this century and opening in the peace and relative prosperity that followed.

Most of the elements of Wolf's interpretation are in his 1957 paper on the closed corporate peasant community. The first half of that paper is an essentially synchronic synthesis of the ideal type. But the second half is devoted to arguments for the historical origin of the closed corporate peasant community in colonial and internal colonial situations where peasants isolate themselves as a defense against the exploitative demands of dominant non-peasants in a capitalist society. With this interpretation Wolf took the closed corporate peasant community out of evolutionary schemes and put it into history—arguing, for example, that its defenses "are neither simple 'survivals,' nor the results of 'culture lag,' nor due to some putative tendency to conservatism said to be characteristic of all culture. . . . They exist because their functions *are* contemporaneous" (1957: 13; emphasis in the original).[6]

G. William Skinner found similar cyclical patterns in Chinese peasant communities. He says:

In short, in the course of the dynastic cycle in China, the rural communities to which peasants belonged went through a characteristic cycle from an open structure during the dynastic heyday to closure during the period of interdynastic chaos. . . . I have argued that the progressive closure of villages and intervillage local systems in traditional China represented the cumulation of rational responses to an increasingly unstable and threatening external environment, and conversely that their progressive opening up represented the cumulation of rational responses to an increasingly stable and benign external environment. (1971: 280)

The vision of change found in Wolf and Skinner also fits many of the changes in Zinacantán after the 1960's. It provides alternatives to the primordialist visions attributed above to Lenin and modernization theorists, especially when interpreting conflict that began during the prosperity of the 1970's, and when assessing the effects of the national economic crisis that began in 1982 when petroleum prices declined.[7]

Ideas About the Economic, the Political, and the Social

Ideas that separate the economic, political, and social status aspects of society have also been of great use in this study. For me, these ideas originate in Weber (1948), but they have become part of the public domain of social science, and have been adapted and used by countless sociologists and anthropologists. Two uses by anthropologists are among those most directly relevant to this study. Fallers (1961) used the distinction between economic, political, and cultural (not social status) aspects of peasant semiautonomy to distinguish sub-Saharan African cultivators from other peasant cultivators. He found African cultivators dependent on and subjugated to the larger society in economic and political life as were peasants in other places, but said that African cultivators did not experience the cultural dependence and subjugation typical of peasants in other places. Skinner (1971) used the distinction between economic, coercive, and normative aspects of closure in Chinese peasant communities to specify response to changes in the outside world.[8] The distinction also appears in more general classifications of societies produced by less Weberian scholars—e.g., in Wallerstein's world-economies, world-empires, and mini-systems (1976a) and Wolf's Capitalist, Tributary, and Kin-ordered modes of productions (1981), and in other typologies, e.g., Polanyi's types of exchange (1957).

Subtleties aside, these concepts label separable aspects of actors' lives and their institutional environments. The economic involves anonymous, far-flung market relations that are inattentive to the actor's social world—the miracle of the invisible hand through which the market as an institutional form transforms economic coercion into the voluntary pursuit of opportunities by "free," socially isolated individuals. The political involves power, public institutions, and power over public institutions. From the point of view of individuals and groups acting in public life, it is the struggle to define what is appropriate behavior, i.e., the negotiation of the institutional forms with which people coerce each other. Social life involves the distribution of respect, social status, and deference as they exist in the relationship of (categories of) people to each other in their everyday lives. The pressures can be subtle, and more pervasive than they are in economic and political life. These basic character}stics of the three concepts are variously displayed in the popular schemes mentioned above.

Although the economic, the political, and the social are separable as ideas, it would be silly to insist that they are separable from each other in practice. Many analysts have noticed that many actors live without differentiating these aspects of their lives, and that concrete societies are best understood using all these perspectives in combination. Political economists have improved our understanding by combining them in an historical approach and, as will be evident in the body of this book, I do not want to lose all the advantages they have identified. Rather, I want to see what can be gained by giving the economic, the political, and the social separate attention.

Finally, I have added a theoretical assertion to the Weberian distinction. In a paper (Cancian 1985) first written in 1981 as the fieldwork reported here was beginning, I argued that as the aspect of society in focus changes, so too does the most appropriate system size. I said that (1) economic life is most directly influenced by events in the larger system, often including the capitalist world-system, and that (2) questions of social status are more completely circumscribed by local patterns of relationships. I left the sometimes awkward political system somewhere in between. There, as here, I protected myself with the nostrum that everything is related to everything else. Nevertheless, I believe that we will learn more if we focus our limited powers more or less widely, depending on the questions being asked. This study attempts to make something of these programmatic assertions.

Plan of the Book

The book is divided into three parts paralleling the scheme just set out. As attention shifts from the economic to the political to the social, the focus narrows from the global to the local.

Part I describes economic change from the 1960's to the 1980's: full-time truckers, merchants, and wage workers, as well as many semiproletarians, emerged from a population that had been almost exclusively corn farmers. The description connects the behavior of individual Zinacantecos to national political considerations and the petroleum-fed prosperity of the late 1970's. In keeping with the scheme just outlined, the analysis focuses on new roles and their relation to the larger political economy, not on the relation of Zinacantecos to Zinacantán or to each other. This framework leaves open questions about class relations in Zinacantán and the status of semiproletarians in local social life.

In Part II the focus shifts to institutions in Zinacantán. Public life that had been oriented to the municipio center and dominated by long-established religious positions was transformed by the creation of many new more diverse and more decentralized public roles; tight control by a political boss gave way to conflicting political parties; and hamlets replaced the municipio as the locus of much public life. It is clear that these changes were responses to the economic transformation described in Part I, to state and church programs initiated outside Zinacantán, and to demographic pressure from within, and that they were shaped by the details of local history. It is not clear whether the conflict that dominated the late 1970's and early 1980's is better understood in terms of emerging conflicts of economic interests among Zinacantecos or in terms of the parallel greater independence from Zinacantán brought by the national prosperity. That is, the frameworks I have associated with Lenin and with Wolf and Skinner (above) both illuminate the events.

Part III describes the ways Zinacanteco men claimed social position, the ways they came to be respected in the community. A complex system of social stratification and an increasingly divided community replaced the unified and unifying dominance of the religious cargo system in the 1960's. Social position became at once more tied to subunits of the municipio and more dependent on economic position in a more diverse and larger outside world. By the 1980's the old association of age, wealth, and public service in religious cargos had virtually disappeared.

Overall, the book sets the analysis of social stratification (Part III) in the transformation of public life (Part II) and both of these in economic change (Part I). However, it seeks to show that while Zinacantecos were moved by economic forces from outside, they continued to build a social world inside, and that the local relationships that constitute this social world are not easy to interpret as simple reflections of outside change.

An Epilogue addresses epistemological questions that underlie my approach. Given the great intensity of recent discussions in anthropology, I want to state my position briefly at the outset. I am bewildered by the currently popular suggestion that once the social origins of science are recognized and our own contributions to what we see are acknowledged, we (the "observers") become more interesting than the "outside world." For all its virtues, reflexivity is subject to itself and, as far as we now know, must be eventually abandoned by those who wish to report on the world or be relevant outside intellectual and academic circles (Karp 1986; Myers 1988; Spiro 1986; Watson 1987). Although we must continue to study processes of social construction in daily life, and must recognize that as knowers we are subject to the same examination (for we have social location and culture too), I am devoted to earnest efforts to achieve intersubjectively verifiable understanding within the social and cultural limitations we share—and to efforts to reduce those limitations by including ever more diverse people in the "we." Anything less and I would have to conclude that my late father gave me bad advice when he urged me to study rather than follow his mason's trade. The houses he built still stand, and still protect people from the weather. I hope that my work is as useful.[9]

PART I /

ECONOMY

Economic change in Zinacantán between the 1960's and the 1980's was linked to regional, national, and international economic processes. Zinacantecos began the period as peasants who traded in local markets while producing the major part of their own subsistence. They ended the period in a variety of more dependent relations to the larger economy. The economic system immediately relevant to them expanded greatly.

The next four chapters explore various faces of this change. Chapter 2 gives background information and statistical descriptions. It looks at work from the local point of view and documents changes in the ways Zinacantecos made their livings. Chapter 3 describes the government activity that was the principal cause of the changes. It is concerned with local behavior of state and national agencies whose actions respond directly to influences ranging from hamlet politics to international petroleum prices. Chapter 4 presents life histories that show how individuals adapted to these changes. Chapter 5 highlights the implications of these findings for comparative questions and for social life in Zinacantán.

In these chapters Zinacantecos are usually seen as individuals pursuing individual careers in the face of the changing larger political economy. As they left farming in the 1970's and 1980's, they were apt to face the larger world alone, and mostly on its terms. Personal ties softened the confrontations, government programs were organized through local political units, and political leaders allocated resources in terms of existing relationships, but there were relatively few local social limits on economic adaptations— especially adaptations made by poor and average individuals who found new jobs outside Zinacantán. Overall, market position became a larger part of Zinacantecos' economic lives than it had been in the 1960's.

This increase in the importance of market position has been common. In a comparison of rural third-world economies, Andrew Pearse noted that rapid economic change often increased income inequality at the same time that the development of institutions that moderate the effects of inequality on people at the bottom lagged behind (1978:202). Thus, market forces increase in importance relative to non-market forces. Such periods may be particularly hard on poor people.

2 / NEW WORK

In the 1960's, Zinacanteco men were corn farmers—they made milpa.[1] Only the young and the poor took wages from others on a regular basis. Virtually every man seeded enough corn to meet the needs of his family, and most men of consequence raised much more than that, for they depended on sales of surplus corn to finance their family and community activities. These men often hired others from outside Zinacantán to help them during peak agricultural work periods, and they seldom worked for others. At that time, wage work on road construction was part of young manhood for many Zinacantecos—but once a man married and established himself, corn farming became the typical way to make a living (Cancian 1972).

By the early 1980's, many Zinacantecos seeded no corn at all. In Nachig, for example, where all but 4 percent of male family heads seeded some corn in 1966, 40 percent had no fields in 1983. Those who depended on wages had to save to buy corn in bulk at harvest time so that their family's supply was assured for the year. The major threat to their economic security was unemployment, not a poor crop. Others did neither wage work nor agricultural work in 1983: commerce and various other activities were their principal sources of income, and their concerns were different from those of farmers and wage earners.

Like most of Part I, this chapter has two purposes: to document economic change, and to provide background for interpretation of the political and social changes documented in Parts II and III. Readers who want a quick overview of economic change may read the first and last paragraph of each section and subsection.

Work before the 1950's

It is important to put the last few decades in historical perspective—especially because the occupational homogeneity of the 1960's might be mistaken for a pure, persistent vestige of the distant past, and the diversity of the 1980's seen as the long-resisted breakdown of ancient tradition. In fact, the homogeneity of the 1960's was quite new. George Collier (1975) and Robert Wasserstrom (1983) have shown that between the Spanish Conquest and the second quarter of this century Zinacantecos often had too little access to land and too little freedom from the economic demands of the dominant Ladino population to permit concentration on corn farming.[2]

Collier's condensed chronology, which concentrates on Zinacantán and the neighboring township of Chamula (Table 2.1), gives a good overview of the years from colonization to the 1950's; it is a useful framework for what follows in this section.

Though Chiapas was distant from colonial capitals in Guatemala City and Mexico City, Indians, especially Zinacantecos, were anything but isolated from the Spaniards. Zinacantán was an important center of long-distance trade before the conquest of Chiapas (Wasserstrom 1983:9), and its location on a major trade route brought it "Spanish settlement from the very beginning of colonial rule" (p. 90). After the conquest, Zinacantecos lost lands to the Spaniards, and could not be corn farmers:

Although they continued to grow maize and beans on rocky hillsides, contemporary reports suggest that by 1750 they survived primarily as *cargadores* (bearers) and *arrieros* (mule-drivers) in the employ of Spanish merchants and landowners. More occasionally, they seem to have accepted merchandise on consignment from *comerciantes* [merchants] in Ciudad Real [San Cristóbal de las Casas], which they then peddled throughout the province. (p. 91)

Describing the situation about a century later, Wasserstrom says:

Between 1838 and 1875, approximately half of the town's residents became tenants or laborers on lowland *fincas* [plantations]. . . . As trade throughout the area rose, however, many Zinacantecos turned away from such employment and chose instead to reside within their community as mule drivers or itinerant peddlers. (pp. 134–35)

Wasserstrom shows that many men died as a result of the travel under unfavorable conditions (Mariano EE),[3] that people moved around within the township as well as across township boundaries during this and other periods, and that the lower, temperate, west-

TABLE 2.1

Collier's Condensed Chronology

16th and 17th centuries
  Clerics and colonists debate the status of Indians
  Mining boom in New Spain
  Rapid decline of Indian population
  Cattle ranchers encroach on Indian lands; their illegitimate claims largely
    validated after 1620
1712 Tzeltal rebellion
1760 *Repartimiento* system of commercial redistribution practiced in highland
    Chiapas
1821 Mexican independence
1824 Chiapas secedes from Guatemala, joins Mexico
1826, 1827 Chiapas enacts colonization laws
1840's Tzotzil groups entitle their communal tracts under colonization laws
1863 Juarez comes to power
    Enactment of Leyes de Reforma strips church and Indian towns of corporate
      lands
    Many Indians forced into debt-indentured labor in lowlands
    Liberals, in power in Chiapas, move state capital to Chiapa de Corzo
1860's Zinacantecos acquire *Ibestik* tract
1869 Chamula Caste War rebellion
1876–1910 Dictatorship of Porfirio Diaz
1891 State capital moved to Tuxtla Gutiérrez
1908 Zinacantecos purchase tract of national land in Grijalva basin
1910 Mexican Revolution begins
1914 Revolutionary forces under Carranza take power in Chiapas
    Ley de Obreros enacted, freeing indentured Indian laborers
    Indians return from indentured lowland labor to the highlands
1917 Mexican constitution adopts agrarian plank with far-reaching land-reform
      provisions
1920's First Tzotzil petitions for land restitution made and largely ignored
1934–40
    Presidency of Lazaro Cardenas
    Land reform begun in earnest
    Chamula scribes participate in labor reforms
    State Department of Indian Affairs established
    Chamulas and Zinacantecos buy up some highland ranches
1941 Zinacantecos acquire ejido donations under land reform
1948 First Chamula stills in operation
1952 Ladino liquor monopolists battle with Chamula distillers until the Depart-
      ment of Indian Affairs intervenes

SOURCE: G. A. Collier (1975: 141–42, table 22).

ern part of Zinacantán (Joigel and Jocchenom) developed different occupational specialties from the higher, colder areas closer to
Hteklum. Those in the temperate area worked as part-time and sea-
sonal labor on neighboring plantations to supplement production
from their own small cornfields, while those in the colder areas concentrated on trade and transport as well as subsistence corn farming
(pp. 135–38). During this period the productive cornfields of the hot,

low Grijalva River Valley below Zinacantán were owned and worked by Ladinos; Indians were laborers there.

The Mexican Revolution of 1910–17 made immense landholdings in the Grijalva Valley less secure (see also G. A. Collier 1987). After the revolution Ladino landowners engaged Zinacantecos and other highland Indians as sharecroppers and renters on their lowland estates—thereby beginning the practices that evolved into the patterns widely followed in the 1960's (Cancian 1972) and described in the next section. According to Wasserstrom, Zinacantecos began lowland corn farming tentatively:

> [T]he 1920's and 1930's may perhaps best be viewed as a period of experimentation, a period in which Zinacantecos tried their hand at lowland farming. For this reason, they preferred at first to plant only one or at most two hectares and to maintain their activities as *marchantes* [traders]. But by the early 1940's, only young men still occupied themselves primarily in peddling. As soon as they had acquired a horse and a little experience, they too rented land in the central basin. (1983:183)

George Collier (1975) seeks to dispel the popular, simplistic image of the passive, dominated Indian mired in tradition. He argues that Indians were and are active promoters of their own welfare—active players within the local political system—in a way that uses and reenforces ethnic identity and makes "tradition" vital. Nonetheless, they occupied the bottom rungs of the regional stratification system. Three passages from his comments on "The Indian in Highland Chiapas History" (pp. 146–54) are particularly useful here.

> It is true that Indians played the role of a subordinated labor force during the latter part of the colony and after independence. Throughout that period, over half of Chiapas's Ladino population lived in San Cristóbal and Comitán, the most important commercial centers. From there they directed operations on countless ranches in all zones to raise sugar, cacao, cotton, coffee, and cattle for trade with Mexico or Guatemala. Indians were usually the labor force on these ranches, particularly after 1856 when Ladinos came to control more and more of the lands traditionally owned by Indian groups. In this period, Indians maintained special relationships to the ranches. Seventy or more Indian families might live as indentured laborers on such a ranch, bound to the land to work off debts. (p. 147)

> In 1914, followers of Carranza entered Chiapas and began the work of the Revolution with anticlerical measures. More significantly, they passed the Ley de Obreros, which abolished company stores and set up a minimum wage, norms for health and accident compensations, freedom of residence, and cash wages for workers—all measures to help free indentured workers. . . . The result was abrupt change in the economy of Chiapas ranching after 1914. With debt-indentured slavery abolished, Indian families left the ranches to return to their former villages. Elder Zinacantecos recall the period as one in which their fathers returned from the lowlands to beg land

and housing from their wealthier compatriots who had not entered into labor indenture, working for them for a period of years and finally purchasing land from them. (p. 149)

Land reform had the additional effect of freeing much of the highlands from Ladino control. An unknown number of their ranches, carved from Indian lands after passage of the Juárez laws, were returned to Indians by the ejido movement. Additional holdings were expropriated to donate to the ejidos, and, in many cases, remaining private holdings were sold outright to Indians by their Ladino owners, who saw no economic future for drastically reduced highland holdings. Thus, land reform transformed Indian communities from a patchwork of small hamlets interspersed between Ladino properties into an area of consolidated and continuous Indian control. (p. 150)

Edel (1966) and Wasserstrom (1983) also discuss these changes at length.

In sum, between the sixteenth-century Spanish Conquest of Chiapas and the Mexican Revolution of 1910–17, there was no consistent dominant or typical economic activity in Zinacantán. Constrained by laws and practices imposed by the Spaniards and their successors, Zinacantecos were traders, laborers, and transporters of goods, as well as subsistence corn farmers. Before the revolution many were forced into indentured labor and residence on lowland ranches in the Grijalva River Valley. The revolution loosened the domination of Ladino landowners, freed indentured labor, and, about two decades later, gave many Zinacantecos control of land in the temperate zones and highlands near their traditional homes. At the same time many Ladino landowners sought to rent fields on the remains of their lowland ranches to Zinacanteco corn farmers. Thus, by the middle of this century many Zinacantecos could become commercial corn farmers.

The 1950's to the 1970's: The Period of Corn Farming

Zinacantecos concentrated on corn farming for at least two decades. Three studies done during that period: (1) give an overview of the lowland farming and other economic activity in the 1960's (Cancian 1972); (2) point out the importance of highland farming (G. A. Collier 1975); and (3) review the expansion of farming activity among some Zinacantecos in the early 1970's (Wasserstrom 1983). Each of the studies shows that the shift to corn farming was consolidated by the 1960's. By then most Zinacantecos maintained lowland fields that they considered their main occupation. At the same time, like most peasants, they did more than work in the fields. Days devoted to ancillary activities like transporting and marketing corn and to unrelated activities like wage labor and trading commonly numbered as many as those actually spent in the fields.

An Overview of Work in the 1960's

In the mid-1960's, Zinacantecos farmed with slash-and-burn agricultural techniques in the lowlands. Few used the weed killers and fertilizers that became standard practice a few years later. The following passage from my study of corn farming describes the situation in the mid-1960's and the important changes during the preceding decade:[4]

AN OUTSIDER'S VIEW OF CHANGE

An oversimplified outsider's version of what has happened might go something like this. In 1956 the Zinacantecos were farming corn on rented lands in the Grijalva River Valley below their homes in the highlands. The area they worked was all within a day's walk of their homes, and at harvest time the corn was packed up to the mountains on muleback. Since most farmers harvested considerably more than was needed for household consumption, they sold the excess in the nearby city of San Cristóbal, usually to local Ladinos (Spanish-speaking non-Indians) and to Indians from corn-poor communities in the highlands. The most economically successful Zinacanteco farmers were those who could withhold their corn from the market until prices reached a peak in August.

Then various branches of the Mexican government began two important programs. A major all-weather road was cut through the Grijalva Valley and numerous feeder roads were built in both the lowlands and the highlands [see maps in Cancian (1972)]. Zinacantecos could now reach fields that had been too distant in the days of mule transport, and some of these fields were substantially more productive than those within walking distance of Zinacantan. The second program established government receiving centers and warehouses for corn near both the old and the new fields. These centers bought corn in wholesale lots and paid a fixed price throughout the year. From the farmers' point of view, the government price usually compared favorably to the San Cristóbal price, especially since the cost of transport from the cornfields to the receiving centers was much lower than the cost of transport to the highlands. Moreover, the farmer could sell in wholesale lots in November or December rather than dealing with uncertain market fluctuations the next summer.

In general, an outsider looking at the situation would have advised Zinacantecos to abandon mule transport and retail marketing in favor of motor transport and wholesaling to the new receiving centers. In fact, this is just what some Zinacantecos did. With each passing year, more and more of them moved their farming operations to the more distant fields, shifted from mule to truck transport, and sold much of their crop to the receiving centers. (1972:2–3)

The role of the farmer changed at the same time. Transportation of the crop, which had involved complex arrangements, including petitioning mule owners with gifts of drink and thanking them at the end of the trip with an elaborate meal as well as payment in corn or cash, was reduced to cash payment to a truck driver who was too busy to linger when the work was done. Marketing could be done wholesale near the fields, leaving the farmer with cash, little corn, and little reason to watch for peaks in San Cristóbal market prices before the next harvest. Corn farming became more a specialized occupation and less a way of life (Cancian 1972 : 130–33).

A few Zinacantecos did other things. A number of men from Hteklum continued family traditions as salt sellers for the region, usually on a part-time basis. Some traded corn in San Cristóbal, and others, who owned several mules, brought coffee from isolated plantations to San Cristóbal. Many young men did wage work on road construction, and some others did occasional wage work in agriculture, but trade and especially farming were considered the appropriate activities for adult men (Cancian 1972: 16–17). Corn farming was normatively dominant in Zinacantán—men were expected to be corn farmers.[5]

The dominance of corn farming was statistical as well as normative during this period. In Nachig, as noted above, 96 percent of the men surveyed (Appendix C) had corn fields of some kind in 1966; 93 percent had rented land in the lowlands. Older men tended to have larger plots—a cross-sectional pattern that is consistent with the life stages suggested above. That is, young men started out as laborers, then farmed small amounts of corn, and finally expanded their fields as family needs increased and their labor resources grew.

In sum then, in 1966 Zinacantecos were agriculturalists, most of whom depended on the sale of surpluses to help support their families. During the decade before 1966, major changes took place in the transporting and marketing of their main crop, corn. Many Zinacantecos found it advantageous to transport with Ladino trucks rather than Zinacanteco mules and horses, and to sell to government warehouses rather than store their corn for retailing when prices rose before the next harvest. During this period, some men bulked, transported, and traded other goods on a part-time basis; a few traded corn on a close to full-time basis; and many, especially the young, worked for wages on road construction and in the fields of other Zinacantecos. Normatively, as well as statistically, Zinacantecos were corn farmers.

Highland Corn Farming in the 1960's

Highland corn production alone did not support most Zinacantecos, especially those in the higher, colder, more densely populated eastern part of the municipio. George Collier (1975) concluded that

TABLE 2.2

Lowland and Highland Corn Farming, Nachig, 1966

	Lowlands	Highlands	Combined
Total men	208	208	208
Corn farmers	193	76	199
Percent with fields	93%	37%	96%
Mean seeded per farmer[a]	3.5	1.4	3.9
Mean seeded per man[a]	3.2	0.5	3.7
Total seeded[a]	668	108	776

[a] Seed is measured in almudes (15 liters of volume). The area required to plant an almud varies with the type of land, but is usually slightly less than a hectare (Cancian 1972: 182–88). An almud produces roughly 1 metric ton of grain.

in Apaz, the westernmost of the eastern hamlets, the limited capacity of highland fields led men to produce 80 percent of their corn on rented fields in the lowlands. He also noted that Zinacantecos living in the land-reform colony of Muctajoc, on the western edge of Zinacantán, had enough land to produce more than 75 percent of their corn in fields near their homes (1975: 37).

Nachig was more like Apaz; Nachig men seeded little in the highlands (Table 2.2). My survey figures for 1966 (not included in the table) show Apaz to be slightly lower than Nachig as regards the size of lowland fields, the size of highland fields, and the proportion of men with highland fields, but the differences between them are trivial compared with the contrast between each of them and Muctajoc. Apaz and Nachig probably represent the rough norm of the eastern hamlets of Zinacantán, while the hamlets to the west are closer to the pattern exhibited by Muctajoc.

In sum, in the 1960's highland corn farming was an important source of income to some men, including many who also had lowland fields, but it was very rarely the principal means of support of a family in the hamlets near Hteklum. It was more important in the western hamlets of Zinacantán, the part of the township that Zinacantecos call "The Cornfields" (see Chapter 6).

Lowland Corn Farming in the Early 1970's

The pattern displayed in the cross-sectional data from 1966 did not last very long. Wasserstrom (1983) showed that Nachig men expanded their operations dramatically between 1966 and 1973 (Table 2.3). He also concluded that this expansion did not result in greater profits for most farmers, and he contrasted the Nachig expansive style with the more conservative "holding operation" (Cancian

TABLE 2.3

Lowland Corn Farming, Nachig, 1966 and 1973 [a]

	1966	1973
Total men	208	212
Corn farmers	193	180
Percent with fields	93%	85%
Mean seeded per farmer [b]	3.5	7.1
Mean seeded per man [b]	3.2	6.0
Total seeded [b]	668	1,273

[a]Data for 1973 from Wasserstrom (1983: 191, table 53). Wasserstrom's data are in hectares. A hectare of land usually takes a bit more than an almud of seed (Cancian 1972: 187–88). Thus, the 1973 figures represent even larger fields in comparison with the 1966 figures.

The number with no corn seeded is an estimate. Wasserstrom (1983) shows 180 men renting in the lowlands (p. 191, table 53), 6% who had become rural or urban workers (p. 194), and "almost 10%" who contracted to work the lowland parcels of others for a fee (p. 196). This is interpreted here as 180 + 12 (5.7% of 212) + 20 (9.4% of 212). Wasserstrom (1985) helped reconstruct these figures. He recalled that the Nachig survey was the first he did in Zinacantán, and that it was not exactly parallel to the Elanvo survey of household heads done later (1983: 193, table 59).

He recalled that corn farming (lowland and highland) was overwhelmingly the dominant occupation of Nachig men, and estimated that all the corn farmers, with the exception of the truck owners (a man, his two sons, and his son-in-law; see 1983: 200), earned the major part of their income from corn farming. He remembered that the truck owners abandoned corn farming a few years later. This concentration in one occupation was in stark contrast to the diversity of occupations in neighboring Chamula, which Wasserstrom also studied with extensive surveys (Wasserstrom 1980).

Wasserstrom's survey was done on a house-to-house basis with the assistance of Nachig men. There were some refusals, and the criteria for inclusion were not parallel to those I used in my 1966 and 1983 work (Appendix C). Thus, I will not use the three sets of data to try to estimate population growth in Nachig.

[b]In almudes. See Table 2.2, note *a*.

1965: 77–78) typical of farmers who lived in the hamlet of Elanvo. Nachig men virtually abandoned nearby farming zones, and moved to more distant areas, which required much higher cash investment (Wasserstrom 1983: tables 51 and 52, pp. 189–90).

In his analysis of this movement to more distant fields, Wasserstrom stressed the traditional connections between hamlet residence and certain lowland farming locations, and the pressure put on these limited amounts of land by the people who moved to Nachig because of its location on the paved highway. As a result, he implied, Nachig men, "unlike their neighbors in Elan Vo' . . . began to rent land at great distances from the highlands" (p. 189). He continued:

Within a few years, however, Na Chij farmers soon found themselves enmeshed in a very difficult and highly complex system of economic relations. Although at first their fields were extraordinarily productive (157 units of maize harvested per unit seeded, according to Cancian), these yields quickly diminished by 30 percent. Moreover, several proprietors, realizing that good lands had become relatively scarce, raised their rents once again. As a result,

Indian tenants paid between 33 and 38 percent of their harvests in rent—an increase which they could scarcely afford. In order to offset such costs, and to augment their own productivity, they pursued the only alternative which remained available to them. Without credit or technology, they preferred not to reduce labor and transportation expenses (as Elan Vo' men did); instead they chose to clear and cultivate extremely large *milpas* which sometimes covered 15 or 20 hectares. By 1973, in fact, most Na Chij farmers had expanded their operations from 2.0 to 6.0 hectares (Table 53). Paradoxically, such strategies increased their dependence upon both Chamula laborers and private truck owners (Table 54). For their part, these shippers, eager to capitalize upon local prosperity and the rising price of corn, doubled their passenger and freight rates. By 1973, therefore, despite the fact that *arrendatarios* [renters] from Na Chij farmed twice as much land as they had in 1966, their net returns remained virtually unchanged (Table 55). (1983: 189–90)

The Elanvo farmers that Wasserstrom surveyed seeded very much smaller amounts: 22 percent had no corn and about 15 percent had more than four almudes seeded (1983: 193). And they rented within the older, nearer areas of the lowlands. Thus, they greatly reduced both the need for paid labor and the cost of transporting people and products (pp. 192–94).

Differing access to transport is probably responsible for the contrasting economic styles that Wasserstrom emphasizes. Because Elanvo was off the paved highway, transport had long put the Elanvo farmer at a disadvantage compared to the Nachig farmer interested in distant locations; at the same time, because of Elanvo's location closer to the lowlands, Elanvo farmers had always had a slight advantage when farming in the older, nearer areas. In addition of course, since these differences had existed for a long time, people who resettled themselves to Nachig and Elanvo probably sorted themselves out according to their preferences for one or the other style of farming.

In sum, Nachig men dramatically increased the size of their farming operations during the decade after the mid-1960's (Antonio AA). In doing so they transformed their style into a riskier one that was heavily dependent on cash expenditures for transport and hired labor. Elanvo men, by contrast, worked on a smaller scale, and were more heavily dependent on their own labor. Other hamlets stood out in other ways, but all three studies (Cancian 1972; G. A. Collier 1975; Wasserstrom 1983) document two common features of Zinacanteco economic life during the period (1950's to 1973) under consideration: (1) the vast majority of men concentrated on corn farming, and (2) corn farming practices changed in response to changes in the environment.

A Decade of Change: Nachig Occupations in 1983

The dramatic shift away from corn farming came in the next decade. The occupational structure[6] of Zinacantán was transformed. By 1983, construction labor, formal government jobs, transport of people and goods, fruit and flower production, and trading in the San Cristóbal and Tuxtla Gutiérrez markets became the main sources of support for many Zinacantecos.

My detailed data are for Nachig. Because of its location on the Pan American Highway, Nachig changed more than some other hamlets. Its men became numerically dominant among Zinacanteco truck owners, and strongly represented among regular workers in government programs. Many of them became masons, construction laborers, and full-time merchants. As far as I can tell on the basis of unsystematic observations, Navenchauc and Hteklum also had many vehicle owners, Navenchauc had many government workers, and Navenchauc, Hteklum, and Patosil surpassed Nachig in the rapidly increasing production of flowers in greenhouses. Many hamlets had full-time traders, but those with easy access to paved roads dominated trade. Other activities, such as cattle raising, were probably more highly concentrated in the hamlets to the west. While no other single hamlet can be taken as representative of all hamlets, the processes I will document for Nachig were widespread in Zinacantán.

Table 2.4 displays the results of the census of occupations done in summer 1983. It is intended for reading, and the rest of this paragraph aims to help the reader evaluate what it offers. The occupations in the table are organized into clusters. Each occupation is classified by whether it is "old" (i.e., was followed by some Nachig men in 1966) or new, and whether the income is usually in fixed wages or variable profits. The data come from principal consultants, who described the economic activities of each man in Nachig (see Appendix C). They described virtually all the men in terms of one or two occupations, and the labels they used were directly parallel to the 22 labels in the table (see notes to the table for exceptions). In five cases the consultants described a third activity. For example, the man who owned a store and showed movies also repaired bicycles as a minor sideline. And the man who peddled popsicles and grew corn also worked occasionally as a construction laborer. In order to get these five cases into the table, I have dropped the occupation that the consultants said contributed the least to the man's income. The statistics in the table are supplemented by Chapter 4,

TABLE 2.4

Occupations of Nachig Men, 1983

Occupation	New/old	Wages/ profit	Alone	With corn	With other	Total
Agriculture (grows and sells)						
1. Corn	O	P	75			75
2. Flowers	Z[a]	P	4	2	1	7
3. Cattle	N	P	1	—	2	3
Trade						
4. Trades fruit/vegs./liquor	O	P	24	16	4	44
5. Operates store	Z	P	2	2	4	8
6. Operates corn-grinding mill	Z	P	—	4	4	8
7. Peddles popsicles/soda pop	Z	P	4	1	—	5
8. Shows movies	N	P	—	—	1	1
9. Trades motor vehicles	N	P	—	—	1	1
10. Distributes Coke/Pepsi	N	P	—	—	2	2
11. Trades imported goods	N	P	1	—	—	1
Labor/crafts						
12. Laborer	O	W	23	77	5	105
13. Mason	N	W	8	6	1	15
14. Carpenter	N	P	1	1	—	2
15. Tailor	N	P	—	—	1	1
16. Fireworks constructor	Z	P	1	1	—	2
17. Adobe-brick maker	O	P	1	—	1	2
Government employee						
18. Reforestation worker	N	W	10	—	3	13
19. Extension agent	Z	W	1	—	—	1
20. Radio-telephone operator	N	W	1	—	—	1
Transport						
21. Vehicle driver	Z	W	10	—	—	10
22. Vehicle owner	N	P	12	2	8	22
TOTAL			179	112	38[b]	329[b]

NOTES to rows, columns and cells: Row 1: A few of these produce beans in quantity. Row 4: Traders of corn, beans, flowers, fruit, and liquor are lumped. Row 5, "With corn" column: One of these has both a store and a corn mill. Row 12: Roughly 10% of these work only in agriculture for other Zinacantecos. Row 22: Many vehicle owners also drive.

[a]These are new to Nachig, but not new to Zinacantán.

[b]Nineteen men, each with two non-corn occupations, make up the 38 cases in "With other" column. The total of 329 is 310 (315 − 5 retired) with 19 counted twice. The paired occupations for these 19 men are as follows (using row numbers to identify them): 2-12, 3-12, 3-22, 4-6, 4-12, 4-12, 4-12, 5-8, 5-18, 5-22, 6-22, 6-22, 6-22, 9-22, 10-22, 10-22, 13-17, 15-18.

where each of the occupations that involves ten or more men is illustrated by at least one case.

Many, perhaps most, Nachig men and their families[7] had some income from still other sources. They may have grown a few flowers, vegetables, eggs, or chickens for sale (José GG), or worked an occasional day for wages, sometimes for a neighbor who needed help. While most production by women involved no transactions outside the household (see especially L. K. M. Haviland 1978: chapter 5), some women made substantial direct contributions to production here credited to men (see Cancian 1972: 52; and Francisco HH herein), and a few women sold tortillas in San Cristóbal or wove for other Zinacantecos and/or tourists. Others, especially widows, also made special orders of the dried tortillas men took to the lowlands when they went to farm. Overall, Zinacantecos, like most rural residents without regular employment, did a variety of things to survive and prosper. Nevertheless, I believe that the activities listed in the table cover virtually all the money and corn income that Nachig people produced outside the household.

The clear conclusions supported by Table 2.4 have been repeatedly anticipated above: by 1983, corn farming was no longer the dominant occupation of Nachig men, and the occupational homogeneity of the 1960's was over. Beyond that, the changes shown in the table are diverse and subject to diverse interpretations. Are we to emphasize that two Nachig men had lucrative, municipio-wide soft-drink distributorships, and that 15 others had formal-sector government jobs? Or, is it more important to note that a majority of Nachig men still had cornfields, and that a vast majority earned virtually all of their income from contemporary versions of "traditional" Zinacanteco occupations: agriculture, trade, labor, and transport? As will be clear in the analysis of the political and social implications of the new occupational patterns in Parts II and III, appropriate emphasis varies with the question asked.

Table 2.5 shows the other side of the occupational transformation—the decline of lowland corn farming between 1973 and 1983. In 1973, 50 percent of Nachig men had five or more almudes seeded, while ten years later 5 percent had as much. After rent was paid, the product of lowland fields farmed by Nachig men in 1983 was barely more than the corn consumed by Nachig residents themselves (see

TABLE 2.5
Lowland Corn Farming, Nachig, 1966, 1973, 1983

	1966	1973	1983
Total men	208	212	310[a]
Corn farmers	193	180	163
Percent with fields	93%	85%	53%
Mean seeded per farmer[b]	3.5	7.1	3.1
Mean seeded per man[b]	3.2	6.0	1.6
Total seeded[b]	668	1,273	507

[a] Five of the 315 men are retired.
[b] In almudes: see Table 2.2, note *a*.

Cancian 1972: 82n., on consumption); the enormous surplus produced in the early 1970's disappeared as new occupations became more important. Moreover, Nachig men who still produced corn in 1983 depended more on inputs purchased in national markets. Thus, while Nachig farmers produced enough to feed Nachig residents, they no longer did it with local resources. Nachig's corn production was, in effect, supported by non-farm work.

Many who continued to grow corn changed their relation to the enterprise. Most importantly, various ways to "own" cornfields while working elsewhere emerged (Manuel BB, Mariano EE, Antonio JJ, Juan KK). The standard of the 1960's—that the farmer or a member of his family set the pace by hoeing the lead row during weeding—succumbed to technological changes and national policies relating to wages and corn prices. Weed killers and plows replaced workers. Contract labor, foremen, and large-scale Zinacanteco farmers, who offered advances to workers much as labor recruiters from Ladino coffee plantations did a few decades before, replaced the very constrained inequality of farmer-worker relations in the 1960's (Cancian 1972). Some Nachig men still resembled the corn farmers of the 1960's, but others who farmed corn in 1983 were as different from the corn farmers of the 1960's as the men who had completely new occupations.

In sum, in 1983 Nachig men were involved in diverse occupations, from corn farmer, laborer, and fruit merchant to mason, truck driver, and tailor (Table 2.4). Even among those who maintained cornfields in the lowlands, diverse combinations of corn farming and agricultural labor with other occupations had shattered the considerable homogeneity that had characterized Zinacanteco economic pursuits two decades before.

3 /   THE GOVERNMENT

The immense increase in public spending during the Echeverría (1970–76) and López Portillo (1976–82) administrations was the principal direct cause of change in Zinacanteco economic life. Construction of roads, dams, schools, and housing throughout central Chiapas pulled and pushed Zinacantecos out of corn farming. The oil boom in northern Chiapas and nearby Tabasco during the López Portillo years also brought huge amounts of cash into the local economy. During each administration, programs designed to diversify and increase agricultural production reached into Zinacantán's hamlets, as did social and educational programs that more directly influenced the internal political events described in later chapters.

These 12 frenzied years of Mexican national life have been repeatedly described and analyzed, especially in light of the economic crisis of 1982 (Cornelius 1985; Riding 1984). Here, I will concentrate on analysis of the local impact of government behavior, and give only the barest outline of events at the national level. The national and international origins of the tide that swept over Chiapas during these years were only indirectly relevant to the Zinacantecos whose lives concern me; the political unrest that stimulated government attention to Chiapas occurred largely in other parts of the state (Benjamin 1989). My principal aims are (1) to show that government activity was increasingly important and pervasive after 1970, and (2) to give details on government activities that most directly influenced Zinacanteco economic, political, and social life.

Background Information

Three areas of Chiapas concern us here (Map 1). First is the high-lands (Altos) area around San Cristóbal de las Casas, where Zinacantán and most other Indian populations were and are concentrated. During the period covered by this study it was densely populated, and exported labor.[1] Second is the central depression including the state capital (Tuxtla Gutiérrez), the Grijalva River, which was the focus of hydroelectric development in the state, and the ranches in the upper Grijalva Valley, where Zinacantecos usually rented lands. Finally, the northwestern tip of the state around Pichucalco and the adjoining parts of Tabasco were important because of petroleum production.[2]

Table 3.1 gives figures on population and surface area. Zinacantán was one of 109 municipios in the state in 1984. Table 3.2 gives the names of the leaders of the three levels of formal government organization—Mexican presidents, Chiapas governors, and Zinacantán Presidentes Municipales (mayors)—from 1960 to 1988. PRI, the dominant political party, normally coordinated nominations across the three principal levels of political organization and won elections. Planning and administration were strongly centralized. While many local programs were administered by agencies headquartered in San Cristóbal, there were important and frequent direct contacts between the political leadership of Zinacantán and state officials in Tuxtla Gutiérrez.

TABLE 3.1

Population and Geographic Area

	Population			Percent annual growth 1970–1980	Area (km²)
	1960	1970	1980		
A. Mexico	37,073,000	51,176,000	69,393,000	3.1%	1,958,201
B. Chiapas	1,210,870	1,569,053	2,084,717	2.9	74,211
C. Altos[a]	NA	171,742	241,011	3.5	3,377
D. Zinacantán	7,650	11,428	13,006[b]	1.3[b]	171
B as percent of A	3.3 %	3.1 %	3.0 %		3.8 %
D as percent of B	0.63	0.73	0.62		0.23

SOURCES: National Censuses: SIC 1963, 1972, SPP 1983; SPP 1981.

[a]For an area of 15 municipios defined as the Altos in a SARH study. PRODESCH (see note 3.10) used areas of 21 and 26 municipios at different times.

[b]It is widely believed that the 1980 population of Zinacantán was very substantially underenumerated. Unpublished PRODESCH reports used 1975 estimates of 13,971 for Zinacantán and 1,811,926 for the state. Appendix B discusses different estimates of 1980 population.

TABLE 3.2

Leaders of Mexico, Chiapas, and Zinacantán, 1958–1988[a]

	National president; state governor	Mayor (Presidente Municipal)
1958–64	Adolfo López Mateos; Samuel León Brindis	1960–[b] Guillermo Pérez 1962–64 José de la Cruz
1964–70	Gustavo Díaz Ordaz; José Castillo Tiélemans	1965–67 José Sánchez Pérez 1968–70 Pedro Pérez Pérez
1970–76	Luis Echeverría Alvarez; Manuel Velasco Suárez	1971–73 Marcos Pérez Gonzáles 1974–76 Mariano Pérez de la Cruz
1976–82 1976–[c] 1977–79[d] 1980–82	José López Portillo; Jorge de la Vega Domínguez Salomón González Blanco Juan Sabines Gutiérrez	1977–79 Domingo Pérez Pérez 1980–82 Manuel Conde Vazquez
1982–88	Miguel de la Madrid Hurtado; Gral. Absalón Castellanos Domínguez	1983–85 Pedro Vazquez Sánchez 1986–88 Juan Sánchez Gonzáles

SOURCES: Sanderson (1984: 109); Almanaque (1984).

[a] In these years national presidents and governors took office in December of the year elected, and mayors on January 1 of the following year. The six-year terms of presidents and governors are thus spread over seven calendar years, e.g., 1970–76. Beginning with 1962 the official term for Chiapas mayors was three years.

[b] Internal political problems (see Wasserstrom 1983: 175) led to Guillermo (Yermo) Pérez's resignation in late 1960 (shortly after my first arrival in Zinacantán). The Síndico replaced him (Cancian 1965: 20).

[c] Jorge de la Vega Domínguez resigned to become Secretary of Commerce in the López Portillo administration.

[d] Salomón González Blanco resigned.

Increases in Government Spending

Rapid increase in federal spending began after the first full year (1971) of the Echeverría administration (Table 3.3).[3]

The government explicitly sought to make income distribution more equal and increase state economic activity, according to Leopoldo Solís, an economist who served in a high post in the administration. Political pressures for change, including those that resulted in the widely publicized 1968 student/government confrontations, were great (Solís 1981: ix–x). Given this, Solís says, a slowdown in the rate of economic growth in 1971 brought about "the spending spree of 1972":

Emergency programs especially designed for maximum employment effects were planned for immediate implementation. Among many other projects intended to increase aggregate demand and restore the dynamism of the country, a program of rural roads constructed by hand was quickly started. (p. 67)

Public investment spending more than doubled in the two years (22.5 bil-

TABLE 3.3

Public-Sector Spending in Mexico, 1965–1978[a]

(Billions of pesos)

	Year					
DIAZ ORDAZ	1965	1966	1967	1968	1969	1970
Total, current pesos	55.6	59.7	66.2	74.2	87.7	96.8
Annual increase (%)		7.4	10.9	12.1	18.2	10.4
In 1975 pesos[b]	119.3					174.4
ECHEVERRIA	1971	1972	1973	1974	1975	1976
Total, current pesos	105.0	132.9	181.4	251.4	365.7	475.5
Annual increase (%)	8.5	26.6	36.5	38.6	45.5	30.0
In 1975 pesos[b]	178.9	213.0	257.7	291.0	365.7	397.6
LOPEZ PORTILLO	1977	1978				
Total, current pesos	642.2	827.0				
Annual increase (%)	35.1	28.8				
In 1975 pesos[b]	411.7	454.1				

SOURCE: Solís (1981: table 3.3).
[a] Federal spending and public enterprises are lumped. Totals are rounded.
[b] Using the implicit GDP deflator from World Bank (1983). It is 39.3 for 1960, 46.6 for 1965, and for 1970 to 1981 it is 55.5, 58.7, 62.4, 70.4, 86.4, 100.0, 119.6, 156.0, 182.1, 218.9, 281.8, and 358.5. The Consumer Price Index is very close to the GDP deflator (within 10%), but varies less; i.e., it is higher in 1960 and lower after 1975.

lion in 1971 and 49.8 billion in 1973) in comparison with the 13 percent annual growth registered during Stabilizing Development [1959–67]. The largest share of the increase was absorbed by spending on transport and communications, which shifted from one-fifth to one-fourth of the public investment budget. (p. 68)

These priorities of the early Echeverría years were clearly reflected at the state level (Table 3.4). The importance of energy development is also clear: even the huge investment in roads (the major component of the SOP/SCT expenditures shown in the table) was consistently surpassed by the investment of the Federal Electric Commission (CFE) for hydroelectric development, and in the second half of the period, by PEMEX expenditures for petroleum extraction. Road building and energy development will be described in detail below.

By the end of the Echeverría years (1976) inflation was substantial, government employment had expanded tremendously, the external public debt was increasing rapidly, and oil was becoming an important component of exports (Table 3.5).

López Portillo (1976–82) inherited an economic crisis from Echeverría, but by 1978 the discovery of new oil reserves and greatly in-

TABLE 3.4
Government Spending in Chiapas, 1970–1976
(Millions of pesos)[a]

	1970	1971	1972	1973	1974	1975	1976[b]
FEDERAL							
Federal government	111.2	176.3	300.3	433.0	1,112.4	642.4	2,159.5
Public works SOP/SCT[c]	86.9	103.7	192.8	265.3	508.6	270.3	677.0
Decentralized agencies	158.0	299.3	361.2	782.7	1,774.2	3,489.4	4,439.4
Electricity (CFE)	134.8	228.7	257.5	524.4	751.0	1,118.7	2,146.7
Petroleum (PEMEX)	3.2	3.6	20.2	122.9	634.2	2,200.0	1,239.9
Other	—	16.4	17.3	41.5	60.5	356.6	232.1
TOTAL	269.2	492.0	678.8	1,257.3	2,946.8	4,488.8	6,831.1
STATE							
Government salaries	17.9	26.5	23.9	25.1	32.3	51.3	92.0
Education	29.2	36.5	70.0	89.5	103.2	150.5	226.7
Public works	39.7	37.7	82.4	89.2	92.1	112.6	66.7
Other	15.1	14.2	13.7	17.5	22.4	38.6	54.2
TOTAL	101.9	114.9	190.1	221.3	250.0	353.1	439.5
Percent federal[d]	12.3%	14.1%	13.6%	15.4%	16.6%	34.0%	40.0%
GRAND TOTAL	371.1	606.9	868.9	1,520.3[e]	3,269.7[e]	4,841.9	7,360.7[e]
In 1975 pesos[f]	668.6	1,033.9	1,392.5	2,159.5	3,784.4	4,841.9	6,154.4[f]
Percent increase	54.6%	54.7%	34.7%	55.1%	75.2%	27.9%	27.1%

SOURCES: Velasco Suárez (1976: tables 28, 70, 71), except that for 1974 and 1975 all federal expenditures have been changed to reflect the totals of 2,946.8 and 4,488.8 (million pesos) given in SP (n.d.: 411). This was done because SP (1975: 59–60) indicates that the total given in Velasco Suárez (1976: table 28) for 1974 was for expenditures in the first trimester of 1974, and that the total given for 1975 was that foreseen as of January 28, 1975. Since the SP figures did not include breakdowns, the proportions found in Velasco Suárez (1976) were applied to the totals in SP (n.d.) to arrive at the figures here.
[a] Rounding error makes sums inexact.
[b] Budgeted, not actual.
[c] Total of lines for SOP and SCT. It is virtually all (more than 95%) SOP, except for 1970, when SCT has a $29.3 million budget.
[d] Income from federal revenue sharing as a percentage of state expenditure. Calculated by Frank Cancian. The largest source of state income was taxes.
[e] The grand totals include expenditures for the PIDER program (see note 3.9) as follows: 1977, $41.7 million; 1974, $72.9; 1976, $90.1. These expenditures are reported in a note to Velasco Suárez (1976: table 28).
[f] See Table 3.3, note b.

TABLE 3.5

Measures of Economic Change, 1970–1983

Year	Annual inflation (%)	Fed. gov. employees ($\times 10^3$)	External public debt ($\times 10^6$ U.S. $)	Oil exports		
				Barrels ($\times 10^6$)	Value ($\times 10^6$ U.S. $)	Percent of total exports
1970	4.7%	530.5	3,206	22.4	40.3	3.1%
1971	4.9	565.1		17.3	34.6	2.5
1972	5.6	610.6		9.4	25.9	1.5
1973	21.3	684.4		8.7	133.9	1.7
1974	20.6	757.5		6.5	133.5	4.7
1975	11.3	849.9	11,537	36.9	468.9	16.4
1976	27.2	896.0	15,930	35.7	560.9	13.1
1977	20.7	1,079.0	20,758	75.4	1,874.5	24.8
1978	16.2		25,615	133.9	3,220.7	31.5
1979	20.0		29,241	194.0	3,764.0	42.8
1980	29.8		33,586	303.0	9,429.6	61.6
1981	28.7		42,642	400.8	13,305.3	68.7
1982	98.9					
1983	80.8					

SOURCES: Cornelius (1985: 92); Solís (1981: 145); World Bank (1983: 317); Buzaglo (1984: 24).

creased exports (see Table 3.5) had dwarfed the economic crisis, and the economy was booming again.

The boom that occurred was based on rising oil revenues and a high level of public and private expenditures. In 1981, public expenditure as a proportion of gross domestic product (GDP) amounted to some 36 percent compared with 29 percent in 1976 and 20 percent in 1970. . . . Real per-capita income during the boom years increased by some 25 percent while unemployment fell. (Wyman 1983a: 4)

The prosperity in Chiapas was part of the national boom, and the fact that PEMEX's share of public-sector spending reached 30 percent by 1978 made the Chiapas experience particularly intense.

Chiapas state government expenditure increased accordingly during the López Portillo years (Table 3.6). It is hard to document spending fully during this period because the pattern of ample, well-organized, annual reports established while Velasco Suárez was governor (1970–76) was not continued. This is not surprising, for de la Vega Domínguez served as governor only a short time (1976–77) before leaving to become López Portillo's secretary of commerce, and his replacement as governor, Gonzales Blanco, was replaced by Sabines at about the middle of the term. The period was politically and financially turbulent, and inflation reached almost 30 percent in 1979 and 1980, and almost 100 percent in 1981 (Table 3.5).

TABLE 3.6

State Government Finances, 1976–1981
(Millions of 1976 pesos)[a]

	1976	1977	1978	1979	1980	1981	Annual average rate of increase
Income							
State resources[b]	201	294	305	365	302	204	4.0%
Federal monies[c]	285	310	425	593	1,360	1,763	48.9%
Total[c]	486	604	730	958	1,662	1,967	33.6%
Percent federal	58.6%	51.3%	58.2%	61.9%	81.8%	89.6%	
Expenditures (percent of total)[d]							
Public works and construction	—	2.3%	22.4%	8.3%	50.5%	57.4%	
Education	—	54.8	40.2	32.2	25.9	21.9	
Other	—	49.9	37.4	59.5	23.6	20.7	

SOURCE: Chiapas (1982a: 214, 221).

[a]Constant pesos as reported in the source. Current pesos went from $486 million in 1976 to $7,948 million in 1981. These are budget figures. High inflation led to even higher expenditures in current pesos, i.e., $11,288 million in 1981 (Chiapas 1982a: 222).

[b]Taxes were the main source through 1981, when some state taxes were replaced by the federal value-added tax (Chiapas 1982a: 215).

[c]Additional federal support under other programs went from 307 million current pesos in 1977 to $1,736 million in 1981 (Chiapas 1982a: 218).

[d]The total budgeted expenditures reported are roughly equal to the income listed above.

The López Portillo years (1976–82) were also complicated by important changes in the fiscal and administrative relations of the three levels of government. Taxation, which had once given the state government substantial income of its own (see Table 3.4), became more concentrated at the federal level, and, as Table 3.6 shows, the state government became more dependent on revenue sharing (Chiapas 1982a: 216). At the same time, a campaign began that sought to decentralize programs and administration from the federal to the state governments, and from the state governments to the townships (Rodriguez 1987). In Chiapas, the Sabines administration (1980–82) experimented with decentralization in the form of block grants to municipios (see below).

The boom years ended when an increasing trade deficit and substantial weakening of the world petroleum market in 1981 brought on the economic crisis of 1982 (see Wyman 1983b). The crisis became public in August 1982, when Mexico announced that it could no longer service its enormous foreign debt.

Many Mexicans, including Zinacantecos, enjoyed the economic prosperity that resulted in large part from the increasing government spending during the Echeverría and López Portillo years (1970–82). The many government programs created jobs and provided services that were new to most people in the Chiapas highlands. In Parts II and III below, this experience of prosperity becomes relevant to understanding behavior during the period.

Government Programs

Government spending took many forms—from high-technology investments in petroleum and hydroelectric power production to construction of thousands of kilometers of rural roads by hand; from telephones, radio stations, and electrification to clinics, reforestation, and extension education for adult women and men. As the stories told in Chapter 4 indicate, Zinacanteco men were touched in a variety of ways by this explosion of activity. Here I will try to connect diverse types of government programs to the changing work patterns described in Chapters 2 and 4, and to the political and social activities described in later chapters.

The four topics covered below represent different levels and types of government involvement in the lives of Zinacantecos. Road construction involved small-scale, locally relevant public works. Dam construction involved huge, centrally organized public investment. The PRODESCH program coordinated most of the development activities in the highlands in the 1970's—including those that reached most directly into Zinacantán and other Indian municipios. The CODECOM program of block grants to municipios galvanized much local energy during a brief period (1980–82).

Creating Jobs: Construction of Roads

Government initiatives in road construction transformed rural transportation in Chiapas in the 1970's. In Zinacantán, new roads connected many hamlets to the Pan American Highway, and opened them for the first time to cargo and passenger service by trucks, microbuses, and (rarely) buses. The road from the Pan American Highway in Nachig to Paste stood virtually alone in the 1960's, but by the 1980's there were roads to almost every hamlet—most of them constructed of stone implanted in a dirt roadbed with the simple hand tools used in the many labor-intensive projects.

Roads in Chiapas more than doubled while Velasco Suárez was governor (1970–76). In the highlands, rural roads tripled, even by the most conservative accounts. In the Grijalva Valley much road construction was associated with the dam projects described below. Table 3.7 shows conservative annual figures for the state and for the highlands.[4]

Road construction created a lot of work. For example, the roads budget for the highlands alone for 1973 was $56,404,800 (Velasco Suárez 1976: 111). This amount would have purchased almost 50,000

TABLE 3.7

Road Construction in Chiapas, 1971–1976

(Kilometers)

	Through 1970[a]	1971	1972	1973	1974	1975	1976
State							
Paved	1,201.0	72.2	92.2	176.8	49.4	47.0	NA
Stone/gravel	1,341.0	55.6	142.2	1,529.4	114.2	164.5	NA
Dirt	552.0	92.6	132.5	206.3	—	157.9	NA
TOTAL	3,094.0	220.4	366.9	1,912.5	163.6	369.4	NA
Highlands[b]	450.0	[c]	194.5	418.5	194.0	181.5[d]	148[d]

SOURCES: SP (1975: 136); PRODESCH (1977: 73); Velasco S. and Matus Pacheco (1976: 222).
[a]Includes roads built before 1970 and through the end of the year.
[b]Highlands figures are totals for the PRODESCH area (see note 3.10). Most are stone/gravel roads.
[c]The figure of 450 km is for roads existing in 1971 (PRODESCH 1977: 71). I have no information on the part of that 450 built during 1971.
[d]Sources differ on highland construction for 1975 and 1976. PRODESCH (1977: 73) listed 181.5 km in 1975 and 148 km (including 89 km of dirt roads) in 1976. Figures in Velasco S. and Matus Pacheco (1976) are 101.0 km for 1975 and 440.5 km for 1976.

tons of corn at then-current official prices, enough corn to feed the entire highlands population of 300,000 for a year (Stuart 1990). Granted that a substantial proportion of even a labor-intensive roads program might have gone to administrative costs, the proportion reaching the workers in the area must have made a great impact.

The construction of roads, and of schools, community buildings, parks, water systems, and other local public-works projects during the same period, gave employment at attractive wages to many Zinacantecos. On these projects, and on the dam construction described below, many learned mason's skills (Manuel BB, Mariano EE, Francisco HH), and some of those emerged as contractors on public and private construction projects during the early 1980's. Thus, the mix of corn farming and unskilled wage labor which had been available for many years before 1970 changed when government programs created demand for skilled construction workers.

Energy Extraction: Construction of Dams

Government investment in energy extraction was especially important during the López Portillo years (1976–82). It had two parts: oil production in northern Chiapas, and hydroelectric production through dams on the Grijalva River in the central depression. Since the construction of dams had the greater direct influence on Zinacanteco economic life, it will receive more attention here.

The Grijalva River hydroelectric system consists of three dams built between 1959 and the 1980's. Their installed capacity, including a fourth dam that had not been built by 1988, will reach about 5,000 megawatts (Velasco S. and Matus Pacheco 1976: 180)— somewhat more than the hydroelectric capacity of Tennessee Valley Authority dams in the 1970's (Columbia 1975: 2714). By 1980, when three-fifths of the planned capacity had been installed, Chiapas had become the site of 20 percent of all the electric generating capacity in Mexico. It had almost 50 percent of all hydroelectric generating capacity in the country, and about 8 percent of the thermoelectric capacity (SPP 1981: 111). The rural backwater that had a generating capacity of less than 18 megawatts (0.49 percent of national capacity) in 1962 (ANDSA 1964: 203) had been transformed into a national resource, the producer of major inputs to the national power network.

The dams and generating plants (Table 3.8) were built at different times (Velasco S. and Matus Pacheco 1976; Rivapalacio 1979). The project popularly known as Malpaso (the Netzahualcoyotl Dam) was built first, between 1959 and 1964. As far as I can tell, this project

TABLE 3.8

Dams in the Grijalva Hydroelectric System[a]

	Installed capacity (megawatts)	Annual generation (gigawatt hours)	Maximum lake size (hectares)
Angostura	920	2,249	63,600
Chicoasén	2,400	5,580	3,000
Malpaso	1,080	3,200	30,000
Peñitas (planned)	400	NA	NA

SOURCES: Velasco S. and Matus Pacheco (1976); Rivapalacio (1979).
[a] As of the late 1970's.

in the northern part of the state mostly affected Tabasco, from where access to the site was easier. It had little direct effect on Zinacanteco work patterns.

The Angostura Dam was built second (between 1969 and 1974). Though it was located in the area where Zinacantecos farmed, few of them (Mariano EE) found work on the project itself. Some (Mariano DD, José GG) worked on related road projects. As far as I can tell, its main effects on Zinacanteco work patterns resulted from the flooding of farm lands. The lake that formed behind the dam (Map 1) eventually covered more than 60,000 hectares and resulted in the relocation of 20,000 people (Almanaque 1984).[5] Zinacanteco renters frequently moved to new plots for other reasons (Cancian 1972), so it is hard to estimate how many were directly displaced by the flooding.[6]

Many Zinacantecos worked at Chicoasén, the third and largest of the dam projects. The stories in Chapter 4, and many fragments of other life stories I heard in Zinacantán, suggest that the demand for labor created by this project pulled many Zinacantecos out of corn farming, and led some of them to acquire construction skills that were not present among Zinacantecos in the 1960's.

Chicoasén ranked as the fifth highest dam in the world when it was being built, and three of the four higher dams were also under construction at that time. Work began in December 1975, four months after the closing of the dam at Angostura. In anticipation of the reduced river flow while the Angostura Dam was filling, a rough road was rapidly built into the Chicoasén site between November 1974 and February 1975, and a bypass tunnel at the site was built between December 1975 and January 1976 (Rivapalacio 1979). By July 1976 Angostura had filled, and the river's flow, which had been reduced as much as 90 percent, returned to normal. This rushed schedule frightened some Zinacantecos who worked on the project (Mariano EE, José GG), but is described positively in Rivapalacio's account:

By the end of 1976 there existed the normal conditions of a project with excellent roads, offices and every necessity for normal work. The two years during which the work was done under difficult conditions and without any facilities is a tribute of the technicians and workers to their country. (1979: 12)

In early 1982, the completion of the fourth dam at Peñitas was anticipated in 1986, and many other hydroelectric projects were under study (Chiapas 1982a: 180–81). All these projects were suspended after the economic crisis began in August 1982; the Las Peñitas project remained suspended in summer 1988.

Petroleum and natural gas production also became much more important to Chiapas during the López Portillo administration (1976–82). Estimates varied,[7] but one assessment of the state's internal gross product put electricity at 9 percent and petroleum at 39 percent of the total (Chiapas 1982a: 182). CFE and PEMEX monthly expenditures for salaries in Chiapas, most of them paid to technicians and administrators who were not permanent Chiapas residents, averaged $160 and $90 million, respectively, in 1981 (Chiapas 1982a: 182), while the entire budget of the state government (including federal revenue sharing) was less than $700 million (28 million dollars) per month.[8]

Work in Villahermosa, Tabasco, the center of the petroleum development, was a constantly present option during this period. Zinacantecos went to work as masons and construction laborers (Mariano EE, Juan KK), and they frequently discussed the higher wages, the disadvantages of distance and higher living costs, and the more dangerous frontier life style that faced those who chose Villahermosa over the relatively placid housing construction projects in Tuxtla. Although the Chiapas and Tabasco oil fields are a mountain range away from the highlands and central depression of Chiapas where Zinacantecos concentrated their work in the 1960's, they influenced the regional economy and, I believe, indirectly affected the work lives of most Zinacantecos who never made the trip across the mountains. Although hard to measure, the influence was certainly large.

PRODESCH

PRODESCH (the Socioeconomic Development Program for the Highlands of Chiapas) coordinated and administered development activities of state, federal, and international agencies in the Chiapas high-lands for many years after it was created early in the Velasco Suárez administration (1970–76). Projects under its umbrella ranged from agriculture, roads, and health to education, electrification, and community development. PRODESCH also maintained the political presence of the government in the Indian municipios. Though it later underwent repeated bureaucratic and substantive transformations and formal renamings, the label "PRODESCH," and the cluster of buildings on a hillside at the edge of San Cristóbal de las Casas, remained the focal point of much of the contact between Indians and the government.[9]

PRODESCH activities were economically important to individuals and groups in Zinacantán: construction projects provided wage work near home, and extension and credit programs led to the greenhouse flower production described below and other new occupations. In Part II we will see that the programs also fostered the creation of new hamlets and new hamlet offices, and became catalysts for political conflict. Here I will describe the establishment and evolution of PRODESCH and other programs and agencies in the highlands, use budgets to give an overview of activities, and describe some specific programs that affected Zinacantecos. Readers who are in a hurry should read only the first and last paragraphs of the next three labeled subsections.

Establishment and evolution of PRODESCH. PRODESCH was established in late 1971. A plan of operation prepared by UNICEF focused on coordinating the actions of state government with 13 federal agencies (mostly secretariats) and five cooperating international agencies. It went into operation in early 1972, and covered 26 municipios with a total area of 7,443 km² and 335,000 inhabitants, respectively 9.8 and 18.3 percent of the state totals.[10]

The executive power of PRODESCH and other agencies operating in the same area varied with different administrations, as did the level of commitment to development activities in the highlands. During the Velasco Suárez administration (1970–76), which created it, PRODESCH reigned supreme, and formally included the state's long-established Department of Indian Affairs as well as the federal National Indian Institute (INI), which had worked in the area on similar programs for many years before (Aguirre Beltrán, Villa Rojas et al. 1975; Velasco Suárez 1971: 46, 48). Relations among the agencies were not always smooth.

Though the López Portillo administration signed a new agreement with the United Nations in August 1977, the role of PRODESCH was cut back while de la Vega Domínguez and Gonzales Blanco were governors (1977–79). PRODESCH became part of the state Secretariat of Economic Development (SDE) created by de la Vega, and INI's role in Indian affairs again expanded.[11]

Political activity blossomed in the mid-1970's in much of the state. Antiestablishment activity, including reported terrorist incidents and guerrilla camps in the jungle areas in the northern part of PRODESCH's area, increased; and tensions continued in Venustiano Carranza, a large population center in the southern part of PRODESCH's area. In 1978, in apparent response to these problems, the Gonzales Blanco administration made a dramatic shift of funding in favor of townships at the northern and southern lowland margins of PRODESCH's area.[12] When he was named to replace Gonzales Blanco as governor in late 1979, Sabines' charge was to manage these conflicts; CODECOM, which will be discussed below, was the principal formal part of his response.

In July 1981, under Sabines, the political side of state activities in the highlands (the Department of Indian Affairs) and the economic side (which was by this time administering PIDER monies in the area) were consolidated under Alejandro Rovelo Burguete, who was simultaneously Delegate of the SDE for the highlands and Director of Indian Affairs. Rovelo had been personal secretary to the director of INI when INI flourished in the late 1970's. In mid-1982, during the waning months of the Sabines administration, a full-scale Secretariat of Indian Affairs (SAI) was established.[13]

The new governor, Absolón Castellanos Domínguez (1982–88), recut the cake. He created a Secretariat of Rural Development (SDR) to replace the Secretariat of Economic Development (SDE), and in it included two sub-secretariats: Rural Development (sub-SDR) and Indian Affairs (sub-SAI). Sub-SAI was headquartered in San Cristóbal de las Casas at the "PRODESCH" buildings, and had Rovelo at its head. Sub-SDR, with headquarters in Tuxtla Gutiérrez, had a delegation in San Cristóbal, with offices adjoining those of sub-SAI. In 1983, Indian Affairs was in sub-SAI, agricultural programs were in sub-SDR, and roads were in SDUOP (Castellanos Domínguez 1983).

In sum, while the "PRODESCH" name officially disappeared during the Sabines years (1980–82), many of the people and programs continued. Extension agents used old contacts to recruit participants for new programs, and, as we see below, Zinacantecos adjusted their requests for government aid to the new reality. "PRODESCH"—i.e., active, highly financed, highly political, government involvement with Indian communities—remained despite repeated bureaucratic reorganizations.

An overview of PRODESCH activities. During the Velasco Suárez administration (1970–76) PRODESCH programs were divided into six sectors. The five listed in Table 3.9 involved construction and/or services delivered or developed in rural communities. The sixth, community organization, was a study unit that had a budget to support staff, but no project budget.[14] Programs continued during the later years of the López Portillo administration (1979–82)—as the experiences of Zinacantecos reported in Chapter 4 make clear—but I was not able to find useful reports of expenditures.

Agricultural programs dominated expenditures in most of the Velasco Suárez (1970–76) years (Table 3.9). Included were expenditures for horticulture and husbandry, soil conservation, credits for fertilizer, various fruit-production programs, reforestation, and the development of a network of CONASUPO stores. All of these programs touched many Zinacantecos at many points over the years (see Chapter 4).

While medical clinic service was by far the largest component of the health-services budgets, the provision of water systems to replace the traditional system of drawing water from open wells was strongly emphasized during the early years—it represented more than 35 percent of the health budget from 1973 to 1976 (Velasco Suárez 1976: 110). Smaller programs listed under health included housing (Manuel BB). The construction of some Community Buildings (Casas del Pueblo; see Chapter 7) was also included under health programs (PRODESCH 1975).

More than half the education budget shown in Table 3.9 went for school construction. Although the state budget (Table 3.4) paid teacher salaries, substantial federal money was put into recruiting new teachers. The influences on Zinacantecos were many: expanded education created jobs in school construction, higher levels of education among young Zinacantecos (José II, Antonio LL), and additional community-service committee posts (see Chapter 7). An Indian-language radio station (XERA) began to broadcast out of a PRODESCH building.

Ninety-seven percent of the 1972–76 PRODESCH communications budget went to roads (Velasco Suárez 1976: 111). PRODESCH also promoted an organization of Indian truckers that helped them break through the bureaucratic barriers that had fostered Ladino control of transportation (Hernández 1984; Loyola 1988). Telephone service

TABLE 3.9

PRODESCH Budgets, 1972–1978, by Sector[a]

	1972	1973	1974[b]	1975	1976	1977	1978
TOTAL (×10³)							
Pesos	60,207	126,809	76,963	126,867	152,321		
U.S. dollars	4,817	10,144	6,157	10,149	11,435	5,532	8.807
Sector							
Agriculture (%)	36.3%	19.2%	35.2%	40.3%	55.4%	37.7%	29.6%
Health (%)	—	14.3	24.3	29.6	17.4	16.4	6.2[d]
Education (%)	26.2	16.8	15.6	13.5	5.0	13.6	6.3
Communication (%)	33.0	45.9	16.3	12.5	14.8	23.2	54.2
Electrification and Industrialization (%)	4.4	3.9	9.0	4.1	7.8	5.9	3.7[d]
TOTAL (%)	99.9%	100.1%	100.4%	100.0%	100.0%	96.8%[c]	100.0%

SOURCES: Velasco Suárez (1976: 108) for pesos and percentages, 1972 to 1976; PRODESCH (1979: 18, 25) for dollars and percentages, 1977 and 1978.
[a] These figures are for investments made by the agencies. Operating expenses (gastos corrientes) are not included.
[b] Not adjusted for presumed error. See Table 3.4, note on sources.
[c] PRODESCH (1979: 18) gives a total of U.S. $5,532 but sums to 5,360.
[d] The 1978 budget uses slightly different categories. The figure listed for "Electrification and Industrialization" is for "Industrialization and Commercialization." The figure for "Health" includes 1.5% for health and 4.7% for human settlements (drinking water) (PRODESCH 1979: 25).

was extended to Indian townships and their hamlets, and a system of regional radio communication was developed. The radio operator in Nachig reflected many new programs: in his new job he provided long-distance telephone service and radio-message relay service from an office attached to the new Community Building on the new park.

Rural electrification took more than 70 percent of the electrification and industrialization budget for 1972–76 (Velasco Suárez 1976: 111). Craft and industrial development took another substantial part.

In sum, PRODESCH had many and diverse programs, so many that it is impossible to mention them all in this overview. The section that follows gives some detail on two programs that reached individuals and small groups.

Examples from Zinacantán. Fertilizer sales by various agencies and greenhouse production of flowers promoted by one agency illustrate Zinacanteco-government interaction in the highlands.[15] Fertilizer became an important agricultural input during the 1970's. By the early 1980's fertilizer was important to the fruit, vegetable, and flower production which had expanded greatly in the highlands, in part because of government promotion efforts. And increased transport costs had driven Zinacantecos out of lowland corn farming and back to highland cornfields, which responded well to fertilizer. After the 1982 economic crisis, these trends intensified greatly.

Four government programs offered fertilizers in the early 1980's. The SARH program served members of ejidos, and another at PRODESCH served farmers who were not members of the ejidos (*comuneros*). Both offered fertilizer on credit, so that the farmer could apply the fertilizer when it was needed and pay for it later with proceeds of the harvest. Applications for credit were usually organized through groups of farmers who formed for the purpose. Both programs required paperwork and formal indebtedness. At INI, fertilizer was available at a discounted price to individuals ready to pay cash. A fourth program coexisted with the others, at least in 1981. It was run by CNC for groups of peasants who applied together for an amount appropriate to the land the members of the group had seeded. The man who told me about the CNC program (a leader of a group that applied) discontinued his effort to get CNC fertilizer after he found that the CNC program could not deliver enough to meet the requests it had solicited. He characterized the SARH, CNC, and PRODESCH programs as essentially the same, and said he went where he received the best attention. In his case that was SARH. Though the programs were technically for different populations, many Zinacantecos had access to all of them through different combinations of friends, relatives, and patrons.

The programs that required applications by groups became enmeshed in municipal and hamlet politics. For example, in 1981 there were two groups in the hamlet of Apaz—one for members of PAN (the opposition political party; see Chapter 8) and another for members of PRI—and PRODESCH documents carried groups called "Apaz A" and "Apaz B." In Navenchauc, according to a PAN member, PAN people were excluded during a long period when a PRI man controlled the local committee post that gave access to discounted fertilizer. In 1981, when PAN managed to put one of its own people in the post, Navenchauc PRI people had to go to a PRI man in Hteklum who had the required access. These programs reflected and perhaps helped consolidate the political factions discussed in Part II.

Zinacantecos rarely obtained and used fertilizer, or other services provided by PRODESCH, in exactly the ways program designers intended. Rather, they determined what products and services were available, and then took actions that would get them desired products or services. For example, a Navenchauc man explained that he and his father had applied for a ton of fertilizer for their cornfields. They thought it might be delivered late, but they were not concerned, because they planned to use most of it on fruit trees. This kind of active use of opportunities provided by government is characteristic of Zinacantecos, and surely of many, if not most, populations in similar structural positions.

Flower production in greenhouses was different from the simple procurement of fertilizer. It involved substantial investment, constant attention to the plants, and coordination with wholesale marketers. The "PRODESCH" program that offered credit and technical assistance flourished in the early 1980's. More than a dozen greenhouses were constructed in Zinacantán Center and Patosil, where climate and availability of water favored them. As I understand it, formal requirements included a cooperative group with responsibility for the enterprise, but actual administration seemed to vary from genuine partnerships to something much closer to individual ownership.[16]

Antonio Méndez (FF), whose story appears in Chapter 4, was operating a greenhouse when I interviewed him in June 1984. Most of the other nine members of his group participated very little in day-to-day operations. The group had applied to SDR in August 1983, and

The center of Nachig, with Antonio Méndez's greenhouse in the foreground, 1984.

a month later they had a $135,000 loan for construction on land that Antonio rented in Nachig (masons earned about $600 per day in Tuxtla at that time). In late February 1984, he was advanced $75,000 worth of plastic covering for the frame that had been built. Each of these loans specified payment in three equal, annual installments.[17]

Antonio lost much of his first crop to frost and replaced it with 7,500 new plants purchased at SDR for $50,000. By June 1984 some of his loans were past due, but he remained optimistic. In August 1985 the plastic roof of Antonio's greenhouse was broken in several places, and the beds were only partially filled with flowers. By 1987 others reported that his enterprise had failed; the useful parts of the greenhouse had been purchased for use in Patosil.

Antonio's case was not typical. Many of the greenhouses that began in the early 1980's succeeded as commercial enterprises, and continued to operate in 1988, the last time I was able to check on them.

In sum, government agencies promoted and facilitated adoption of new crops and new technologies by Zinacantecos and others in the area. The agencies sometimes competed with each other, and Zinacantecos took advantage of this competition.

CODECOM: Block Grants to Municipios

CODECOM made block grants that completely changed the organization and financing of local public-works projects in Chiapas. Control of projects was passed from state and federal authorities to mayors (Presidentes Municipales) and municipio committees called the Municipio Development Foundation (Patronato de Desarrollo Municipal). This decentralization of operating control led to great local political turmoil that will be discussed in Chapter 8. Here I will focus on CODECOM as a government program.[18]

The Sabines administration made the first CODECOM grants in February 1980. The grants were made to committees normally headed by the mayor (Presidente Municipal). Local authorities planned and executed projects, and asked for additional funds after those granted had been expended and accounted for. They were encouraged to anticipate additional grants. For example, when he distributed more funds in June 1980, Sabines remarked that grants would be from $1 million to $15 million at a time, and that municipio committees could expect another grant three or four months later.

The program sought to create and draw on local talent, and to replace state and federal government initiatives and administration with local initiatives and administration. In keeping with this goal, in November of its first year, CODECOM published a manual (Chiapas 1980) helpful to municipio officials administering CODECOM funds. It included statements by López Portillo and Sabines about the goals of the decentralization, samples of relevant official documents needed by local officials, and architect's drawings for potential projects, such as bridges, parks, schools, and water systems.

While CODECOM reflected a national policy of decentralization, it was also a major component of Sabines' effort to deal with political unrest in Chiapas, especially problems in rural, lowland jungle areas. He was named governor in large part because of the expectation that he could be effective in dealing with the problems.[19] Thus, the radical nature of the CODECOM program stemmed from local political pressures as well as from central government policy initiatives.

By the end of the program, the state had disbursed $1,318.5 million (more than 50 million dollars at the 1981 exchange rate) and had recorded $513.4 million of municipio matching contributions in labor and raw materials (Chiapas 1982b). Zinacantán received a total of $11 million (about 440,000 dollars at the 1981 exchange rate, half that by mid-1982) over the three years (1980–82) of the program, and is listed as having contributed $9.8 million in labor and materials.[20] Official records (Chiapas 1982b, 1982c) show more than 100 projects in Zinacantán, ranging from parks and schools to local government buildings, basketball courts, church repairs, and a plant nursery; major projects are listed and illustrated with photos in Chiapas (1982d). Records kept by the secretary of the Zinacantán committee from January 1980 to June 1981[21] show compatible expenses, plus listings for acquisitions of smaller items like sound apparatus and marimbas for hamlets.

CODECOM transformed the office of mayor in Zinacantán, and in most other Indian municipalities in Chiapas. Though the previous mayor of Zinacantán (Domingo Pérez) solicited major public works from the Gonzales Blanco administration, he handled very little cash.[22] Except for $50,000 once received from the state for pipe for a water system, Domingo Pérez estimated (and a PRODESCH official confirmed) his annual budget at about $5,000—enough for some filing cabinets, chairs and tables in the town hall. By contrast, his successor received $7 million in grants during his first year in office, and personally controlled the disbursement of these funds to contractors.

In sum, CODECOM brought two great changes to public-works programs in Chiapas. It increased local autonomy in project selection, and it put local officials in charge of unprecedented amounts of project funds. That problems arose in Zinacantán and other townships receiving CODECOM grants is not surprising. In Chapter 8 we will see that this radical political initiative proved to be a double-edged sword.

Summary

Two kinds of government activity influenced Zinacantán's economy and political life in the 1970's and early 1980's. Direct programs of social and economic intervention increased dramatically during the Echeverría administration (1970–76) and continued in various forms through the López Portillo years (1976–82). In the late 1970's, exploitation of Chiapas' hydroelectric potential and petroleum reserves brought immense investment in infrastructure, thus creating additional pressures that pushed and pulled Zinacantecos out of corn farming and into wage labor, skilled construction trades, civil service jobs, and commerce.

Most of the direct programs in the highlands were coordinated by PRODESCH, a state-level agency with national and United Nations collaboration that was founded in the early 1970's, and continued through various reorganizations and relabelings into the 1980's. The programs involved familiar combinations of activity in communications, health, agriculture, education, and community development. Investment in roads, schools, clinics, and community buildings created well-paid work in the highlands, and provided new foci for hamlet-level and municipio-wide political activity (see Part II). New schools and agricultural extension programs changed the young men who came of age in the late 1970's (see Chapter 4). The roads, in combination with an organization of Indian truck owners, encouraged greater Zinacanteco participation in commerce and transportation. By the end of the 1970's, Chiapas had been transformed from a technological backwater into the producer of about half the hydroelectric energy (one-fifth of all electric energy) generated in Mexico, and a major producer of petroleum. The construction of roads, dams, and public housing in the lowlands outside of Zinacantán, and the demand for services created by the petroleum exploitation, indirectly put even greater pressures on Zinacanteco work patterns.

Given their large scale, either the direct socioeconomic development programs or the energy exploitation activities would have had substantial effects on Zinacanteco life. Together their effects were immense. They not only transformed Zinacanteco work and influenced internal political events; they also created a widespread and genuine prosperity that, I believe, affected the ways Zinacantecos related to each other. Their effects on individual economic lives are explored in the chapter that follows, the political effects are the focus of Part II, and the effects on community social life are analyzed in Part III.

4 /   ECONOMIC CHANGE
IN LIFE HISTORIES

his chapter presents the stories of eleven Nachig men who participated in the economic transformation of the 1970's. The stories provide a perspective that is absent in both the aggregate statistics presented in Chapter 2 and the descriptions of government activity in Chapter 3. They represent the complexity of the changes more forcefully than the two other approaches I have chosen to use, and they provide some insurance against simplistic interpretation of statistical trends and government activities. Zinacantecos, like most people, have minor roles in creating the economic situations they face, but, as these stories show, in their struggle to attain personal goals they become active participants in them.

The experiences of these eleven men duplicate those of many others who lived in Zinacantán and the region during the same period. I selected these men to represent the variety of new occupations and the differing levels of wealth and income within Nachig, and I favored younger men, because I knew relatively few of them from previous field work and because much has already been published on individuals from older generations (see Cancian 1972).[1]

The interviews were done in spring 1984, and the ethnographic present in the accounts refers to that period. Usually I opened the interview by explaining my interest in how work had changed since I first visited Zinacantán in 1960—especially since the time when I studied corn farming in the late 1960's. I said that I would like a storylike account of how he, the man being interviewed, grew up, and how he learned to work.

Most of the accounts are preceded by two introductory paragraphs. The first gives some background on the individual. The second points to some important features of the case, and is also meant to serve in lieu of a conclusion at the end of the case. Seven of the eleven accounts include extensive first-person descriptions. Manuel Sánchez (BB) responded elegantly to my opening general request, and his first-person account is close to a direct translation of what he said at the beginning of our interview. In the other cases, I interpreted, edited, and reshaped the longer, more detailed stories told by the men. Although I sometimes created the sequence and selected the content from a much richer account, I always tried to (1) maintain the storyteller's personal style, and (2) avoid putting a conclusion of mine into his mouth. Where the man's own words did not permit straightforward editing, I constructed the account in the third person. Useful details of the man's experience—for example, Antonio de la Cruz's (AA) comments on living in Tuxtla and Manuel Sánchez's (BB) account of becoming a mason—are summarized in the endnotes for his case. Each case ends with a brief description of the man's situation in later years. Most readers will want to read selectively in both the text and the endnotes.

The stories are ordered by the age of the teller, from 48-year-old Antonio de la Cruz (AA) to 20-year-old Juan Pérez (KK). This order highlights changes in education and occupational choices available to young Zinacantecos in the 1960's, 1970's, and early 1980's.

Antonio de la Cruz (AA), Age 48, Popsicle Seller

Antonio de la Cruz and his wife have four living daughters. The eldest, age 22, is married. Many years ago his family lived on inherited land near his brother's family in Nachig. Then he bought land in Hteklum and lived there for a number of years. By the time he wanted to return to Nachig six years ago, new households established by his brother's sons made the family land very crowded, so Antonio bought his present (18 × 20 m) plot and built a house on it.

Antonio's story illustrates the troubles that befell some of the Zinacantecos who greatly expanded their corn production when roads and government buying programs made expansion practical in the late 1960's. His economic life changed dramatically when he had a very bad crop and stopped farming corn. Now, in 1984, he has begun to plant corn again. Because he has no sons, it will be difficult for him to adopt the mixed strategy that Manuel Sánchez (BB) is now using. Antonio's story also records the path that still leads some men from neighboring Chamula and other highland townships to seek work on coffee plantations on the Pacific coast of Chiapas. The

Antonio de la Cruz while he served as Juez Rural in Nachig, 1988.

job that he held for years in the state capital, Tuxtla, is the kind that has led some Zinacantecos to leave their homes in the highlands permanently.

His Story

My father died when I was small. I didn't know him. I was left herding sheep with my mother. She wouldn't let me go to school. The education committee came and told me to go to school, but she would not give permission, and I obeyed her. That's why I can't read or write or sign my name.

I learned to make milpa [see note 2.1] with my older brother; but there I was, stuck at home. I was afraid when I saw people like you—people who spoke Spanish. So I thought, alone, "I won't learn anything as long as I stay here."

I talked with a couple of other boys who were also kept at home, not allowed to go looking for work. We had heard about Don Erasto Urbina. He had been mayor of San Cristóbal, but he also sent people to work in the coffee plantations. So we went to him and told him we wanted work. He questioned us, asking if we were sure we wanted to go far away, for Zinacantecos never go there. We said yes, and he accepted us for a group that was leaving soon.

We went far away, beyond Tapachula; and after three months I returned home with $350 (I forget what they paid per day then). My mother had been crying because I had disappeared. But I explained to her that I went to work so that I could have money, so that I could buy clothes I needed. She was happier, but made me promise not to go again.

After that I went to Tuxtla [Map 1] to work, and I made milpa. I must have made milpa ten or 12 times, including five or six years with Yermo. We went to Porvenir, San Vicente, and Acala together.[2]

In 1968 I had 22 hectares of milpa, but it didn't rain. I lost a lot. In all I got just seven tons of small grain corn that people didn't want to buy at regular prices. The owner looked at the milpa, and did not charge me rent.

So I stopped making milpa, and I went to Tuxtla to find work. I worked for about three years as a laborer, and then I entered a popsicle factory—where I worked for 14 years.[3] I stopped making milpa all that time. For a while I planted some potatoes in Nachig, but it didn't work out very well.

This February I left the popsicle factory and came home. I seeded milpa on ejido I had borrowed from my brother—one almud at Pih, near Yermo's land. I worked on this from March to June, and I would have had to go back to Tuxtla when the milpa work was done, but then I found this work in reforestation and entered it just a few weeks ago. [This was contract tree-planting work for the government. Antonio was not a formal employee of the government.]

In August 1985 Yermo reported that Antonio was still working on the reforestation project. Apparently work was regular, but the administration was not, and workers often did not receive their pay on time. When I saw him briefly in 1987, he was working as a night watchman on a road-construction job near Nachig. In 1988 he told me that he had had that job for only two two-week periods, for he had been named to office (Juez Rural Suplente; see note 7.1) in Nachig in late 1986, and had to be present to serve during alternate two-week periods during 1987 and 1988. In 1988 he was making milpa during his off periods and looking forward to the end of his term, when he could again seek a regular job.

Manuel Sánchez (BB), Age 47, Farmer and Mason

Manuel Sánchez was born in the municipio of Chamula in 1936, and was raised in Nachig by a Nachig woman. Though some people remember his Chamula origins, he is now a Zinacanteco—in dress, in behavior, and in the expectations of other Zinacantecos. He married a Nachig woman, and they have eight living children. Manuel is the third-ranking curer (shaman) (Vogt 1969: chapter 20) in Nachig, and thus spends some of his time in private and community rituals. He has also passed two religious cargos (see Part II and Chapter 10).

Manuel's story illustrates some of the many changes government activity brought to Zinacantecos. In the early 1970's, he worked on public works and learned to be a mason. Under another government program, he was given most of a new house for his family (see Chapter 7). His semiproletarian mix of corn farming and wage work was dealt a severe blow by the economic crisis of 1982.[4]

His Story

I am an orphan. Six years after I was born I was given away. My father left my mother. He went with another woman. My mother struggled to bring me up for six years. She had a friend, a widow, and I went to live with her. I took her as my grandmother, for I didn't remember that my mother had given me away. So I took my grandmother as my mother. I grew up with her.

I went to school when I was about nine years old. I lasted a year in school. Then I came here to San Cristóbal, and I encountered a woman in the barrio of Santa Lucia. I stayed a year with her. So I left her house when I was 11, and went back to live with my grandmother again.

That's where I learned to talk Spanish a bit. That's where I learned to talk, to pray and cross myself; that's where I learned all sorts of things.

Then, when I was 12, I began to work jointly with a man named José, José López. He had three sons. With him I learned to work in agriculture. I worked with him for two years, from age 12 to 13 to 14.

Then I started to make my milpa alone. I began with half an almud. I began doing the weeding alone, working alone. I did it with nothing, just to have something to eat. So, the harvest came. José had four animals, and he took my harvest to the house for me. From the half almud of seed, the harvest was 42 almudes. So my grandmother was happy. With the corn she produced chickens and pigs, everything. Now she didn't have to buy corn. She had sustenance for her animals. So, that's why she was happy.

Then the next year, when I was 15, they left the milpa they had been working. There was no place for me to work. So, when I was 16, I went with a man from Paste named Manuel Gómez. There I worked for another two years. I was bigger, and I did more. I seeded an almud. The work was hard. It lasted three, four, five weeks. Then they left the land, and I stopped working there too.

So, I started working on the road, at the time that they were paving the road to Comitán. That's when I started to work. When I was 17. So I started to work. Then, a compadre [ritual kinsman] *of mine—now he is my* compadre; *he was my uncle then. He said, "Look son, it's time to start looking for a wife. You are alone. What will happen to you if the lady dies. You will be alone. It's better to look for a wife—so that you will live happily. Now you are earning a bit." "Yes, Uncle," I said, "that's fine."*

Holy Week was near. So I went to him, and brought him a gift, and said, "Look, Uncle, what will be needed?" He said, "We'll prepare it." "But, I won't have enough money," I said; "Will you lend me a bit?" "Surely," he said, "I'll lend you $50." That was something then, it was not like now. That's how I asked for my wife. And, I courted for three years. He helped me marry her.

Thus, I became a man. So, then I continued to go out to work. I stayed six years on road work, six years. Then, being married, I started to work with SAHOP [on roads]. There I worked another three years. Then I came back and joined my father-in-law, for there was a sickness. He gave me a little money so that I could work in the lowlands on corn. We were very poor. We had no house, nothing. We had no children.

So, with money from my father-in-law I made some milpa. But it was not sufficient. Sometimes there was too much heat, wind, and it did not yield. There was a loss.

So, it was not going well, and at that time they invited me to work in other places. That's where I learned to be a mason. I learned to plaster, to lay bricks, to lay blocks, to build with stones.[5] *Thus, I learned, a little at a time, to be a mason. And, now I know how to do it a bit. I work on houses. That's how I got to the present. Now that I am about 47 years old.*

Now I have a son who is 21. I got married when I was 21.

I am still working like that. I make milpa and I do mason work. Thus, I do two things. When it is rainy, and material can't be brought to the jobs, then I go to work on my milpa. That's how I'm passing the time, with poverty. That's how I'm passing the time. That's all. That's how it is. That's how my life is.

In late August 1985, Yermo reported that Manuel had just gone off to the lowlands to seed beans. Except in periods of intense agricultural work like this one, Manuel continued to work as a mason, and sent his sons to do milpa work. In 1988 he was still combining mason's work with farming. His two grown sons were not yet married, and he had large fields.

Juan López (CC), Age 43, Farmer and Laborer

Juan López resides near the Nachig church with his wife and four living children. The eldest, a 17-year-old girl, is followed by an 8-year-old boy and two younger children. Juan was a member of the first Church Committee (about 15 years ago), a member of the School Committee about six years ago, and is presently a member of the Ejido Committee in Nachig.

Juan is the poorest man I interviewed, and, though he spoke Spanish fairly well,[6] the least articulate. Because his account of his work history was fragmented, I have used the third person in all the text below. His story illustrates the work patterns of Zinacanteco semi-proletarians who have not changed much in response to changed economic opportunities and constraints in the region. A few are even less involved in the new work than Juan; they limit themselves to their own farming and wage labor in the fields of other Zinacantecos, a combination that was frequent in the 1960's.

His Story

Juan was born on June 24 [the day of San Juan] about 40 years ago. He spent five years in school and seems to have finished the second grade. When he began school, Nachig had one teacher. When he finished, there were two. His father was poor, so he left school and went to work.

When he married about 20 years ago, he was making milpa in the lowlands. He stayed in one place for five or six years, and was still working there when his eldest daughter was born. Then he worked at Candelaria [Cancian 1972: zone 9] for two years. Both his father and Yermo were working there at the same time [about 1967–68]. After that he didn't farm for a year or two, then took it up again for one year at another place in the lowlands. Then he stopped farming for four years. For the past six years he has been farming exclusively on his ejido land in the highlands. Most years he farms two almudes. The most he did, he says, was two and two-thirds almudes one year at Candelaria.

He has done construction work as a mason's helper repeatedly, but never for very long at a stretch. This year he has done none so far [up to July 31, 1984]. Last year he worked in San Cristóbal for a few weeks, but did not go to Tuxtla because of his duties on the Ejido Committee. The year before that he did go to Tuxtla.

When there was work at Chicoasén, he went there to work. After two weeks he got sick, returned home, and stayed there working on his land. His longest period of work as a laborer seems to have been two months in Chiapa de Corzo during the repairs after the earthquake [1977].

He says that other people work as laborers much more regularly than he does. He does not seem to be rushing about looking for work, and has some income from flowers and apples on his land [0.8 hectares] *in Nachig.*

In 1987 and 1988, Juan was combining corn farming and retailing fruit from one of about 20 stands that had sprung up in Nachig to serve passing motorists. Though he produced some of the fruit, most was bought in San Cristóbal; he was a part-time trader.

Mariano Hernández (DD), Age 42, Vehicle Owner

Mariano Hernández is a rich and well-connected man. His father, who died in 1981, was Yermo's younger brother, and a powerful leader in Nachig. Mariano's younger brother is the Pepsi distributor mentioned in Chapter 2. Mariano and his wife, who is from a large and prosperous family, have seven children. He is the richest man I interviewed, and though a few men are clearly richer, he is one of the richest men in Nachig.

Mariano's upbeat story represents the successful son of a successful man. Despite limited literacy, Mariano used contacts and family resources to profit from economic change. His father was the head of the reforestation program in Nachig in the late 1970's, and thus was the key broker between local people and government resources (in this case jobs). Mariano himself became president of the committee that administered CODECOM funds in all of Zinacantán, and is a leader of and broker for owners of vehicles transporting people in Zinacantán.

His Story

My father sent me to school. I stopped going because I wanted to work—to have money to buy clothes and other things. I went to Tuxtla to get work, and I worked for a few days. All the work was by piece rate, and it was hard. The day's work was hard to finish.

I went home and told my father that I wanted to leave the work. He said, "Fine, come to the lowlands to make milpa with me." We did this for a few years, but then it was hard to get good land.

I went back to work in Tuxtla, and I got a good job—not an office job, of course—a job as a mason's helper. I got $9 a day, which was

Mariano Hernández with his truck, 1988.

good, for they were paying $2.50 in San Cristóbal and in Nachig. I worked a year or more there, and the boss saw that I was doing a good job. He assigned me to overseeing materials, and I worked another year at that—making $15 per day.

Then the contractor finished the work and was moving to another job at a place beyond Tuxtla. My father didn't want me to go so far away, so I returned to making milpa with him for a year. But it didn't work out well. So I went to the state road agency. They always have work. They sent me to Concordia [a project related to the Angostura Dam] *to work, and asked me if I could do mason work. I couldn't, but I knew a little about dynamite work. So I worked with a dynamite crew. I earned $25. I stayed there two years, and I was earning $35 or $40 per day by the time I left.*

Then I looked for my wife. I got married, and my father gave me a piece of land for my house, and I built a house.

I was going to look for work in Tuxtla, but my father-in-law told me to leave that work, and to come to the lowlands and make milpa with him—so I did.

We had good land, at Montehiltik, below Vega de Chachí [Cancian 1972: zone 8]. *The first year I cut three hectares of reforested land, and the harvest was good. I got two tons per almud, and I sold the corn* [to the government] *at the Flores Magón receiving center* [see Cancian 1972] *and brought the money home. The next year I cut another three hectares, and the harvest was good again, and I sold the corn again* [he said the price was $940 per ton].

I found that I had $25,000 saved. So I bought a corn grinding mill, and I left my wife to run it, and went to make milpa again.

After that year of milpa I got bored with milpa, and I talked to somebody at INI about getting corn out of the receiving center and selling it in Nachig. I got a store, a CONASUPO store, with corn and beans and sugar to sell. They didn't pay by the day. They paid a commission. It was $50 for every ton of corn sold. After a while I was selling 16 tons per week. Sometimes during the summer when corn was in short supply I would sell as much as five tons in a day.

Then the reforestation program came to Nachig, and I went to work for it for two years, planting trees. I would work from 6 A.M. to 2 P.M. in reforestation, and then go to the store to sell. By then my son was learning to sell in the store too. And I was paying work-ers to make milpa for me where my father-in-law was working.

I saw that I had $100,000, and thought about what to do—what to buy with it. I had a friend in San Cristóbal who had a microbus, and I asked him how much he wanted for it. He said $200,000, and he took the $100,000 down and $10,000 per month for the rest. All went well, and I finished paying for the microbus.

I had another $200,000 by then, and I wondered what to do with it. By then I was driving. I knew how to do that work. I went to the Ford agency and asked how much it would be for the vehicle I now have. They said it would be a million pesos [it turned out to be $645,000 plus interest]. They took $200,000 down, and I got to-gether a group of people to sign as security for the loan—and paid it off at $35,000 per month.

Now my sons drive. Both of them finished sixth grade. They were both born during Holy Week. The older one will be 18 next year, and the younger one will be 16. When the older one left school, he learned to drive. It's not like it was before. He didn't do agricultural work. He had an accident driving, but it wasn't his fault. It was the other driver's fault. We fixed the microbus and continued to work with it.

Mariano was named Head of the Church Committee (see Chap-ter 7) for the 1986 to 1988 term, and had to spend a part of most days in Hteklum. In summer 1988 he, with his sons, was still in trans-portation. By then he had a microbus and a 3-ton truck. One of his sons worked as a driver for his brother.

Mariano López (EE), Age 35, Mason

In 1972 Mariano moved to Nachig from Elanvo (Map 2). At the time he was courting his wife, and working in Concordia in the lowlands. He said it was scary to leave Elanvo at midnight or 1 A.M. to come to the road in Nachig where he found transport to work each Monday. He talked to his mother and she was not happy about moving. He asked his prospective wife, and she said yes. His father-in-law wanted to come too. They bought a piece of land together, and at first lived together—where his father-in-law's house now stands on the road to Paste near the Pan American Highway. Later, Mariano bought the land across the street, built a small house, and started work on his present house. In 1980 there was a chance to buy more land, and he told his brother, who had married in 1978 and was still in Elanvo. His brother wanted to come and they bought the land together. They support their widowed mother. She lives with Mariano sometimes, and sometimes in Elanvo with her dead husband's younger sister. Mariano and his wife have a son, nine, a daughter, seven, and a son, four. Another son died as a baby two years ago.

Mariano's story illustrates a popular path to economic success during the years of expansion brought by government construction projects, and the anecdotes with which he embellished his account of skills acquired and jobs held show the way the work is embedded in social relations inside and outside of Zinacantán. The onerous parts of his work life changed dramatically—from tending mules that hauled coffee through the mud from distant plantations during his youth to riding small planes through storms to distant construction sites in recent years. Much of what Mariano says documents the difficulties and dangers many Zinacantecos face when they leave home to work.

His Story

First I was a traveler, a muleteer. We went to Yahalón and places like that to get coffee. It took a week, and it was raining and muddy. You earned $40 per muleload. My father had ten mules, but sometimes they could take only eight loads. That's how it was long ago. I suffered a lot.

When my father died I was about ten. I went with my uncle. When the work with the mules was done we went to the lowlands. We planted corn, and beans, and squash, and chile. We had a shack there, so the suffering wasn't so bad. The suffering in the lowlands is the food. It's hard tortillas, and vegetables.

I studied for one year in school. That's when my father died, so there was no one to maintain me in school. I didn't learn Spanish there. My uncle taught me. He would not talk to me in our language, he would talk to me in Spanish. Then he died [about 1975].

Mariano López in work clothes, 1984.

About when I was looking for my wife the mules died, so I started working on construction. That was about 15 years ago.

First I worked on the road—when they built the road to Paste. It was 1970. At first I was just digging, then they saw that I worked well, and they put me on breaking stone for a month. Doing that your hands swelled from the blasts, but I lasted for a month. Then they called me and put me on leveling the road. And then, later, when we were working on the road to Elanvo, I worked on construction of bridges.

In 1972 I was working as a gang boss in Chamula, and the work ended. They wanted to take me to work far away, but I didn't want to go. So I went to work as a mason's helper in Tuxtla, and then in Concordia for the CFE [that built the nearby dam at Angostura]. *This is when I got my wife.*

When they were building the new clinic near the gas station in San Cristóbal, I went there to work as a laborer, and earned $35 per day. After a while I asked a mason to teach me the work, and he did. I worked there ten months, and by the end I was doing mason's work, but they were still paying me as a laborer.

After the work on the clinic I went to Tuxtla. I got only work on sidewalks. They were paying only $40 per day, and there was no place to sleep. I heard that there was work at Chicoasén at better pay, and I thought about going there.

I was sleeping in a covered area near the market, and I ate some raw tomatoes that gave me diarrhea. There I was, stuck. There was no toilet around. So I went out into an open area, behind a post, on a pile of dirt. The cops came, and asked me what I was doing, and

I explained. I said, look, take all my money, but don't take me to jail. So they took all I had, $30, and let me go.

That night I left for Chicoasén. I had heard that the truck left at 2 A.M. I got myself in a corner of a dump truck, and when the gang boss said that only people who already had jobs could go, I said nothing.

When we got there I went to the supervisor and asked for a job. He said his jobs were all full. He needed no one. Then he called the gang boss and bawled him out. The gang boss said, "I told them. He probably didn't understand." I said, "I didn't understand what he said. I'm an Indian."

I told the supervisor I had no money and nowhere to go, and I hung around bothering the poor man. At 10 A.M. I had a job, and I worked there a year and a half in 1974 and 1975. At first I worked as a mason's helper, but then as a mason, earning $64 per day, then $85, $90, and finally $100. First I worked on the church at Nueva Usumacinta [a relocated town that was being moved out of the area to be flooded by the dam]. Then I moved to other relocated towns in the same area: Juy Juy and then Carmelo.

By that time it was easy to get work, and I didn't have to suffer as much.

Then I went to Veracruz to work for about three months. One of the engineers from Chicoasén took me. I worked on an engineer's house. After that I returned and worked in Chiapa de Corzo for six months, on the reconstruction after the earthquake. That was 1977. Then I went back to Veracruz for a year and a half, working on houses for gringos at Laguna Farallón. We built nice houses, and they liked them. It was a big lake by the sea, like Navenchauc, but much bigger.

In 1979 I got some contracts putting up small houses in Tuxtla, and a guy found me on the job and had me build a house for him. I was dumb, and told him that I was earning $100 per day. It took me six months to finish his two-story house, and then I built a 14.5-m well for his compadre. After that I worked at Colonia INFONAVIT Grijalva [a very large government housing development] for six months.

IMSS-COPLAMAR was building clinics in communities, so I went to Zequentic and asked the foreman, Alfonso, for a job. He said sure, and put me to work. I told him I preferred to work by piece-work, and that was fine with him. I was earning $170 per day, and I started at 7 A.M. and would be done by about 11 A.M.

They needed people to build clinics in other places, and asked me if I could do a clinic alone. I said, sure, but it will be far from home, so I want to get paid a bit more. They gave me $200, and I went to San Andrés and did a clinic.

Then I was taken to Paste to install some factory-made roof panels. I could see that the masons had put the bolts in the wrong place when they poured the concrete, so, right in front of the engineer, I told them to take the work down and change them. They got pissed, especially because I just came in from outside and started to order them around. But the engineer was pleased with my work, and asked if I wanted to go to another place.

First we went to the Tuxtla office, where he showed pictures of the projects I had completed (for they always kept pictures of the projects); then we went to the Soyaló-Bochil areas to build clinics. Alfonso was there too, and he got mad because I got a clinic right on the road, and he was assigned to one in the middle of nowhere. He was drinking a lot, and I wasn't. I just told him that it was luck, that we'd have to see how it came out the next time.

Then I was sent to Alvaro Obregón to build a clinic, and the work pretty much ended. I worked for another month. They gave me work as part of an inspection team. I went around with a metal tape-measure ruler and checked work done by others. It was not all good, and I had to see that it was corrected.

I didn't like that work very much. It was rainy a lot, and we had to go many places by airplane. My wife and my mother told me to quit. They said the plane might crash. So I quit and went back to work at INFONAVIT Grijalva. I worked there for all of 1981.

In 1982 I went to work in Villahermosa for two months. I needed work done on my teeth, and people said it was cheaper there. I earned $600 per day, and spent $5,000 for my teeth, and still brought some money home. Then they came from San Cristóbal to ask me if I wanted to work on a project there. It was Architect Fernando and Don Ticio. I don't know why they came to me, but I had built a bath for one of them before.

I worked for them for ten months and built five houses. When I started, the first house had been badly built, and they wanted me to fix that. I left it for last. I built the other four right and left the repairs for last.

I quit there on December 25, for I had my cargo[7] in Nachig during 1983. I received it the twenty-ninth of December of 1982 and turned it over to my replacement on the twenty-ninth of December of 1983. During the year I couldn't work much. I worked if there was work around Nachig, but I couldn't go to Tuxtla. There always seemed to be something to do for the cargo: sweeping the church, looking for musicians or other helpers, changing flowers every 15 *days. And then, we made four visits to other fiestas with the Virgin: first to San Sebastián, then to Zequentic, then the Fiesta of San Lorenzo, and finally the Fiesta of Guadalupe in Navenchauc.*

On January 2 of this year I started working in Tuxtla. I went to look for a job, and they gave me one right away. I asked the Sacristans to schedule the dismantling of the altar from my cargo for a Sunday, so it did not interfere with my work in Tuxtla.

Now I'm on vacation, for a week or two, whatever I want. I get vacation because I have been working for six months. I get one week or two, and the same at the end of the year. During the vacation the pay is the minimum salary of $700 per day. When I'm working I usually get overtime, so I earn $1,200 or $1,500 per day.

[Mariano now works as a supervisor of masons and spends little time working with his hands. He says that he had not missed a day since the beginning of the year. In Tuxtla he shares a room provided by the company.]

In October 1984, Mariano left his job in Tuxtla and sought work in nearby San Cristóbal, so that he could commute from home to work on a daily basis. He was lonely in Tuxtla, he said. He felt abandoned. His family hardly knew him, for he returned on Saturday afternoon and left on Monday morning. Besides, it was expensive in Tuxtla—eating out, going to the movies to pass the time, and sometimes drinking up a lot of money. Now, he said, he is just home after work. When he was interviewed again in August 1985, Mariano was earning $1,200 per day in wages working on private house construction in San Cristóbal, and thought he could be earning $2,500 in Tuxtla.

Mariano seeded four almudes of corn in 1985. "It is better not to buy corn," he said. Though he went to the location and worked some, he said he really can't do that kind of work—that he does not handle a machete well. He has hired "campesinos" (peasants) to do the work, buying corn to pay those who do not want a cash wage. He says daily wages in the temperate zone, where his land is located, are currently $500 or one almud ($560 at current market prices) and meals.

In July 1988 Mariano was working as a mason in San Cristóbal.

Antonio Méndez (FF), Age 30, Truck Driver and Flower Grower

Antonio Méndez lives in a modern, three-room house on a very small plot (11 × 15 m) that he purchased by the side of the highway.

His family land is far from the road, so he and his two brothers live on separate, purchased plots near the road. His older brother is a carpenter, and his younger brother (José II; see below) runs a store. Antonio and his wife have three daughters. His wife's father owns a truck.

Antonio's story illustrates the radically different set of alternatives presented to Zinacantecos who came to adulthood in the early 1970's. With a little more schooling, and many more wage-work opportunities, Antonio soon found himself with no cornfields. Only recently, like Mariano EE, did he begin to plant corn again. Antonio's story also illustrates the risks involved in taking government and other loans for investment in new types of projects.

His Story

Antonio was born June 30, 1954. He completed fourth grade in Nachig about 1968, when there was no fifth or sixth grade.

His father, a corn farmer who died in 1981, taught him to work. He worked in the lowlands with his father. Then, in 1971, he worked on the road from Nachig to Zinacantán [Antonio kept documents like pay slips and union cards that help date his jobs]. *In 1976 he worked at Chicoasén for about a year. He also worked on construction in many other places, he says, but never for very long in one place. Around 1977 he sold flowers in the Tuxtla market for about a year.*

Antonio Méndez, 1984.

Then he worked as an assistant on a truck, and learned to drive. He began as a driver in 1978 when his father-in-law bought a truck, and most of his work as a truck driver was for his father-in-law. He also drove a microbus for someone else for a year [1981]. With the truck he went as far as Villahermosa, Tapachula, and Oaxaca, and once to Mexico City. He earned $3,000 per month, free and clear. Now drivers earn $15,000 per month, plus meals.

Antonio had one hectare of corn seeded in the lowlands in 1984, but he did not actually work on it, or even always go to supervise work. His father-in-law employed a Chamula foreman, who recruited and supervised laborers, and Antonio's fields were managed under the same arrangement. His father-in-law just goes to the lowlands to drop off his laborers. Though Antonio did not have a milpa in 1981, 1982, and 1983 while working as a truck driver, he did have milpa before that, and he planned to seed two hectares in 1985.

In mid-1983 Antonio quit as a driver and began to construct a greenhouse for producing flowers. The construction of the greenhouse is described in Chapter 3. Although many people in the ceremonial center, and in the nearby hamlet of Patosil, seem to have succeeded under the greenhouse program, Antonio did not. Whether, like Antonio de la Cruz (AA), he will work for others for many years remains to be seen. His father-in-law's wealth may help him start again.

In August 1985 Antonio was working as a microbus driver, and various people told me that he was hard to find at home and owed many people money. In July 1988 he was working as a truck driver, and, according to both Yermo and his brother José II, he was often hard to find in Nachig.

José Gómez (GG), Age 29, Laborer

José Gómez grew up an "orphan." His father and mother separated when he was about eight. He, his younger sister and brother, and his mother left his father's house in an adjoining hamlet and returned to Nachig, where they settled on his mother's land. First they borrowed a house on an adjacent plot, and then they built their own house. In the early 1970's he built his present ample adobe-brick, tile-roofed house on his mother's land. They all lived there, and his wife joined them when he married in 1976. His mother died in 1977. When his sister married about five years ago, she moved away for some months, then she asked for land to build a house near his and he gave it. Last year his brother found a wife and built the third house in the yard. He now lives with his wife in the house he built. The first of their two sons was born in November 1977.

José's path is different from Antonio Méndez's (FF). With less schooling and fewer family resources, José has become a fully proletarianized semiskilled laborer. While his land, both on his houseplot and away from it, adds something to his income, his family's survival depends almost completely on his construction work.[8] The major household expenses he lists—corn, wood, and curing (health)—are listed as most important by others as well.[9]

His Story

My mother's younger brother took me to the lowlands and taught me to work. We had milpas at Las Limas, San Vicente, El Rosario, and places like that. I went to school, but there was no one to maintain me. My mother suffered a lot getting food for us. I missed a lot of school when I went to the lowlands; when I came back I didn't know what was going on. I left after three years, when I was in the second grade. Now I read and write some Spanish. Tzotzil is hard to write. Sometimes I practice in Tuxtla after work.

When I left school I went directly to work on the road to Paste [about 1971]. I worked on it until it reached Paste, and then I worked some on the road from Nachig to Hteklum. My uncle [MoSisHu, Mariano DD's father] advised me to save my money and to build a house. After those jobs I built the house where I now live.

Then I went to Tuxtla to work for some months; then to Concordia, when they were moving the town out of the way of the flooding from the Angostura Dam. After that I rested some and went to work at Chicoasén for a year. First I was a plain laborer. Then they saw that I arrived regularly and didn't drink, so I got a helper's job in the tunnel. I learned to work with reinforcing steel rods. In the end they gave me a better job. I put the bags of cement into the mixer—to go with the sand and gravel that arrived on a belt.

I left because the work was dangerous, especially the ride there on the curvy road. A lot of people were hurt, and I told my mother about the accidents. She got worried, and told me not to go, for who would maintain her if I got killed. I had some money so I went to make milpa in Villa Flores, then two years in another place. My first son was born when I worked at Villa Flores.

Then I went to work in San Cristóbal on the INFONAVIT project. We built 91 houses and I worked there eight months. The project was done and the foreman was transferred to Tuxtla. I went with

A government-sponsored housing project under construction, Tuxtla Gutiérrez, 1988.

him, and I have worked for him three years straight in Tuxtla [José did not lack work in 1983]. *Now he puts me to work on steel reinforcing rods most of the time. I get $1,000 a day* [at this time day laborers got $600, and helpers for masons working by contract got $800 and were expected to work longer and harder than day laborers]. *The company, Constructura Calpan, has built more than a thousand houses in Tuxtla.*

In August 1985 José had a regular job on a government housing construction project in Tuxtla. In 1988 he was still doing semi-skilled construction labor.

Francisco Pérez (HH), Age 29, Farmer, Trader . . .

Francisco Pérez, the older of Yermo's two sons, is a prosperous and active young man. He has been married to the daughter of a rich man for more than nine years, lives in a house that is attached to Yermo's, and has four living children. He worked with me on several occasions between 1981 and 1984; thus his story is not strictly comparable with others in this chapter.

His story is included here to illustrate the mixed strategy that some Zinacantecos follow. Francisco is very different from Mariano

López (EE), the mason, and José Gómez (GG), the laborer, both described above. They have good jobs that, they say, result from their records of reliability. Francisco does not take jobs that tie him down. When I interviewed him (July 1984) he was active in corn farming, and in vegetable and fruit production, as well as in chicken raising, and had recently done some trading of corn and beans and some mason work.[10] In the last two years, he said, he had worked as a mason only in the highlands (not in Tuxtla) and had done more trading of corn and beans. At the time of the interview he was thinking of taking a mason's job in another hamlet for a couple of weeks, for he could not get corn and beans at a price that made trading attractive. His wife sometimes helps him in retailing in the San Cristóbal market, and takes an important role in the new chicken enterprise.

His Story

I stayed in school four years, and did three grades. There were not more advanced grades at the time. Then my father came and talked with the teacher, and I left school. I had learned to read and write.

Then, for many years, I made milpa with my father. After a while I started looking for a wife. My father and I made milpa and looked for work where they were paying good wages. Then I learned to be a mason, and we went to work at Chicoasén. The foreman there was good. He let me work even though I wasn't a very good mason then. I stopped working at Chicoasén four or five months before I got married. At that time I gave my earnings to my father and he handled all the money. He gave me money for clothes and other expenses when I needed it.

I was married with both a church and a civil ceremony. After three years of living with my parents, we had one child. I asked to set up a separate household, and my father was very good about it. We had 40 bags full of corn, and he gave me 20 of them, and some money and some beans. We also got a house [next to his father's] and dishes and pots to set up our kitchen.

So I started making milpa alone. In order to get ahead faster I went with my father-in-law, for he knows more Spanish and he knew where there was good land. I seeded 11 hectares, and it was going well, but then the winds came and ruined most of it. I barely got four hectares of decent crop. I also seeded beans, but that didn't work out too well. They got yellow.

That's when I learned to trade in corn and beans. Now I do some trading, and some mason work, and I have a milpa on my ejido land. Also, I fattened some chickens for sale.

Francisco Pérez, 1984.

Late in 1984 when there was demand for flagstone to pave the churchyard in Hteklum, Francisco began producing it from a quarry near Nachig. He found there was a good market for flagstone outside Zinacantán, and, by August 1985, he had cut back on many other activities (including chicken production) to concentrate on flagstone.

In June 1988, he moved to his land across the Pan American Highway from his father's house, so that he could have more space for his chicken and rabbit production. Though he still sold some flagstone, the quarry's future was uncertain, for a group of Nachig men had just bought the land where it was located, and individual plots had not yet been allocated. Francisco was also buying Zinacanteco clothes woven by Nachig women and taking them to Tuxtla to sell at wholesale for the tourist trade. And he was almost ready to have his fruit trees grafted with plums.

José Méndez (II), Age 26, Storekeeper, Government Employee

José Méndez, Antonio FF's younger brother, was born February 5, 1958. José was the first man I interviewed in May 1984. When I approached him with Yermo, who introduced me, he startled me by appearing from his house dressed completely in Ladino clothes, quickly agreeing to be interviewed, and then pulling a date book out of his shirt pocket to check his commitments and eventually to re-

José Méndez, 1984.

cord our date some days later in San Cristóbal. As part of the interview, he gave a list of dates for major events in his life in recent years.[11]

His Story

His parents separated when he was small. They beat him a lot before they separated, his siblings said. He grew up with his older sister, but felt awkward in her home, for he could not order her to take care of him. Once, he left Nachig to seek another life in Tuxtla, but while he was there he dreamt that he was called back to Zinacantán by the Mayores [the messengers of the cargoholders in Hteklum], *and he awoke desperate to be home again. Now he would like to travel, but he would always come back to Nachig.*

When he was about 20 he was married to [lived with] *a woman for about four months, but it did not work out. She did not obey him, so he left her. One day, when he was at PRODESCH, he met his present wife* [who was and is a SARH employee, the only female government employee in Nachig].[12]

He had a series of government jobs [see the chronology in note 4.11] *and resigned from the last one early in 1982, after he had entered as Mayordomo in Nachig, for he could not carry the job and the cargo at the same time. When he finished the cargo in December 1982, he was unemployed. In April 1983 he took a week-long*

*course on management of CONASUPO-COPLAMAR stores. Eighteen
people started the course. He was among the 13 who finished, but
there were only eight jobs available for the graduates—and his application was turned down because he did not prove that he completed military service* [local, part-time, universal training]. *In May
1984 the job paid $29,000 per month plus per-diem expenses when
traveling. In October 1983 he set up the private store that he now
runs.*[13] *He also gives injections of medicines every afternoon to
those who want them* [a skill learned in connection with his IMSS-
COPLAMAR job].

*José lives in a small house attached to his store with his wife and
son. Two previous children, a son and a daughter, died as infants.*

In 1985 José was still operating his store. He had, after May 1984,
a brief term as a Sacristan in Nachig, but left the post in the midst
of a controversy about his behavior. By 1987 he had built a multiple-
room cinder-block house with a concrete slab roof, still ran a store,
and was seeking a permanent government job. In 1987–88 he worked
some months as a substitute teacher, but said that he got impatient
with the children, and didn't want a permanent teaching job. He
hoped that in December he would get a permanent job at SARH,
where his wife still worked. Like many other Nachig people (about
20 in summer 1988), he and his wife also retailed fruit (often purchased from other townships) from a stand on the highway in front
of their house.

Antonio Lopez (JJ), Age 25, Government Employee

Antonio is a young widower. He married Yermo's daughter in June
1981, and she died of fever while pregnant in March 1982. She had
completed four years of school in Nachig, and was working there as
a preschool teacher. Antonio now lives alone in a house he built a
few feet from his parents' house. His mother feeds and cares for him,
and he spends a few nights each week sleeping where he works.

He is a full-time employee of the SARH reforestation program, and
is included here to represent Zinacantecos who are direct-hire government employees—in contrast with those working for government contractors, like Antonio de la Cruz (AA), José Gómez (GG),
and others who do construction work.

His Story

*I studied in Nachig. I was one of the 16 members of the first class
to graduate from primary school* [sixth grade] *in Nachig. It took me*

eight years of study, and I was 17 when I graduated in June 1976.

The next year I started secondary school in San Cristóbal on Saturdays and Sundays, but after I began working in the reforestation program in March 1977, it was too hard to keep up. So, I got a completion certificate for the first year, and quit.

Three others (all young men) from the first graduating class also went to San Cristóbal to study. Two are now teachers in Bochil, and the other, the son of Antonio López,[14] *the corn trader who is a Sacristan in Nachig now, is in law school in San Cristóbal. His father gives him money. He doesn't come to Nachig much.*

I helped my father with his milpa during school vacations. Once I worked on construction in San Cristóbal for two weeks, in 1975 I think, from 6 A.M. to 6 P.M. for $24 per day. It was hard. And I went to Chicoasén to work on house construction twice during vacations.

I got my job on the reforestation program by asking José Hernández [father of Mariano DD]. *There are 33 Nachig people working at the nursery at Rancho Nuevo* [many too young to be included in Table 2.5], *35 or 40 Navenchauc people (including two from Apaz), and three from Chiquinibalbo. No other Zinacantecos work there, but there are people from San Cristóbal, Chamula, and Comitán. There are 123 or 124 people in all. Now there are no Nachig bosses. José Hernández died. His son* [the Pepsi distributor] *quit, and so did his son-in-law* [the owner of the truck that delivers construction workers to Tuxtla on Monday morning].

At first we had to work hard—when we were doing reforestation in Nachig—but now most of the reforestation is done. I work in the nursery, from 7 A.M. to 2 P.M., and the work is not very hard. We water, and transplant, and sometimes go out and collect seeds in the woods. Things like that. I go to Rancho Nuevo on Monday morning and return to Nachig on Wednesday. Then I go Thursday morning and return Friday. The one-way fare is $90.

For four or five years I signed annual contracts, but now I am permanent.[15] *There are rumors that the nursery will be closed, and that they will send us to Pichucalco or Villa Flores or Comitán. If there are no other opportunities, I'll have to go. It's a good job.*

Antonio speaks about his job in a somewhat melancholy, discouraged way. "There is nothing more," he says. "There is no way to advance." Many 25-year-old Zinacantecos—especially those, like Antonio, from prosperous intact families who can help them—are seeking opportunities to improve their economic situation. At present Antonio feels that his job is so good that he can't do better; and that seems to be discouraging, at least sometimes.

In August 1985 Antonio was still working in the reforestation program. His nominal semimonthly pay had doubled to $18,000. In July
1988 he was still with the reforestation program. In January 1988 he
had remarried, and stayed in his house, near that of his parents.

Juan Pérez (KK), Age 20, Mason and Farmer

Juan Pérez is Yermo's younger son. He married four years ago and
has two sons. He and his family live jointly with his parents. He
farms jointly with his father and gives his income as a mason to his
father, holding back a bit for personal expenses when he needs it.

Juan's story demonstrates the difficulty of simple classification of
individuals. He is "traditional" in living jointly with his father, yet
literate and skilled in non-farming work. Clearly semi-proletarian
in that he depends on both farming and wages to an important degree, he is also very active as a contractor of the labor of others in
both agriculture and construction. Juan is from an elite family and
appears headed for elite status, at least in the economic sense. But
many features of his adaptation look like those of Manuel Sánchez
(BB), who is much older, and much poorer. Whereas Manuel is a
curer, Juan is a Catechist (see Chapter 7).

His Story

Juan finished primary school in Nachig in 1979, and attended sec-
ondary school in San Cristóbal on weekends for a couple of months,
but he found that he couldn't manage it on a part-time basis. So he
quit to dedicate himself to work.

He worked in Chicoasén as his father's laborer [Yermo worked as
a mason], *seeing how the work was done. Then he worked for two*
more years in Tuxtla learning to be a mason. When he could work
alone he made trips to Villahermosa to work as a mason. The trips
lasted a month or two each. The last one ended just before the erup-
tion of the Chichonal volcano in April 1982.

For a while he was a contractor on the big Tuxtla housing project.
He got $16,000 per house from the general contractor and recruited
mason contractors to whom he paid $14,000 per house. He had
seven or eight masons working for him and made $7,000 to $8,000
per week during that period. Then they changed the system so that
engineers who work for the general contractor deal directly with
the working mason contractors.

In summer 1983 there were no big construction jobs in Tuxtla, so
Juan concentrated on milpa work with his father. The following

October he took up flower trading as a regular occupation. The only
work available in Tuxtla was on private projects that paid $500 to
a mason working a 7-to-5 day.

When he traded flowers, Juan would leave Nachig about 4 A.M.
arrive at the San Cristóbal market before 5, buy flowers [mostly
from Chamulas], *leave for Tuxtla by truck about 7 : 30, arrive at the*
Tuxtla market about 9, sell his flowers, and return to Nachig in the
afternoon. Some days, he said, he made only expenses, or $300 or
$400. On good days he was able to make $2,000 to $3,000.

Early in 1984 he stopped the flower trading and got a job on the
INFONAVIT *Grijalva project in Tuxtla. As a mason contractor* [i.e.,
doing individual houses on a piecework basis] *he earned $27,000 per*
house. He paid his regular laborer $4,000 for six 7-to-4 days per
week. [The same man earns $600 per 7-to-3 day working for others
when Juan is busy with his milpa.] *Because the work on a standard*
6 × 11 m house takes 10 to 12 days for Juan and his laborer, Juan
can earn considerably more than the $1,000 paid daily to masons
who work from 7 to 3 for daily wages.[16]

When he was interviewed [May 30, 1984] *he had taken a few days*
off to work with his father on their milpa.

Before the 1985 cornfields were seeded, Juan asked his father for
separate land, land he could work independently. Yermo gave him
half of their joint land, and Juan paid workers to farm for him, while
he continued to work as a mason in Tuxtla. In 1986 Juan tried to sell
some marijuana[17] for a Zinacanteco who produced it. The contacts
he made in San Cristóbal were government agents, and in November
Juan was jailed in Tuxtla for a seven-year term. According to Yermo,
the jail, which is only for drug offenders, is a large enclosed area
within which many prisoners have their own houses. Families may
visit and stay overnight, and Juan, like some other prisoners, has his
own one-room house, which he bought from a man who was released. In summer 1988, Yermo expected Juan to be released in early
1990, after serving half the seven-year term.

5 / IMPLICATIONS OF
ECONOMIC CHANGE

The changes described above are familiar. Many third-world populations have gone from production for household use to monetized economic life, from subsistence to commercial agriculture, from peasant to proletarian work roles. Above I have documented these changes in Zinacantán; below I want to make a bridge to broader concerns by discussing some issues commonly associated with this kind of change: (1) proletarianization; (2) income and income distribution, monetization, and standard of living; and (3) life-cycle and generation effects. Then I will highlight the issues carried forward to Parts II and III.

This discussion concentrates on the period before the economic crisis of 1982. The crisis led to the cancellation of many government projects and sidetracked many of the economic trends described in Chapters 2, 3, and 4. As the shock of 1982 became the "permanent crisis" of the mid-1980's, government programs again grew to substantial levels. In the period covered by this study they never regained the dominant economic role they had in the 1970's.

Proletarianization

In situations like the one studied here, men (families) who have lived mostly from agricultural production and/or from pre-capitalist craft production often become dependent on wage work (Cancian 1989). They sell their labor; i.e., they are proletarianized.

From the aggregate point of view, these changes are almost always a matter of degree: some families depend on wage work, others do not. Where a population is almost completely proletarianized, the

TABLE 5.1

Occupations by Source of Income, Nachig, 1983[a]

	N	Percent of total	Second occupation None	Corn	Other
Those who earn wages					
Laborer	105	31.9%	7.0%	23.4%	1.5%
Mason	15	4.6	2.4	1.8	0.3
Government employee	15	4.6	3.6	—	0.9
Vehicle driver	10	3.0	3.0	—	—
TOTAL	145	44.1%	16.1%	25.2%	2.7%
Those who do not earn wages					
Corn farmer	75	22.8	22.8	—	—
Trader	70	21.3	9.4	7.0	4.9
Vehicle owner	22	6.7	3.6	0.6	2.4
Other[b]	17	5.2	2.4	1.2	1.5
TOTAL	184	56.0%	38.3%	8.8%	8.8%
GRAND TOTAL	329	100.0%	54.4%	34.0%	11.6%

[a] Calculated from Table 2.4. Except for the N column, cells contain percentages of the total (329) cases. Each case is 0.3%.
[b] Includes rows 2, 3, and 14–17 in Table 2.4.

case is relatively clear and simple. For example, the people of Chamula, the municipio adjoining Zinacantán, had long been land-poor and dependent on agricultural labor and craft production (Pozas 1959; G. A. Collier 1975; Wasserstrom 1980, 1983), and Wasserstrom (1983: 200ff.) found a very heavy concentration of proletarians in Chamula's population in the 1970's.

Zinacantán is one of the less simple cases. The vast majority of Nachig men were not proletarians in 1983: only 16 percent earned wages and had no other work (Table 5.1). Among the wage earners, laborers (men like José GG) were the most completely proletarian. Masons usually depended on wages, but sometimes worked by contract (Mariano EE, Juan KK). Many drivers had incentive arrangements that supplemented their wages, and some had opportunities to skim something from the fares they collected. Government workers had salaries and a security of employment that set them apart from most wage workers (Antonio JJ). In sum, even the wage earners had a variety of relations to the source of their wages.

While most Zinacantecos did not become full-time wage workers, on the whole they became much more dependent on the sale of their labor. Like other Latin American peasants, many of them became "semiproletarians" in the 1970's. While peasants usually depend mostly on their own production, and proletarians usually depend mostly on the sale of their labor, semiproletarians are those who cannot survive without substantial efforts in both farming and wage work. Table 5.1 shows that about 25 percent of Nachig men mixed wage labor and corn farming.

Students of Latin American peasantry (de Janvry 1981; Pozas and Pozas 1971) have found the concept "semiproletarian" useful in theories relating part-time rural labor migrants to the development of urban capitalism. In these theories semiproletarians are seen as labor that is reproduced and maintained in the countryside without cost to the employer. This interpretation points to important features of the rural-urban relationship and is very useful in understanding the functioning of the larger system that includes rural people.

The concept is less well developed when the focus is behavior in the rural setting, as contrasted with the regional or national political economy (Cancian 1989). Semiproletarians do not simply represent a midpoint on a continuum from peasant to proletarian. Given the mixed nature of their adaptation, it is not clear which of their multiple roles will pattern their behavior when they are in a rural setting.

In sum, the direction of change is clear. Zinacantecos in Nachig in 1983 were much more proletarianized than they had been two decades before. But they were not very proletarianized by absolute standards or in comparison with other highland Chiapas populations like the Chamulas. The majority of Nachig men who worked for wages in 1983 were semiproletarians who combined construction work with corn farming to support their families. The ambiguous status of semiproletarians in the rural social structure complicates analysis: it is not clear whether their behavior will be (1) unique to semiproletarians, (2) like that of proletarians, or (3) like that of peasants. I will return to these issues in Part III.

Income and Income Distribution, Monetization, and Standard of Living

The economic transformation described in Chapters 2, 3, and 4 raises questions about the quantity, distribution, and kind of Zinacanteco income and wealth.[1] Have income and income distribution in Zinacantán been changed by the new occupational structure? Have those at the bottom of the economic ladder been impoverished (immiserated) by changes that drove them out of farming and into the labor market? How has the change from corn to cash income changed everyday life? Are Zinacantecos in general better or worse off?

The real income of wage workers increased about 20 percent between the early 1960's and the early 1980's. While the real increase in cash wages is hard to measure because of inflation, Zinacantecos often paid agricultural workers in kind (i.e., in corn). In the early 1960's these workers earned about five almudes per week (Cancian 1972: 130); by 1980 they earned at least six almudes per week. This increase is roughly comparable to the national real per-capita income increase of 25 percent during the boom years reported by Wyman (1983a: 4).[2] Workers who traveled to the lowlands to work in fields were (over the entire period) customarily provided with meals and transport costs as well as cash or corn wages.

Cash wages for unskilled construction work were usually much higher than cash agricultural wages in the 1980's. Before the economic crisis of 1982 they were usually about twice agricultural wages. The ratio decreased to about 1.5 to 1 in 1983, 1984, and 1985.[3] It is hard to tell if unskilled construction workers cleared more than agricultural workers, whose transport and maintenance were paid, but many Zinacantecos seemed to prefer construction labor to agricultural labor. In the early 1980's, construction labor was easy to get and provided more continuous employment than agricultural labor.[4]

The gap between richer and poorer Zinacantecos increased between the 1960's and the 1980's. The rich benefited from opportunities in transport that did not exist in the 1960's. Until the 1970's, when the expanding economy and government programs (Chapter 3) opened trucking to Zinacantecos, Ladinos had controlled all aspects of motorized transport. The few Nachig men who succeeded in purchasing, operating, and paying for more than one vehicle in the 1970's probably became richer than any Zinacanteco in the 1960's. At the same time, some households (e.g., those of women living alone) with no direct access to the cash economy were probably worse off in absolute terms.

Documentation of the changed income distribution is hard to find—I have no good measures of absolute income and wealth for samples of Zinacantecos over time—but many changes were obvious. While multiroomed adobe houses were rare in the 1960's, multiroomed masonry houses equipped with television sets were not unusual in the 1980's. At the other end of the scale, while fewer families lived in wattle-and-daub houses, they were not rare in the 1980's. Among the rich, the trucks themselves represented wealth with few if any parallels in the 1960's, and the many men with formal-sector skilled construction jobs (José GG, Mariano EE) or civil-service jobs (Antonio JJ) had secure, high income streams that had few counterparts in the 1960's.[5]

Differences based on type of work also contributed to social differentiation. They changed the ways Zinacantecos related to each other. For example, rich men, who had been buyers of labor in the 1960's, became sellers of transport in the 1980's. Rich men in corn farming abandoned the old norm of hoeing along with workers in the fields and took to bookkeeping, truck scheduling, and the hiring of foremen to represent them in the fields (Mariano EE, Antonio FF). Both rich truck owners and poor construction laborers were required to maintain relations with many people and institutions outside of Zinacantán. In sum, there were changes in the social relations of work as well as in the distribution of income.

Between the 1960's and the 1980's, Zinacanteco economic life became more monetized. The most important change came from the shift out of corn farming. In the 1960's farmers produced basic subsistence for their families. Although farming (Cancian 1972) and community ceremonial obligations (Cancian 1965) involved cash inputs, there was a strong preference for producing rather than purchasing the corn consumed in the household. Another important change came from the increased availability of truck and bus transport among the hamlets of Zinacantán, and from Zinacantán to San Cristóbal, Tuxtla, and the farming areas in the lowlands. Riding replaced walking in many everyday situations. In both these areas, Zinacantecos had much greater personal control over meeting their basic needs in the 1960's than they did in the 1980's.

Changes in women's work created more need for cash. For example, in the 1960's there were no corn-grinding mills in Nachig, but by 1983 there were eight, and it was normal for women to have the day's corn for tortillas ground at a mill, rather than getting up before dawn to grind it by hand as they had done in the past. Standard household articles, like pots and cups, changed, and the availability of inexpensive ones decreased (L. K. M. Haviland 1978). During the same period almost all men, to some degree, replaced clothes that had been woven and sewn at home by women with purchased Ladino-style clothes. Perhaps most important, as population increased it became harder for women to find fuel wood on communal or unattended lands near population concentrations (like Nachig); and more families began to pay for firewood, and for transporting it to their homes from the distant places where it could be found (José GG).[6]

Overall, these changes increased the standard of living in Zinacantán. Men no longer made onerous walking trips to their lowland fields (Cancian 1972: 131–32), or long walks to the San Cristóbal market and meetings in Hteklum. Women were spared the drudgery of grinding corn, routine weaving, and, in some cases, gathering wood. Houses improved; water was piped in. There is little doubt that the "average" Zinacanteco enjoyed more manufactured goods in the early 1980's than he or she did 20 years before, and many other aspects of life were more convenient and required less physical effort.[7] On the other hand, the "average" household had become more dependent on cash income, and at least some jobs in construction demanded continuous intense physical effort that was rare for agriculturalists (Antonio AA).

In sum, Zinacanteco income and wealth was transformed in quantity, distribution, and kind between the 1960's and the 1980's. On the average, Zinacantecos became more prosperous and more dependent on cash income, and the difference between the rich and the poor became greater.

Life Cycle and Generation

Life-cycle and generation effects account for some economic differences between men of different ages. Life-cycle effects in their simplest form take place in historically stable systems where seniority is important. In such systems men change economic roles as they get older; they often control more resources (including the labor of others) as their seniority increases. Generation, as I am using it here, is important when there are historical changes, for then the moment at which a young man comes to maturity may affect his economic life course.

Three careers described in Chapter 4 illustrate the effects in Zinacantán. As a child, Mariano EE learned to be a muleteer and farmer, but as he came of age and sought a wife in 1970, he shifted to construction work. The expansion of government programs in the 1970's enabled him to acquire mason's skills while he was young, and he stayed with that work into the 1980's. In the mid-1980's, citing the stress and expense of weekly commuting to Tuxtla, he began to work regularly in San Cristóbal, and to hire others to farm corn for him. His shift to nearby construction work permitted him to organize the farming effort.

Manuel BB, who was about 12 years older than Mariano EE, was more deeply committed to family and corn farming before he had the opportunity to become a mason. While he kept a hand in each occupation, he favored corn farming over construction. By the mid-1980's, his sons were old enough to help him in farming. Antonio AA was still older and had no sons. He abandoned corn farming after a disastrous crop in the late 1960's, and he spent many years working in a popsicle factory in Tuxtla before he returned to Nachig in the 1980's and began farming a bit.

These three cases suggest both generation and life-cycle effects, as well as other influences on work histories. The two younger men had more opportunities to learn construction skills, and all three were involved in corn farming as they grew older. It seems likely that their recent increased dependence on corn farming was not solely due to life cycle, for the crisis of 1982 made all Zinacantecos conscious of the undependability of wage work.

The occupational transformation that took place between the 1960's and the early 1980's was largely a generation effect. Because younger men did not take it up as they came of age, corn farming was reduced from the universal occupation to one followed part- or full-time by only 60 percent of Nachig men. Table 5.2 shows that in 1983 only 38 percent of men under 35 farmed corn, and that less than 10 percent of them were devoted exclusively to corn farming. (In 1966, 89 percent of men 25–34 years old had cornfields in the lowlands.) Though a few men over 40 abandoned corn farming for other occupations, more than 75 percent of them still farmed corn in 1983.[8] I have separated 35-to-39-year-olds from 40-to-44-year-olds in the table, because this seems to pinpoint the period when the shift took place. As the preceding chapters have shown, in the early 1970's, when those 35 to 39 in 1983 had most likely been settling down to regular work, there was a substantial increase in alternative employment. Thus, the census reflects the massive onset of government inputs fairly precisely.[9]

TABLE 5.2

Occupations by Age, Nachig, 1983[a]

Age group	Percent of men in age group					Counts	
	Corn	Corn only	Labor	Trade	Other	Total occupations	Total men
25–34	38.4%	(7.1)%	46.4%	19.6%	33.6%	155	112
35–39	46.2	(7.7)*	48.7	28.2	23.1	57	39
40–44	76.1	(28.3)	39.1	26.1	8.7*	69	46
45–54	80.6	(38.9)	36.1	18.1	6.9	102	72
>54	80.5	(56.1)	26.8	12.2	4.9*	51	41
OVERALL	60.3%	(24.2)%	40.6%	20.3%	18.7%	434	310

[a] Occupations in Table 2.4 are lumped into four categories as follows: Corn (row 1), Trade (4–7), Labor (12–17), Other (2, 3, 8–11,18–22). The 124 (434 − 310) men with occupations in two categories are counted in each of them.
*Cell count less than 5.

After the economic crisis of 1982, many men took up highland farming (Collier and Mountjoy 1988; and my interviews).[10] There were (1) shifts of corn farmers from the lowlands to the highlands, (2) shifts to farming (of corn, flowers, fruit, and vegetables) by men reducing their commitment to wage work, and (3) entries into farming by young men who found alternative employment less attractive than it had been in the 1970's.

It is clear that the 1970's produced a new generation of Zinacantecos who worked outside of agriculture—a trucking-and-construction generation. When this study ended it was not yet clear what the interaction of personal development and historical change brought to the generation that came of age after the economic crisis—that is, in the middle and late 1980's. They (Antonio JJ, Juan KK) were even better educated than the trucking-and-construction generation, but in many ways they faced more limited opportunities.

In sum, the greatest part of the aggregate occupational change between the 1960's and the 1980's was made by men who came of age during the 1970's, when government programs created many new economic alternatives to corn farming.

Summary

Between the 1960's and the 1980's, many Zinacantecos became dependent on wage work, some as proletarians and the majority as semiproletarians. Some found secure government jobs, others increased their activity in commerce, and a few did very well in trucking and the transportation of people. Both cash income and cash expenditures increased during the period, especially because fewer and fewer men were farming corn. The rich got richer while many others stayed poor, making the income disparity within Zinacantán greater, at the same time that the demise of corn farming as the universal occupation created other differences among men. Those who came to working age in the 1970's accounted for most of the occupational change.

There are two major issues to carry forward from this analysis of economically driven change to the analysis of political and social relations in Parts II and III of this study. First, quite simply, how are we to think about semiproletarians? While they are an important category from the point of view of the national political economy, the category's utility in the analysis of rural political economy is basically untried. Second, what about the diverse relations of production in which Zinacantecos became involved? Did the new occupational categories constitute classes in any meaningful sense? Did the demands of the new occupations lead Zinacantecos to relate differently to public life and to each other?

A final more general concern stems from the profound nature of the transformation that took place during the short time period covered by this study. Zinacantecos went from a very limited range of contacts with the larger economy in the 1960's, when they were primarily corn farmers, to a much more intense and diverse range of contacts in the 1980's. In one sense this is easy to describe. I have compared Zinacanteco work in the 1960's and the 1980's by classifying the work done by Nachig men and comparing the frequency of different occupations in the two periods. In another sense this comparison is difficult if not impossible, because work relations changed so profoundly. For the most part they came to involve much greater dependence on the larger political economy—such that work roles whose labels survived from the 1960's to the 1980's may well have different social implications in the two periods. We will understand the work roles better when we know more about how they fit into Zinacantán's political and social life.

PART II /

PUBLIC LIFE

Many Zinacantecos say the trouble began in 1976 when Domingo Pérez was named the PRI candidate for Presidente Municipal (mayor). Marcos Pérez and some other important people got mad and formed an opposition party. Soon, minor disputes between individuals could not be settled if the individuals belonged to different parties, because they no longer respected the same judges. Tax collection for fiestas broke down, because men would not pay hamlet officials who were members of the other party. At some fiestas there were two bands, one from each party. As time went on, the parties suffered internal splits, and there were three and eventually four bands at the major fiestas. On top of this there were fights, jailings, and disputes over the control of the town hall. Later, police were sent to protect the Presidente from the opposition, and the governor had to intervene to maintain the operation of the civil registry. In one hamlet, water service was cut off in opposition neighborhoods. In another, children went to the public school controlled by their father's party, even if it meant a long walk to the other side of the valley. Throughout Zinacantán, access to jobs and other benefits of government programs depended on party affiliation.

It is easy to agree with Zinacantecos who say that "politics" began in the summer of 1976. The dramatic, open conflicts that began then dominated public life in the late 1970's and much of the 1980's. The period of close community control of internal conflict that had lasted at least two decades ended. By the early 1980's, political conflict had replaced the price of corn as a favorite topic of conversation.

From another point of view, the change began long before 1976, and the political events of 1976 were only a reflection of forces in the local, regional, national, and international political economy.

These forces included the state and the church outside of Zinacantán, economic interests at various levels, from the international petroleum market to the struggles among Zinacanteco truckers, and the activities of local leaders and their supporters. The four chapters that follow take this broader view.

I will begin with local institutions—in part because this arrangement makes it easier to lay out many details needed to interpret the public conflict. Chapter 6 focuses on public roles and political units in the 1960's, and Chapter 7 focuses on the institutional decentralization that took place in the 1970's. These chapters provide both the institutional vocabulary of political struggle in Zinacantán and a description of the change that preceded the open conflict described in Chapter 8. Whereas Chapters 6 and 7 are organized around institutional forms, Chapter 8 is organized around the events of three local administrations (1977–85), beginning with that of Domingo Pérez (1977–79). Chapter 9 uses data on demographic change and service in religious positions (cargos) to assess the trend towards decentralization and the forces for and against localism.

First, a brief look at some concepts relevant to the analysis of local politics. I take politics to be the struggle to define and interpret the institutions that constitute a political unit, in social terms a community. The struggle is constant—Comaroff and Roberts (1981: chapter 1) and Dahrendorf (1968: chapter 6), among many others, review related ideas. Institutions are continuously contested, negotiated, reproduced, and invoked—but the struggle is not of constant intensity or scope. Sometimes communities slowly adjust institutions to pressure from within. Sometimes discontent is bought off or repressed. Sometimes the community itself is at stake. Where I can distinguish them, I mean to emphasize historical changes rather than routine repetitive political processes of adjustment.

Politics as organized conflict, as factionalism, existed in Zinacantán long before the events described above (Vogt 1969: 284–87), but the older patterns can be distinguished from the severe conflict, the new politics, that developed in the late 1970's. I do not want to characterize the former as normal and the latter as pathological, nor the former as the mythological creation of a functionalist vision of social science and the latter as a more fundamentally realistic characterization of the conflict and contradictions in a situation like Zinacantán's. Rather, I want to argue that almost any observer would find the late 1970's very different from the late 1960's—that there was important change in the late 1970's. The likelihood that different observers would see the change in different ways depending on their social positions and frameworks is of less concern to me here.

I also want to argue that behavior during the first period was more constrained by tradition and custom—that Zincantecos generally felt that things were going along as they should. Change and conflict were pervasive but not dominant. As I suggested in Chapter 2, the custom and tradition I speak of have no relation to ancient tradition or aboriginal custom: they are the traditions and customs of the 1950's and 1960's—those that were, in their details, perhaps formed in the 1930's and 1940's (see G. A. Collier 1975, 1987, 1989; Wasserstrom 1983). Thus, I want to distinguish my approach from those that thoroughly historicize their accounts and underplay the difference between periods of cultural continuity and periods of uncertainty and cultural transformation, between adjustment and adaptation to small environmental changes and wrenching change.

If the concept of culture is worth anything in this situation, we must be able to assert that culture defines the expectations of its bearers, and that they are aware of differences between events that meet their expectations and those that require them to change their expectations. Culture also has to be at least somewhat sticky in the face of change. When local institutions yield to material forces internal and external to the community, people notice change. It seems to me they are often upset, and sometimes they actively try to conserve a past that is no longer attuned to new political and material realities—Conrad and Demarest (1984) and Cancian (1989) review related ideas.

What does this mean for how I will look at political life in Zinacantán in the 1960's, 1970's, and 1980's? I have chosen to discuss it in terms of both institutions and events in order to represent both the sticky and the new, i.e., both the restriction of action by institutional forms and the creation of institutional forms through action. I can then hope that the shifting loci and balance of constraint and assertion will become apparent—i.e., that I will be able to show, at once, the waxing and waning of community through time and across places. Stickiness, contradictions, and temporal cycles must all be represented.

6 /   PUBLIC LIFE

IN THE 1960's

This chapter describes the institutional frame-work of Zinacantán's public life in the 1960's, and assesses both the degree of political centralization and the rate of institutional change during these years. It gives background for understanding and interpreting the change and the conflict described in Chapters 7, 8, and 9. The description has two parts. The first covers public roles, civil and religious positions, and related political activity, and is largely based on earlier work (Cancian 1965). The second covers the political units that made up the municipio—Zinacantán Center (Hteklum) and the hamlets (Map 2)—and depends more heavily on new research.

Public Roles

In the 1960's there were three kinds of formal roles in public life: civil officials, religious cargoholders, and native curers (Cancian 1965: 15; Vogt 1969: 288). Table 6.1 records some basic facts about them. Powerful informal political leaders made up an important fourth category. The following long quotation (Cancian 1965: 24–27; written in the 1962 ethnographic present) from an introductory chapter of my study of the religious cargo system serves two purposes here: (1) it gives an overview of Zinacantán's public life in the 1960's, and (2) it insures, to a small degree, that the present study will take account of the earlier interpretations.

RECRUITMENT FOR POSITIONS IN PUBLIC LIFE

The manner in which a person is differentiated from all other people in his community and placed in a specific role can be very complex. This is especially true in a society such as Zinacantán, where kinship does not give

TABLE 6.1

The Three Sectors of Public Life in the 1960's[a]

Sector	Term (years)	Expenses or remuneration	Adult men participating (percent)
Curers 100–150 persons[b]	Life	Paid in goods	5–10%
Civil officials 1 Presidente Municipal, 1 Síndico, 9 Regidores (civil),[c] and 4 Alcaldes Jueces	3	No significant pay or expenses	5–10
Religious cargos 55 cargos, on 4 levels[d]	1	Substantial expenses	70–90

[a] After Cancian 1965: 15, table 1.
[b] Ranked by length of service.
[c] In 1962 for the first time (number corrected).
[d] The figure 55 includes eight Mayores, who function in the civil government as well as in the religious cargo system. It includes only two of the four Apaz cargos listed in Table 6.3 (see Cancian 1965: 164, note 3).

substantial clues to the placement of a person in the community-wide social structure. Here I will try to describe only the most obvious and basic procedures by which an individual is recruited for a position in public life.

Curers recruit themselves in a manner unique in the realm of public life. They learn of their calling in a series of dreams in which they see the native deities who live inside the mountains. Once they have had such dreams, they report to a senior curer for their interpretation. The interpretation reveals whether the dreamer should become a curer. It is believed that a person who is called and does not become a curer will die.

Because the civil officials are responsible for representing the community in relations with the Ladino government, they need facility in Spanish. Most of them speak some Spanish, though an examination of the incumbents over the past few years indicates that this is crucial only for the top officials—Presidente, Síndico, first Regidor, and first Alcalde Juez. As the administrators of justice in the community, they must command the respect of those who come to them for settlements. They do so mainly by their ability to make appropriate comments and present a reasonable perspective when a case is brought before them.

Under Mexican law all these officials are elected by popular vote. Like the manner of service in office, this requirement is adjusted to local conditions. As specified by law, there is a nominating meeting before the election. Before, during, and after this meeting, candidates are discussed and groups are formed in support of candidates. For weeks there is talk about who will be chosen. . . .[1]

In fact, the candidates of the political boss . . . have been elected for a number of years. However, the opposition is always active. This activity reached a peak in 1952, when about half a dozen younger relatives of the major opposition leaders appeared at the town hall carrying guns and demanding that the Presidente be unseated. Their protest did not carry, but opposition leaders are always talking of similar moves that will remove the incumbents with whom they are dissatisfied.

Most of the important civic decisions are made by the political boss and his close associates, while the civil officials settle disputes and carry on the official contacts with the Ladino government. Thus, though authority usually increases with age in Zinacantán, the civil officials may be relatively young and unimportant men. It is not uncommon to have a Presidente in his late 20's. Of the six Presidentes who served between 1952 and 1963, four were younger than 30 when they entered office. . . .

Formally, all [religious] cargoholders are appointed by the six *moletik* [Elders] (the four Regidores and the two Alcaldes Viejos), who are responsible for seeing that all positions are filled and that the required ritual is carried out. They communicate their appointments to the individuals some months in advance so that they may make the necessary preparations for entering a cargo. This has been the system of recruitment for religious offices as long as the oldest informants can remember. The [Elders] supported by the community have the power necessary to coerce individuals who are reluctant to undertake the expense and obligation of a cargo. An appointee who is able to resist the persuasion of six old and respected men, and who is willing to endure the mark that refusal may leave on him in the eyes of the community, may appeal an appointment to Ladino officials in San Cristóbal. They will issue an order stating that it is illegal to force a person to serve a religious cargo, and the appointee will be free.

For the last ten years men in great numbers have been requesting appointment to cargos of their choice. By 1961, the practice of requesting cargos had become so popular that the [Elders] held waiting lists as long as 20 years for some positions; that is, some men had requested specific cargos for the year 1981. . . .

CAREERS IN PUBLIC LIFE

The reputation a man makes in the three sectors of public life in Zinacantán is the face he presents to the community. Only a handful of adult Zinacantecos go through their adult years without participating in at least one of the three.

The curers receive the most distinctive type of respect for their participation in public life. Their reputations are usually greatest in the hamlets where they live, but the most important curers are known throughout the township. Their all-important resource—the power to communicate with the native deities and cure sickness—provides them with their renown. Only a small percentage of Zinacanteco adults are curers.

The civil officials, with the exception of the Presidente, do not necessarily continue to receive respect after they have served their terms of office. However, most of them are men who can continue to command respect for the same qualities that originally caused them to be selected for public office. Only a small percentage of Zinacanteco adult males hold civil office, and those who do not know Spanish are usually excluded completely from such service.

The cargo system is the only sector of public life in which almost all Zinacanteco males participate in some degree.[2] The cargoholder . . . receives a very special kind of prestige and respect, which is principally dependent on the amount of money he spends in the service of his cargo or cargos.

The public service of the curer is usually known to a limited number of people, and service as a civil official is limited to a small proportion of the population. The cargo system, on the other hand, provides a single standard by which all adult males may be compared on their participation in public life. For this reason (and others to be discussed later) the cargo system is the key to the community-wide social structure of Zinacantán. Cargo service is the most important single determinant of a man's position in the community.

The few individuals who do not take any roles in public life are usually at the bottom of the social scale in Zinacantán. In some cases, men who participate as civil officials or curers find themselves excluded from the cargo system because their other roles preclude the accumulation of money necessary to pass a cargo—but this is rare. A few men who for some reason never accumulate the funds for a cargo consistent with their self-image find alternative paths to prestige in curing and civil offices. Some gain prestige through informal political activity. In most cases, however, men who are successful curers and civil officials also participate in the cargo system. A man's reputation in the community is a composite of that made in the performance of various roles. The outstanding men are characterized by important participation in two or three sectors of public life.

Native curers (Vogt 1969; Fabrega and Silver 1973) will not be discussed in detail. Their numbers are small—and though they participate in various communal ceremonies each year, most of their interaction is with individual patients and their families. Below I will concentrate on (1) formal roles in civil government, then (2) the related formal and informal political leaders, and (3) the religious cargos associated with the saints of the Catholic Church.

Civil Offices

In the 1960's, officials of the civil government were principally concerned with public works, the administration of justice, and relations of the community and its members with the Ladino world outside. Zinacantán was an independent political entity under Mexican law, and the organization of the civil government was dictated by that law. Table 6.2 lists the civil officials and indicates changes that took place during the 1960's. For the most part, this section briefly paraphrases the description in Cancian (1965: 16–21).

The Presidente was the principal authority in the municipio (much like the mayor in the United States) and was its representative in dealings with the larger governmental system. The Síndico usually functioned as his alternate, and the Alcaldes Jueces (judges) were formally responsible for settling disputes. There were also men, usually young, who served as policemen and errand runners for the senior officials, and were called Mayores. They bridged the civil and the religious systems, for while most of their service was in the civil

TABLE 6.2

Civil Offices in the 1950's and 1960's[a]

	Late 1950's		Late 1960's	
	Number	Term (years)	Number	Term (years)
Municipio level				
Presidente Municipal	1	2	1	3
Síndico	1	2	1	3
Alcalde Juez	4	2	4	3
Regidor Civil	None[b]		9	3
Comandante	None		2	3
Mayor	6[c]	1	8[c]	1
Ejido Committee	Many[d]	3	Many[d]	3
Hamlet level				
Principal	1–3	1	1–3	1
Cobrador[e]	1	?	2	3
Agente Municipal	(Navenchauc only)		(Navenchauc only)	
Ejido Committee	1–2[d]	3	1–2[d]	3
School Committee	3[f]	1	3[f]	1

[a] Role names for civil office are in Spanish, except for committees, which will have descriptive names in English. Most committees had a Head, Secretary, and Treasurer (Presidente, Secretario, and Tesorero). Some also had other members.

[b] As noted in the text, religious Regidores filled the roles of these officials. Where context does not distinguish them from religious Regidores, the "civil" is used to identify them.

[c] See Note 6.6. Sometimes, especially in later years, additional men volunteered for and served as Mayor.

[d] The Ejido Committee had a Head, a Secretary, a Treasurer, and various members who were effectively delegates from hamlets. As far as I know, hamlet members, where possible, adjudicated disputes involving hamlet residents. As noted elsewhere, there were two Ejido committees in Zinacantán.

[e] The Cobrador (Tzotzil: *tsom tak'in*) collected funds for public works, thus freeing the Principales to concentrate on their long-standing duties involving other taxes.

[f] School committees were attached to particular schools and organized at the hamlet level. They became more important as the number of schools grew (Table 7.2).

realm, it counted towards progress in the religious cargo system (see below).

Members of the Ejido Committee were not officials in the same sense as those described above—both because their roles required less time and because the ejidos did not include all of the families in Zinacantán and were strictly speaking not part of the municipio's government. Civil government and the ejido were connected through the Head of the Ejido Committee, who was the political boss of Zinacantán during this period (see below).

Three changes are reflected in Table 6.2. (1) As of January 1962, state law changed the term of the Presidente Municipal and a number of other officials from two to three years (before 1952 the term had been one year). (2) A convenient fiction under which men chosen to be religious Regidores (see below) served also as the legally installed civil Regidores ended in the early 1960's when the Presidente (Yermo) was forced to leave office (Wasserstrom 1983: 175) and was replaced, under the law, by the incumbent First Regidor, a man who did not speak Spanish and could not effectively fill the office. (3) In 1965 the Presidente appointed two men as Comandantes, with authority to carry guns and to accompany the Mayores when difficult arrests had to be made (J. F. Collier 1973: 33).

Most of these officials were divided into two alternating groups: one group served a 15-day term while the other "rested" and attended to personal business.

At the hamlet level, the Principales and Cobradores made announcements, delivered messages from officials in Hteklum, and collected taxes (see below). Hamlet elders, who held no formal office and served no fixed term, were much more important than the formal hamlet officials listed in Table 6.2. They settled disputes informally and provided political leadership (see especially Vogt 1969; J. F. Collier 1973). Navenchauc was the only exception to this pattern of informal leadership at the hamlet level. There the Agente Municipal had responsibilities for local matters that paralleled those of officials in Zinacantán Center.[3]

Geographical distance created other differences between hamlets. People close to Hteklum could easily participate in municipal affairs and use the formal judicial system—they could easily walk there, do their business, and return home in one day. People from the western edges of the municipio faced longer walks, expenses for transport along the Pan American Highway, and, in some cases, the need to find a place to sleep in Hteklum. Thus, as Jane Collier has shown (1973: 66), those living nearer to Hteklum used the municipio court at a higher rate than those living in distant hamlets.

In sum, in the 1960's formal civil government in Zinacantán was for the most part centralized in Hteklum, and informal leaders were crucial to public life in the hamlets, especially those farthest from Hteklum. Early in the decade, state law changed terms for many offices from two to three years. The creation of new offices for Regidores Civiles, and the elimination of the fiction through which religious Regidores filled the offices, were the biggest changes of the decade.

Political Leaders

Most political power in Zinacantán was concentrated in the hands of one man, Mariano Hernández Zárate, from the 1940's until his grip was loosened in the early 1960's (see Vogt 1969: 285–87; Wasserstrom 1983: 173; Tax 1947). He came to power as the leader of land-reform efforts.

Over this formal organization lies a political power structure that has also changed over the years. Little is known about the situation before the turn of the century and up until the 1920's, but it can be guessed with some assurance that the political powers of the Ladino world had a much firmer and more direct control over the appointment and election of officials in Zinacantán than they do now [1962]. Within the community, according to informants, there has been a series of political leaders. Most reports indicate that there were usually two or three men who held great political power in the community. These were usually men who could speak Spanish and manipulate the Ladino world as well as maintain the respect of Zinacantecos. In the late 1930's there seem to have been three such individuals at one time. Two are now dead and the third is often seen in the role of elder statesman when Ladino officials appear in Zinacantán on business.

Through the 1930's and especially in the early 1940's the national land-reform program of Mexico was making great changes in Zinacantán. The township and its people were eligible for much new land under the reform laws. The man who led the community in its demands for land emerged as a solitary political power in that period and maintained his hold on the community until very recently (Edel 1962). Until the incident which resulted in the impeachment of the Presidente in 1960, that old leader was a political boss in the full sense of the word. The impeached Presidente became the center of an opposition group that caused the leader to be jailed early in 1962. He was free within a few months, but his hold on the community was shaken. He is an older man and his probable successors do not seem fully capable of replacing him. It is difficult to predict how the political situation in Zinacantán will develop. (Cancian 1965: 21–22)

In sum, Mariano Hernández Zárate controlled the Ejido Committee and the PRI party apparatus that selected candidates for major civil offices in the municipio (see Chapter 8). In both cases, he often did it through the officially registered heads of these activities, who were his political allies. As the 1960's ended, both the ejido organization and the local PRI drew the attention of politically powerful men, but no new leaders of close to Mariano Hernández Zárate's power had emerged.[4]

Religious Cargos

In the early 1960's, Zinacantán's cargo system had four levels arranged in a hierarchy (Cancian 1965: 29). A man had to serve a year in one of the first-level cargos to begin his career. After that, he was eligible to serve one of 12 second-level cargos, then one of six third-level cargos, and finally one of two fourth-level cargos. First service usually did not occur until the age of 35 or 40, and years of "rest" between service periods were required to earn the enormous amounts of money necessary to sponsor fiestas. Thus, many men who hoped to compete for the limited number of offices on higher levels died before reaching their goal.

There were substantial differences in the prestige and respect associated with different cargos. Both the authority invested in the particular cargo and the cost of performing the ritual associated with it contributed to the prestige (Cancian 1965: chapter 8; Chapter 10, below). For example, the Mayordomo Rey was in charge of a chapel in the ceremonial center. He had to spend considerably more than $10,000 (measured in 1960 pesos) in the course of a year's service. In 1960, agricultural laborers earned $5 per day plus meals, and an ordinary Zinacanteco farmer was lucky to clear $1,000 from a year of farming (Cancian 1965: chapter 7), so most Zinacantecos could not aspire to serve as Mayordomo Rey. The Mayordomo San Antonio spent about $3,000, and his principal duties involved ceremonial patterns directed by someone else. Thus, a man who served as Mayordomo Rey acquired much more prestige because he had more authority and spent more than one who served as Mayordomo San Antonio. A man's prestige in the community usually increased with service in a second and subsequent cargos, and men who began their careers in prestigious first-level cargos were more apt to continue to the higher levels (these paragraphs paraphrase Cancian 1974a: 164–66).

Table 6.3 lists the cargos by level, location of the church or chapel to which they were attached, and type. The specific Mayordomos and Alféreces are identified by the saints with which they were associated (Cancian 1965: 30), and most were served in pairs (senior and junior). For example, there were two Mayordomos of San Antonio and two of Santo Domingo. A complete list of cargo names is given in Table D.1.

In the 1960's, most of the ritual activity associated with cargos took place in Hteklum, and most cargoholders from the hamlets maintained a house there during their period of service. All the cargos served in Hteklum were established before the 1950's.[5] A group of researchers led by Sol Tax (Tax et al. 1947) found them all in late 1942, except for two (one Mayordomo and one Alférez of San Sebastián). These two were added between 1943, after Tax left, and 1946, when Manuel Pérez Gil served a cargo with them. Pérez, who served his first cargo in 1936, told me in the early 1960's that no cargo had ever been lost, i.e., discontinued. Thus, except for the addition of Mayores[6] (Table 6.2), the cargos served in Hteklum were stable from at least the mid-1940's to the mid-1960's.

TABLE 6.3

Religious Cargos, 1930's to 1960's[a]

(Type and number)

	Level	Number of cargos			
		1930's	1940's	1950's	1960's
Served in Hteklum					
Mayordomos	1	11	12	12	12
Other mayordomo-type	1	8	8	8	8
Mayor[b]	1	6	6	6	8
Alférez	2[c]	13	14	14	14
Regidor	3	4	4	4	4
Alcalde Viejo	4	2	2	2	2
Alcalde Shuves	[d]	1	1	1	1
Served in hamlets					
Salinas	1	2	2	2	2
Navenchauc	1	—	—	2	2
Apaz	1	—	—	—	4
TOTAL		47	49	51	57

[a] Most terms were one year; a few were less. Four first-level cargos and Alcalde Shuves served at specific fiestas during only a part of the year. Some Alféreces, Regidores, and Alcaldes Viejos had duties before and/or after their year in office. Many people served as auxiliary personnel (in formal roles) and helpers of cargoholders (Cancian 1965: chapter 5). Among them, four Sacristans, two Musicians of the Alféreces, and two Scribes were the most important, and their duties most time-consuming.

[b] See Table 6.2, note c.

[c] Two Alféreces were regularly served on higher levels (Cancian 1965: 31).

[d] Alcalde Shuves was served without regard to previous service, was usually filled by an older man, and was always his last cargo.

By the end of the 1960's, there were eight cargos served outside of the ceremonial center. Before the 1950's, the only cargos served outside of Hteklum were those in Salinas. They marked the special status of Salinas as a source of salt (Cancian 1965: 36, note 5). Then, in the early 1950's, a church was built in Navenchauc. A few years later two new Mayordomo positions were created to care for it (Cancian 1965: 37, 164; Vogt 1969: 252). The Apaz church and cargos were added in the early 1960's (Cancian 1965: 37, 164, note 3; Vogt 1969: 252).[7]

In sum, the religious cargo system was fairly stable from the 1930's to the 1960's. In the 1930's, it included 45 cargos served in Hteklum and two in Salinas. In the mid-1940's, a Mayordomo and an Alférez of San Sebastián were added to those served in Hteklum. In the late 1950's, two Mayordomos were added in Navenchauc, and a few years later four new cargos were added in Apaz. By the late 1960's, eight Mayores usually served, making the total cargos 57, with all those outside Hteklum being served at the first level.

Political Subunits: Hteklum and the Hamlets

Zinacantán's status as a political and ethnic unit precedes the Spanish conquest (Vogt 1969: vii), and Hteklum's status as the ceremonial center is probably as old, for the Spanish chose it as the site for a convent shortly after the conquest (Vogt 1969: 18). In the early nineteenth century a census showed half the population concentrated around Hteklum (the *cabecera*, or seat of government), and listed many smaller populations, including a number of the hamlets present in the 1960's (Wasserstrom 1983: 96). The colonial and pre-revolutionary political economy greatly influenced changes in population distribution and organization (Wasserstrom 1983).

In the 1960's, Zinacantecos divided their municipio into about 20 subunits, most of them formally designated as hamlets with Principales. The size and formal status of these subunits changed because of (1) territorial expansion and political activity connected with land reform, (2) population movements due to construction of the Pan American Highway, and (3) other political and economic factors discussed in the chapters that follow. Here I will first describe the effects of land reform and the highway, then draw on Zinacanteco tax lists to document the status of particular places in the 1960's.

Land Reform and the Pan American Highway

Land reform greatly expanded the land available to Zinacantecos; it put Zinacantecos in control of most of the land that a few Ladino families had held inside the municipio (Edel 1966). Land-reform efforts began in the 1920's, increased under the Cárdenas administration (1934–40), and brought practical access to much of the land by the mid-1940's. Two ejido units resulted (Map 3). One included the people of Hteklum, Vochojvo, Patosil, Salinas, Nachig, Paste, Elanvo, Navenchauc, and Apaz; it was headed by Mariano Hernández Zárate, the political boss mentioned above. These hamlets had 6,070 hectares under their control before land reform, and received 7,040 more. Their ejido land came from the Ladino ranches of San Nicolás, Yalentay, Pig, Shucun, San Antonio, and some others.[8] The second ejido, headquartered in Jocchenom, received 5,030 hectares—thus close to doubling the area of the hamlets to the west. It was under separate leadership (Edel 1962).

Land reform did not affect all the hamlets equally. Using Edel's data, Wasserstrom (1983: 171) estimated that 86 percent of the families residing in the western hamlets (the Jocchenom ejido) received land. For the hamlets closer to Hteklum, the figure averaged about 40 percent of the families. The difference apparently resulted from

The band playing during a procession at the Fiesta of San Lorenzo, 1971.

the hesitancy of people in the eastern hamlets to join the agrarian movement and to pay the contributions that supported the long struggle that preceded allocation of the land. In Navenchauc, where there was a clear division between the agrarian activists loyal to the leadership in Hteklum and a group opposed to the movement, only about 20 percent of the families received land. Navenchauc was further splintered because some of its residents joined the Jocchenom ejido group.

Land reform produced dominant political leaders and consolidated some regional divisions within the municipio. It did not make Zinacantecos independent farmers, because Ladino owners usually kept the best land and control of the water, and because population growth after the allocation meant that ejido plots usually did not fully support families (Wasserstrom 1983: 171–72). Its greatest effects on the economic life of the 1960's came because it broke the hold of large landowners in the Grijalva Valley and led many of them to rent to Zinacantecos.

The Pan American Highway (Map 2) was completed and paved in 1950. It replaced the old unpaved road which went from Tuxtla Gutiérrez, through Salinas and Hteklum, to San Cristóbal. The highway opened commerce and gave advantages to the hamlets located along and near it, and made Hteklum less important. By the 1960's, when the old road fell into disrepair, Hteklum found itself at the end of a

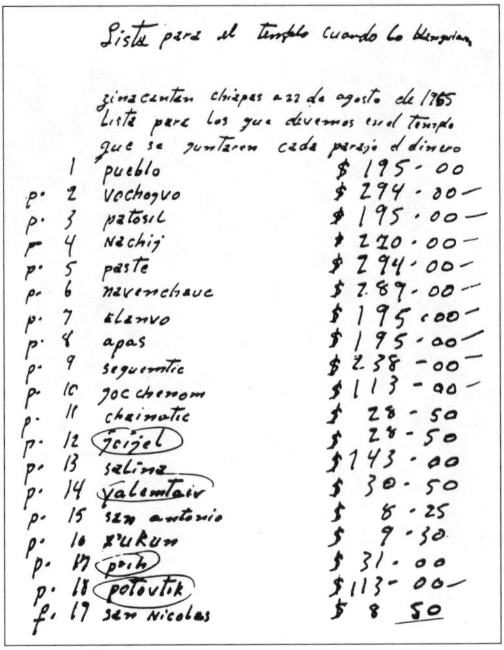
Lista para el templo cuando lo blanquian

zinacantan chiapas a 22 de agosto de 1965
Lista para los que devemos en el templo
que se juntaron cada parajo el dinero

	1	pueblo	$ 195 - 00
p.	2	vochojvo	$ 294 - 00
p.	3	patosil	$ 195 - 00
p.	4	Nachij	$ 220 - 00
p.	5	paste	$ 294 - 00
p.	6	navenchauc	$ 289 - 00
p.	7	elanvo	$ 195 - 00
p.	8	apas	$ 195 - 00
p.	9	seguemtic	$ 238 - 00
p.	10	joc chenom	$ 113 - 00
p.	11	chainatic	$ 28 - 50
p.	12	jcijel	$ 28 - 50
p.	13	salina	$ 143 - 00
p.	14	yalemtaiv	$ 30 - 50
p.	15	san antonio	$ 8 - 25
p.	16	x'ukun	$ 9 - 30
p.	17	pech	$ 31 - 00
p.	18	potovtik	$ 113 - 00
f.	19	san Nicolas	$ 8 50

Fig. 6.1. Public works tax list, 1965.

rocky road (Vogt 1969: 29–30); its monopoly on easy communication with the outside world was over.

Tax Lists: The Organization of Cooperation

During the 1960's, Zinacantecos paid taxes for three main purposes: (1) fiestas, (2) public works, and (3) the municipio secretary's salary. The last was paid monthly (Vogt 1969: 281–82), fiesta taxes were levied for each of several (about seven) major fiestas each year, and public works were undertaken less frequently. Fiesta taxes, which paid for the hire of a Ladino band from outside Zinacantán, were set by an ad hoc committee named to administer the part of each major fiesta not sponsored by cargoholders.[9] Public works such as bridge construction or repair of the churches were also administered by ad hoc committees.

Each ad hoc committee developed a budget, calculated each hamlet's share according to the number of taxpayers residing there, and assigned the Principales (who kept lists of individual taxpayers) to collect the total required from their hamlets. This was done in cooperation with the Presidente, and with the help of political leaders and others who had the skills necessary to make the calculations.

The lists used by the ad hoc committees provide two kinds of data: an indication of what places had official status in Zinacantán, and, since the hamlet shares varied with the number of adult male residents, a measure of the hamlets' relative population size. The list in Figure 6.1 was created by the ad hoc committee in charge when the church was whitewashed in 1965. It includes 19 places, and the amounts due from their residents. Table 6.4 displays information from three tax lists (including the one in Figure 6.1), a population estimate for 1965, and the number of Principales recorded by Vogt.[10]

TABLE 6.4

Hamlets on Tax Lists in the 1960's

Hamlet[a]	Tax List[b]			Estimated population 1965[c]	Principales (Vogt 1969)
	Fiesta		Public work 1965		
	1962	1965			
Hteklum	−	−	X	694	[d]
Vochojvo	−	−	X	1,047	2
Patosil	X	X	X	694	2
Salinas	X	X	X	509	1
Nachig	X	X	X	962	3
Paste	X	X	X	1,047	2
Elanvo	X	X	X	694	2
Yalentay	X	X	X	109	1
Pig	−	X	X	110	1
Navenchauc	X	X	X	1,029	2
Apaz	X	X	X	694	2
Zequentic	X	X	X	848	2
Jocchenom	X	X	X	402	2
Joigel	X	X	X	102	1
Chianatic	X	X	X	102	1
Potovtic	−	X	X	402	1
San Antonio[e]	X	X	X	29	0
Shucun[e]	X	X	X	33	0
San Nicolás[e]	−	−	X	30	0
Total population				9,537	

SOURCES: Appendix B; Vogt (1969: 162).

[a] The ordering of hamlets on tax lists reflects geography (Map 2), history, and size. New units and small units tend to be at the end.

[b] X = present; − = absent. The specific lists are described in more detail in Appendix B.

[c] The 1965 population was estimated by averaging total municipal population from the 1960 and 1970 national censuses [(7,650 + 11,428) ÷ 2 = 9,539], then distributing the total in proportion to the hamlet shares shown in the 1965 tax list shown in Figure 6.1. See the text and Appendix B for background.

[d] Vogt (1969: 162) lists hamlets only. Hteklum had two in 1942 (Tax et al. 1947: 52).

[e] San Antonio, Shucun, and San Nicolás were not usually seen as hamlets.

Hamlets and Superhamlets

In the 1960's, Zinacantán's subunits were 15 hamlets, Hteklum, and three small places that did not have hamlet status (Table 6.4). Here I will describe them briefly, note some changes during the 1960's, highlight some features relevant to the changes described in Chapters 7, 8, and 9, and conclude the section with a description of the hamlet clusters or "superhamlets" indicated by the groupings in Table 6.4. Vogt's chapter "Settlement Patterns" (1969: 155–79) gives a rich picture of the 15 hamlets (plus Hteklum), including comments on distinctive features of each one and aerial photos of several of them.

Hteklum was distinctive because it was both the ceremonial and political center for the entire municipio and a hamlet to its permanent residents. In Spanish it was referred to as the center (*cabecera*), not as a hamlet (*paraje*). Vochojvo was officially a hamlet—though much of its population was settled contiguously with Hteklum, and many of its residents lived as close to the church of San Lorenzo as many Hteklum residents did. When fiesta taxes were calculated, Vochojvo shared a special status with Hteklum: together they paid for certain decorations for the fiesta, and were exempted from the hamlet taxes used for the band (Table B.4). As the list for public works shows (Figure 6.1, Table 6.4), they paid regular taxes on other occasions.

The nearby population of Patosil was a regular hamlet, as was Salinas, which is somewhat more distant from Hteklum. Salinas, which had been on the route from Tuxtla Gutiérrez through Hteklum to San Cristóbal before the completion of the Pan American Highway, had special status because of the cargos based there (Table 6.3) and because ritual activities took cargoholders from Hteklum there during the Fiesta of Rosario in October (Cancian 1965: 218).

Nachig, which straddled the Pan American Highway to the south of Hteklum, and Paste and Elanvo, farther to the south, all had regular hamlet status, and had substantial populations, at least since 1940 (Appendix B).

The next group of hamlets in Table 6.4 includes two large established hamlets (Navenchauc and Apaz) and two smaller ones of more recent origin (Yalentay and Pig). Navenchauc was the largest hamlet listed in the 1940 census (Appendix B), the site of cargos established in the 1950's, and the only hamlet with legally recognized civil officials (Agentes Municipales). As such it had a measure of independence from Hteklum.[11] Apaz, set near the escarpment south of the

highway (see especially G. A. Collier 1975), established its own religious cargos in the 1960's—thereby making itself one of the three
hamlets with local cargos.

Yalentay and Pig came into existence as the result of the land-
reform programs. In the 1940 census (Appendix B) they were listed
as private properties (*finca* and *rancho*, respectively). In the intervening years, parts of them were made into ejidos and parts were sold as
private plots to Zinacantecos. In the 1960's they were the smallest
populations recognized as hamlets. Pig, as comparison of the two
fiesta tax lists in Table 6.4 shows, was not officially recognized as a
hamlet until the mid-1960's.

The hamlets to the west are connected by their participation in
the Jocchenom ejido, and by their distance from Hteklum. In the
early 1960's, four hamlets in the area were listed on the tax lists:
Zequentic, Jocchenom, Joigel, and Chainatic. Potovtic apparently
achieved official status at the beginning of 1965 with the new municipio government (Table B.4). The hamlet shares shown in the tax
lists suggest that Potovtic was created by a division of Jocchenom,
because their combined share of taxes in early 1965 is equal to Jocchenom's share on a list drawn up in late 1964 that excluded Potovtic (Table B.4, columns B1 and A3).

San Antonio (south of Paste), Shucun (south of Elanvo), and San
Nicolás (near Vochojvo) were small population clusters created in
the process of land reform (Edel 1966; Vogt 1969: 28). They were not
official hamlets and had no Principales. The people of San Antonio
and Shucun collected taxes informally and took them to the Principales in Paste and Elanvo (respectively) for delivery to Hteklum.
Though I have no direct information on the status of San Nicolás, it
may have held special status parallel to Hteklum and Vochojvo (see
above) during this period.

Recognizing clusters of hamlets is useful, especially as an aid to
the discussion in Chapters 8 and 9. These clusters have no official
status, and vary with the purpose of the grouping. John Haviland
(1977: 19–21) suggests a grouping into "superhamlets" that reflect
geographical and historical connections. In constructing his clusters,
he cites George Collier's work showing disproportionately frequent
ritual kinship ties between certain hamlets. The first three of the
clusters I use in Table 6.4 match three of Haviland's superhamlets,
and the fourth lumps the three superhamlets that he identifies in
the western part of the municipio. As the estimated population figures show, the western hamlets in my fourth cluster have the smallest population of the four.

Two clusters will be particularly useful in discussing political events in the chapters that follow. Hteklum, Vochojvo, and parts of Patosil formed a natural area within easy walking distance of the church of San Lorenzo. Because of this, their residents had informal, but special, access to public life in Hteklum. I will call this area the "Center," and use the term, capitalized, to refer both to the political and ceremonial center that is confined to Hteklum and to the larger population that has easy access to these activities; I will explicitly distinguish the two uses only when it is important to do so.

The second important area coincides with the fourth cluster in Table 6.4. Zinacantecos, especially ones from the Center, have a term they regularly use for these hamlets to the west that are united by membership in the ejido of Jocchenom. It is the "Cornfields" (*Chomtik* in Tzotzil, *La Milperia* in Spanish). The term is descriptive: the more extensive land per person and the lower altitude make local corn farming much more important in these hamlets. I will use the term Cornfields, capitalized, to refer to this area in what follows.

Summary

This chapter describes the major institutions of public life in Zinacantán in the 1960's: the civil offices, the religious cargos, and the hamlets. It also notes the role of political leadership, the ejido movement, and the construction of the Pan American Highway in changing these institutions.

Two characteristics of the institutions and their recent history need summary—so that they may be compared with the situation in the 1970's that will be described in the next chapter. First, in the 1960's and the immediately preceding decades, the institutions of public life were dynamic and changing. Civil and religious offices and hamlets were added, and customs surrounding their roles in Zinacanteco life were modified. Yet, as we will see, the rate of change was moderate by comparison with what was to come.[12]

Second, public life in Zinacantán was relatively centralized in the 1960's and the immediately preceding decades. Formal leadership was concentrated in the township offices in Hteklum, and in the ejido officials—Mariano Hernández Zárate in the hamlets nearer the Center, and other leaders in the Cornfields, the hamlets to the west. Most civil officials and religious cargoholders moved to the Center during their periods of service. Decentralization of public life had not yet begun.

7 / INSTITUTIONAL DECENTRALIZATION IN THE 1970's

Public life was transformed in the 1970's. New hamlets were created, and many new civil offices and religious cargos were established in the hamlets. Hamlets became much more independent from Hteklum, and from the municipio-wide civil and religious systems. Overall, the changes of the 1970's dwarfed those that took place in the 1960's.

Hamlet organization and civil offices changed in three ways. First, the informal leadership and dispute settlement that prevailed in the 1960's was replaced in many hamlets by Agentes Municipales appointed by the Presidente Municipal and by formal staffs that served with the Agentes. Second, the expansion of schools, electricity, and piped water during the same period led to the naming of many new hamlet administrative committees. Finally, in keeping with new land-tenure laws promulgated under the Echeverría administration, new committees were formed to take care of land problems formerly handled by the Presidente. All the new officials were given tax exemption during their service and for a period after service.

Religious offices also expanded during the 1970's. Churches, like those in Salinas, Navenchauc, and Apaz, were built in several other hamlets; and in three hamlets, mayordomo-like cargos and Sacristans were soon created to service the saints in the churches. During the same period the Catholic Church recruited native Catechists to make the Church's teaching more directly accessible to its members. All these new officials were also exempt from taxes.

In addition, during the 1970's many hamlets divided into two or more parts, and thereby created more settings for local activities.

This chapter describes the decentralization of the formal institutions of public life in two ways. First, I will take advantage of my extensive work in Nachig. The narrative about what happened there is connected to Yermo Pérez's career in public life and, in some places, to the careers of the men whose stories make up Chapter 4. Then I will present an overview for the entire municipio—using interviews with key figures and data from documents, especially tax lists. While case materials suggest that the story of each hamlet is different, the summary of new hamlets and new hamlet offices presented in Tables 7.2 and 7.3 shows that the outcomes were often similar.

The Transformation of Local Institutions in Nachig

Nachig's history illustrates three processes that occurred in other hamlets as well: creation of new hamlet offices, adjustment to the growing burden of hamlet-level service, and fission into distinct and independent hamlets. Nachig had a relatively long record of contact with the outside world. The hamlet was close to Hteklum (about an hour's walk) and San Cristóbal. The opening of the Pan American Highway about 1950 brought San Cristóbal even closer (15 minutes by auto). It also led people from outlying hamlets to move to Nachig, where they could be near the road (Mariano EE), and gave Nachig people access to commercial and agricultural opportunities that were not available to people from many other hamlets. During the decades discussed here, Nachig was one of the larger hamlets of Zinacantán, and one of the first to make contact with outside institutions.

Creation of New Public Roles

Table 7.1 lists Nachig public roles in the order in which they were created. In the early 1960's, Nachig had four formal local roles: Principal, Cobrador, School Committee Member, and Representative to the Ejido Committee, which was based in Hteklum. They involved about ten men at a time (Table 7.1); their duties are described in Chapter 6. The Principales existed well before the other local offices, and went back decades. The Cobrador post was created in 1951; Yermo was its first incumbent. The School Committee probably came during the Cárdenas administration (1934–40) with the first school, a two-room building for which Nachig people contributed the construction labor. Late in the 1950's, Yermo served on the School Committee that received a new five-room school built by the state. The Ejido Committee existed in 1941 (Tax et al. 1947: 70; Edel 1966); Yermo served on it in the late 1940's.

In the 1960's, when the hamlet elders, including Yermo, could not

TABLE 7.1

Nachig Public Roles in the 1960's and 1970's

Position or committee	Number of incumbents	Term (years)	Date established
Positions earning tax .exemption and rest			
Principal	3	1	Before 1950
School Committee (state)	3	1	Before 1950
Ejido Committee	2 or 3	3	Before 1950
Cobrador	2	3	1951
Light and Water Committee	2	1	1960's
Agente Municipal	3	3	1974
Vocal	3	3	1974
Communal Land Committee	2 or 3	3	1977
School Committee (federal)	2	1	Mid-1970's
Mayordomo	2	1	1976
Sacristans	4	1	1976
Catechist	2	Life	1977
Positions not earning tax exemption and rest			
PRI Steering Committee	3	6	Long ago
Basketball President	1	Not fixed	1970's
Basketball Captain	1	Not fixed	1970's
Fiesta Committee	3	One fiesta	Early 1970's
Church Committee	3	2	Early 1970's

resolve a dispute, it was taken over the mountain to the Presidente in Hteklum. Nachig's formal offices, especially Principal, Cobrador, and Ejido Representative, also linked the hamlet to Hteklum, as did the service of Nachig men in religious cargos.

The first wave of decentralization came with the construction of a church in the late 1960's. The project began when a local priest recruited representatives of many Indian municipios to meet with church groups in Mexico City. All their expenses except the bus fare were paid by the Church. Yermo and his brother José were among the four representatives from Zinacantán. They met with nuns from a Portuguese order who were particularly interested in Nachig (which means "Sheep House" in Tzotzil) because of their connection to the Virgin of Fátima, who had appeared to Portuguese shepherds. The nuns offered to build a church in Nachig, and eventually bought land and paid for both the materials and labor needed to construct it. Yermo and a number of other Nachig men told me that José led the local organization of the project, and saw it through an early period when many people opposed it.

José's older son, Mariano DD, headed the first Church Commit-

The hamlet of Nachig from the air, 1964. At the lower left the Pan American Highway leaves the valley in the direction of San Cristóbal.

Election day, July 6, 1988, in the Nachig plaza. The scene extends across the bottom photo on facing page. (Note that the front of the microbus at the right appears at the left in the facing photo.)

The center of Nachig, 1991. The church (on the highway at the right) was built where the three trails enter the highway near the center of the 1964 photo, facing page. (Photo by Lauren Greenfield, courtesy of the National Geographic Society)

The center of Nachig, looking from the parking area in front of the plaza across the Pan American Highway to the church, 1988.

tee, serving with a Treasurer and a Secretary. At first, Mariano said, they just took the expenses out of their own pockets. Soon, according to Manuel BB, the Sacristans found the expenses burdensome—so people talked of establishing cargos for the church.

Beginning in 1976, two Mayordomos Virgen de Fátima were named and served on a calendar-year basis. José, who was still alive at the time, appointed them. During the second year, 1977, Manuel BB was Senior Mayordomo, and his junior partner was a man who became Senior Alcalde Viejo in Hteklum in 1987. Later Mariano EE and José II also served the cargo.

A second wave of decentralization began with the Velasco Suárez and Echeverría administrations (1970–76). Their programs (Chapter 3) soon reached Nachig: a Community Building (Casa del Pueblo) was built just across the Pan American Highway from the church while Marcos Pérez was Presidente of Zinacantán (1971–73), and a plaza was developed in front of it. Nachig suddenly had a formal public center. Yermo recruited Nachig men to work on the Community Building, and was the government's contact for a coordinated program that subsidized 18 private houses for Nachig men, who worked at least 100 days on its construction. Both Yermo and Manuel BB received houses under the program.

By the mid-1970's, Nachig had its own Agentes Municipales (who did formal dispute settlement in the Community Building) and Vocales to run errands for them. According to Yermo, he and his brother supported the effort to get an Agente for Nachig, for the two of them were spending more and more time doing informal settlements for the growing local population. Nachig named three men to the Agente's position—as did some other hamlets that thought the work would be burdensome—so that each man could serve for two weeks, and then have four weeks off.[1]

The presence of the Agentes led to additional duties for local officeholders who had preceded them in the expansion of Nachig's public life. Under the new system the Principales and members of the School Committee and the Light and Water Committee (see below) were required to appear at the Community Building each afternoon during their periods of service. José GG, who was on a School Committee in 1984, said that he and other younger men who migrated to wage jobs and had to lose wages while serving their turn agreed to serve for two calendar weeks; that way they could be at work on Monday when free. The Agentes served 15-day periods on the monthly calendar.

Sometime between the late 1960's and the early 1970's, electric power was brought to Nachig, and a water system was built to replace the wells scattered throughout the hamlet. The Light and Water Committee (Patronato de Luz y Agua Potable) was formed to administer these services and to collect fees for the Federal Electric Commission (CFE)—thereby adding two new local offices.

Finally, in the early 1970's, Echeverría's reform of land-tenure laws led to the formation of a Communal Land (Bienes Comunales) Committee with responsibility for settling land-tenure problems on communal (*comunal*) lands, and a parallel "vigilance committee" responsible for controlling fires and the cutting of timber and firewood. Nachig named two or three representatives to these committees each year.[2]

In sum, between the mid-1960's and the mid-1970's, the number of civil officials in Nachig more than doubled, and a Community Building and public park were built. Most of the new officials increased the local autonomy of the hamlet; some created direct connections to government agencies outside of Zinacantán. During the same period, a local church was built, and local cargos like those of Salinas, Navenchauc, and Apaz were established. Table 7.1 summarizes these changes and some other details about public roles in Nachig.

Growing Burdens of Service

The growing number of hamlet offices was felt as a burden for many reasons. More service was required of individuals; they served more frequently; they were subject to recruitment at both the hamlet and the municipio levels; and they suffered when officials at the two levels competed for them. The tax burden on those not serving increased because so many were exempt from taxes during and after service. And the time demands of service were made more onerous by the rigid schedule required of many men who were wage workers.

Antonio AA's service as Second Principal in 1980 illustrates some of these extra burdens. In the 1970's, as in earlier decades, it was difficult for an individual to refuse appointment to any office. Antonio was present when he was named at the hamlet meeting in November 1979, but he said nothing: "When the meeting says John Doe will enter, it's as if he has already entered. It's obligatory." During 1980 Antonio had to be in Nachig every Sunday, and during his "on" period he had to be at the Community Building every afternoon to "accompany the Agente." Even during his official "off" periods he found it hard to get to his job in Tuxtla, for there were also obligations (like the year-renewal ceremonies by the hamlet's curers, Vogt 1969: 160) that required all Principales to be present. Antonio could not work enough to support his family, and he borrowed money during his year of service. In his case, and those of other migrant wage workers like José GG, who served on the School Committee, obligations to the new local administration every afternoon added substantially to the burden of service. Corn farmers and merchants suffered less.

The hamlet restrained the expansion in two ways. One was simple and of local importance: some of the cargos created in the 1970's were eliminated by the early 1980's. The Auxiliador de Agente cargo that had been served during the 1977–79 period, when Yermo was Agente Municipal, was discontinued. So too was the separate School Committee established when the local preschool (Jardín de Niños) had been opened. Its demise came at a regular semiannual hamlet meeting, where appointments were made and cooperative work like street and path maintenance was planned. The assembled crowd discussed the way the tax burden for fiestas fell more heavily on a smaller and smaller number of men not exempt from taxes,[3] and decided to discontinue the committee.

The second reaction to the growing burdens of public service had more far-reaching effects. It changed the relations of Nachig to Hteklum, and set a precedent for other hamlets. The problem came to a head in 1981, when the Elders called on Nachig to name a local man as one of their Scribes.[4] At that time all men had rights to a "rest" from taxpaying after a period of service,[5] but they were not protected from appointment to another position, and they were especially vulnerable to the argument of authorities in Hteklum, who might not recognize service to their hamlets. The Scribe named at the Nachig meeting agreed to serve, but he demanded protection from other appointments during his service and a guaranteed period of rest after service. The meeting generalized his request into a hamlet policy, and Nachig leaders got the Presidente Municipal to endorse the hamlet meeting's resolution and the Elders to recognize its validity. The Nachig Rest Resolution of 1981 unambiguously established the equal status of hamlet-level and municipio-level service, and guaranteed tax exemption and freedom from other service on both levels to men who served on either level.

In sum, although framed in terms that protected individuals from the burdens of service, the Nachig Rest Resolution established the right of the hamlet to demand service of its residents even when that meant that they would not be available to serve in Hteklum. Thus, it undermined the traditional authority of Hteklum and enhanced the independence of the hamlet.

The Creation of New Hamlets

The strains associated with growth and decentralization also led to the creation of new hamlets. In the late 1970's, Nachig split into three parts: Nachig, Jechtoch to the east, and Jechchentic to the west (Map 2). Though distinct processes, the splitting off of Jechtoch and Jechchentic both involved localism inspired by government projects (Chapter 3) and the political conflict that will be discussed in detail in Chapter 8.

Jechtoch made a relatively clean, simple break from Nachig. Its area was not included when the Nachig piped-water system was built in the late 1960's, since it was on higher ground and could not be served by the original installation. The difference in interests created by this government program, plus an influx of people from the adjacent hamlet of Vochojvo, sharpened the definition of the area.

When Domingo Pérez entered as Presidente in January 1977, Jechtoch people generally sided with the opposition that was led by Marcos Pérez, a Vochojvo man (Chapter 8). A Jechtoch man entered as a Nachig Agente in Domingo Pérez's administration (along with Yermo), but within a month he had resigned. Soon, with the help of Marcos Pérez, Jechtoch people began two local projects that confirmed the separateness of the area. They sought cooperative labor from the entire hamlet of Nachig for construction of a separate water system, but the help was refused (apparently on the grounds that the original system was by this time capable of supplying Jechtoch as well). So they built the system themselves (with government technical advice and materials). At about the same time in 1977, the Agente who had resigned and two other men organized a successful petition for a school. Again, only Jechtoch people contributed labor.

At this point Jechtoch began collecting taxes separately from Nachig, and sent them to Hteklum through the Principales in Vochojvo—thus supporting the political opposition while Nachig supported Domingo Pérez, the Presidente. In early 1979, after two years of this makeshift arrangement, Jechtoch got its own local Principales and emerged as a hamlet.[6]

The separation of Jechchentic from Nachig was less definite and more conflictful. Jechchentic had more connections to Nachig: they were united by the original water system, Nachig children attended the federal school in Jechchentic, and Nachig adults served on the

School Committee (for many years after the break began; José GG).
And terrain more clearly separated the Jechchentic population from
potential allies in other hamlets.

The open controversy between Jechchentic and Nachig began, as
it did with Jechtoch, when Domingo Pérez entered as Presidente.
Many Jechchentic people cooperated with Marcos Pérez and his followers. And they stopped contributing to the Fiesta of the Virgen de
Fátima, Nachig's patron saint. According to Yermo, Nachig people
let the failure to contribute pass in 1977; they waited a year to see
if things would calm down.

Things did not calm down. The issue came to a head during Holy
Week in 1978. Anticipating the hamlet meeting that was to take
place, Yermo, as Agente, contacted the leader of Jechchentic and requested that they rejoin Nachig. The leader responded that he would
ask his people at their meeting. On the meeting day Nachig people
could see the Jechchentic meeting from their own meeting, which
was taking place a few hundred meters away, but they could not tell
what was being said. Afterwards, the Jechchentic leader reported
that he had forgotten to discuss the topic. The Nachig men assembled again, and that same day they went to Jechchentic and cut the
pipes leading from the public water supply to the houses of opposition members. Only those who had continued to pay taxes in Nachig
were spared.

The turmoil continued for many years, as we will see in later
chapters.[7] Jechchentic became one of the "hamlets" defined by a
combination of party membership and place of residence: as time
passed some Jechchentic people switched parties and paid taxes to
Nachig Principales, while some Nachig people paid taxes to Jechchentic Principales. When water service to opposition members in
Jechchentic was cut off, Nachig Agentes and the Water and Light
Committee had to deal with the clandestine attempts to use the
water: they reprimanded a woman for giving water to her mother-
in-law (who was of the other party), and jailed a man after he was
caught connecting to the public system after dark. Although its intensity varied, the conflict continued into the 1980's.

Summary of the Discussion of Nachig

The number of hamlet offices in Nachig expanded rapidly in the
1970's (Table 7.1). The construction of the church in the late 1960's,
recruitment of Sacristans to care for it, and the naming of Mayordomos beginning in 1976 led to local religious activities involving
many volunteers as well as those who filled the formal roles. The

construction of the Community Building and the jail in Nachig accompanied establishment of a formal local government headed by Agentes, and this local activity made some older offices, like that of Principal, more burdensome—especially because the wage work to which many Nachig men devoted themselves in the 1970's did not allow the flexible schedules possible when corn farming was dominant in the 1960's. Though Nachig and its people maintained multiple ties to Hteklum, the formalization of hamlet organization made it increasingly possible and necessary to live public life at the hamlet level. By the late 1970's, the hamlet itself began a painful process of separation into three parts.

The Transformation of Local Institutions in All the Hamlets

Public life decentralized throughout Zinacantán in the 1970's. New places were recognized as hamlets, new offices were created, churches were built, and mayordomo-like cargos were established.

The hamlets differed at the outset, and they followed diverse paths into these transformations of local institutions. Vochojvo and Paste, large hamlets like Nachig, fissioned into two or more hamlets. Navenchauc, the other large hamlet of the 1960's, divided into political parties that often operated as separate units, but the hamlet retained one official name and its people jointly conducted some of their activities. Many of the changes in Nachig came later to other hamlets. On the whole, all the hamlets went in the same direction, but their pace and their situation in the early 1980's differed. In what follows I will first present an overview of changes in hamlet organization and civil offices, then describe changes in the religious cargo system in the hamlets.

Hamlet Organization and Civil Offices

Table 7.2 presents an overview of change in all the hamlets. About a dozen new place names (indented in column A) were added to the 19 found on a public-works tax list in 1965 (see Table 6.4). Most of the names belong to new hamlets that had their own Principales and appeared on tax lists in the early 1980's. For the most part they were long-established places and neighborhoods that took on official status. Notes to Table 7.2 (and see especially text note 7.16) give details on the formal status of the places, and on differences among consultants on these matters. I believe that many of these changes have parallels to the processes involved in the fission of Nachig.

TABLE 7.2

Hamlets, Agentes, and Schools[a]

Hamlet[b] (A)	Fiesta tax lists[c]			Agente named (E)	Agencia built (F)	School built (G)	Built by (H)
	1973 (B)	1980 (C)	1983 (D)				
Hteklum	a	X	X	—	—	Early[a]	?
Vochojvo	a	X	—	—	—	1965[a]	Fed.
Vochojvo Alto	—	—	X	—	—	a	Fed.
Vochojvo Bajo	—	—	X	—	—	a	Fed.
Patosil	X[a]	X	X	—	—	1954	INI
San Nicolás	—	X	X	—	—	1980	Fed.
La Selva	X	X	X	—	—	1983	Fed.
Salinas	—	X	X	—	—	1977	Fed.
Petztoj	—	X	X	—	—	1979	Fed.
Tierra Blanca	—	—	—	—	—	Early	?
Nachig	X	X	X	1972	1972	Early[a]	?
Jechtoch	—	—	X	—	—	1979	Fed.
Jechchentic	—	—	X	—	—	1979	Fed.
Paste	X	X	X	1972	1970's[a,d]	1955	INI
Shulvo	X	X	X	—	a	1972	Fed.
Elanvo	X[a]	X	X	1974	1980	1956	INI
Chajtoj	a	X	X	a	1981	1979	Fed.
Yalentay	X	X	X	—	—	1956	INI
Pig	X	X	X	—	—	1977	Fed.
Navenchauc	X	X	X	1960's	1960's[d]	Early[a]	?
Apaz	X	X	X	1974	1970's[d]	Early	?

| | Fiesta tax lists[c] | | | | | | |
Hamlet[b] (A)	1973 (B)	1980 (C)	1983 (D)	Agente named (E)	Agencia built (F)	School built (G)	Built by (H)
Zequentic	X	X	X	1972	1970's[d]	Early	?
Jocchenom	X	X	X	1972	1980	1956	INI
Joigel	X	X	X	—	—	—	INI
Chainatic	X	X	X	1971	1980	1956	INI
Potovtic	[a]	X	X	1972	1980	1969	Fed.
Joigelito	—	X	X	1972	[a]	1956	INI
Chiquinibalvo	—	—	X[a]	—	—	1972	Fed.
San Antonio[e]	X	X	X	—	—	—	—
Shucun[e]	X	X	X	—	—	—	—
Jocotal[e]	—	X	X	—	—	—	—
Bomchen[e]	—	—	X	—	—	—	—
Avanchen[e]	—	—	X	—	—	—	—

[a] Notes on sources and details not in the table or the text are organized by column and printed as note 7.16.
[b] Names of places not on 1965 tax lists (Table 6.4) are indented.
[c] During the period covered, X indicates present and — indicates not present.
[d] Indicates that I used indirect evidence to reach this conclusion. Other entries are based on direct statements or on documents.
[e] Not usually seen as a hamlet.

Two non-routine changes are recorded in the tax lists (Table 7.2, columns B, C, and D). First, the special tax status of Hteklum and Vochojvo (Chapter 6) continued from the 1960's through 1973, but was eliminated by 1980. Second, the appearance of Bomchen and Abanchen on 1983 tax lists resulted from political polarization similar to that that created Jechchentic; both were groups of people defined by political affiliation and residence in or near the places from which they took their names.

The appointment of Agentes in nine hamlets (column E) was the most important organizational change of the early 1970's. According to Domingo Pérez, it began in 1971 when some people from the Cornfields that were organized under a single ejido official asked that an Agente be appointed for their hamlet. Other hamlets followed, and soon virtually every place with a 1965 population of more than 100 (Table 6.3) had its own Agente, and many soon had some kind of official local building (Table 7.2, column F).

Both the Agentes and many of the building projects were initiated while Marcos Pérez was Presidente (1971–73).[8] Pérez, a particularly effective and well-connected man, combined with the Velasco Suárez administration (including PRODESCH) to make the basic changes that decentralized Zinacantán's civil organization. It is hard to separate Pérez's role from the impetus of outside forces like PRODESCH, whose efforts also changed many other municipios, but it is widely agreed that the next Presidente in Zinacantán was not as effective in soliciting government resources.

Schools (columns G and H) were important markers of hamlet identity. Some of the larger hamlets had schools before the 1950's. The Hteklum school was probably the first, because Hteklum had a large Ladino population when the road between Tuxtla Gutiérrez and San Cristóbal passed through there (i.e., before the completion of the Pan American Highway about 1950). Tierra Blanca still had many Ladino residents in the 1980's; it may have had a school before the hamlets that were dominated by Zinacantecos. My guess is that the "early" schools in the large hamlets (Navenchauc, Apaz, and Zequentic) were built in the late 1930's or early 1940's along with the Nachig school. A federal school was built in Navenchauc in 1958, making it the first hamlet with two schools. Most of the seven schools added to the federal system in the 1970's were in places just achieving hamlet status, as were the four added in the 1980's in places near Hteklum.[9]

Many factors contributed to the construction of buildings and the establishment of new offices at the hamlet level during the period

The chapel, public buildings, and the basketball court in Chajtoj, 1984.

covered in Table 7.2. They included increasing population, government agencies seeking to expand their services and influence, local leaders seeking areas of influence, and political conflict (Chapter 8). PRODESCH, for example, had standards that encouraged the provision of services to local populations of 250 or more. As in Jechtoch, the resulting new schools led to definition of local communities that would contribute labor for construction and would supply members for the School Committee. Other agencies sought out local groups to form cooperative societies for a variety of agricultural programs (Antonio FF). It is hard to separate the various influences, and inappropriate to do so, for each of the activities provided alternatives to Zinacantecos seeking identities for their local communities and independence from Hteklum.

Land tenure was the focus of other changes during the same period. Under the agrarian code that was revised during the Echeverría administration there were three kinds of land tenure: communal land (*comunal*), ejidos, and small properties (*pequeñas propriedades*). All three types existed in Zinacantán, and all three were involved in the changes.

Most of the populated land east of the Cornfields was communal land. While officially held jointly and administered by an organization of community members, communal land was treated as private property by most Zinacantecos; in Nachig there was little if any land not officially assigned to individuals. Before the revision of the agrarian code in the early 1970's, the Presidente Municipal established boundaries, recorded transfers of ownership, and settled inheritance disputes. Then, as noted above, Communal Land Committees were established to administer activities and to protect the common interest in the land. Their organization paralleled that of the ejido, with an administrative committee, a vigilance committee, and regular meetings of the full membership at which problems were discussed. The committee expanded the number of offices that Zinacantecos had to fill and the number of meetings they had to attend.[10]

Under the law, small properties were essentially private holdings subject only to size restrictions. Large land holdings like the few Ladino-owned ranches still in Zinacantán fit into this category, as did the smaller private holdings of Zinacantecos who had purchased ranches (like Yalentay) that had not been distributed in land reform in earlier decades (Map 3). Though Zinacantecos formed associations of owners to purchase and administer these lands, they held the land as individuals, and service to the associations did not earn tax exemption. Relatively few Zinacantecos owned small properties. For example, less than 15 percent of Nachig men in the 1983 census ($N = 315$) owned plots in the areas of Pig[11] and Shucun that had been purchased from Ladinos. More Nachig men acquired land in nearby San José Bocemtenelte in 1988. The purchase of Ladino land that survived land reform occurred in other parts of the municipio, including San Nicolás and La Selva.

The most important influence of land-tenure laws on hamlet organization came in the early 1970's, when residents of the Cornfields opted to organize the entire area as an ejido. In doing so they incorporated all local residents and land—including parcels that had been private communal land—thereby expropriating lands owned by members of other hamlets.[12] This move took land from many residents of the eastern hamlets who had inherited land in the Cornfields, and created political antagonisms that lasted into the 1980's.

In sum, civil offices were greatly decentralized in the 1970's, and many new hamlets were established. The formalization of hamlet government and the activity associated with new schools, Communal Land Committees, and other government programs greatly increased the number of people serving in hamlet offices, and substantially decreased the dependence of hamlets, old and new, on Hteklum.

Religious Cargos

Between the late 1960's and the early 1980's, four hamlets created new religious cargos, doubling the number of cargos served outside

Hteklum (Table 7.3).[13] With the addition of churches and cargos in Nachig, Paste, and Elanvo, the proportion of Zinacantecos living in hamlets with their own cargos also doubled, and reached 60 percent of those living outside the Center (Table B.4). During the same period, four other hamlets built new churches, and created new ways of caring for them and their saints. Finally, in the late 1970's the Catholic Church recruited Catechists in all the hamlets that had churches.

The decentralization of religious activity had more diverse origins than the spread of Agentes and other hamlet officials. The Navenchauc church was built in part in response to Protestant missionary activity (Cancian 1965: 164). Like Nachig's church, it had active encouragement from Catholic Church officials outside Navenchauc. Apaz's church depended more on local initiative, and, I think, on competition with Navenchauc. Since Zinacanteco accounts of the origin of hamlet churches seldom mentioned other hamlets, it is hard to assess the contribution of such competitive sentiments. Nonetheless, the dates of the construction of churches and the establishment of cargos in Nachig, Paste, and Elanvo suggest that the events are related.

Lorenzo López, a Paste resident who was Senior Alcalde Viejo in 1975, gave the following account of the construction of the church and the establishment of cargos in Paste:

An old man in Paste had a private saint, a Virgen de Rosario that he had gotten from the church in Hteklum many years before when he was a Mayordomo [see also Wasserstrom 1983: 234]. He kept it in his house, but did not care for it well. It had no clothes, and it got smokey. Then some people built a small building for it near his house, but it was still like a private saint.

One year during Santa Cruz [when people were doing neighborhood ceremonies; Vogt 1969, and Chapter 11, below] the old man had the little house locked and would not allow people to enter to pray. The people came to me and said they wanted to have a church. José Sánchez, who was Presidente, said it was fine if we wanted to build a church, and the material was prepared. By this time the old man had died, but his son agreed to give the saint to the church. Another man, Mariano Méndez, had a San Pedro Mártir in his house and agreed to give it also.

We brought in a sculptor from another town, and he set up in the little house where the Virgen de Rosario was and refurbished both saints. By the time he had finished his work, the church was ready and both saints were brought to it. It was the Fiesta of Rosario in October—the same fiesta celebrated in Salinas.

When everything was ready, a Head of the Church Committee was named. He collected money for the fiesta—about five pesos per person—each year.

TABLE 7.3

Churches and Cargos in the Hamlets[a]

Hamlet (A)	Church built (B)	Cargos since (C)	Number of cargos (D)	Committee[b] (E)	Sacristans (F)	Catechists (G)	Flowers changed by (H)
Salinas	ca. 1859	ca. 1850	2	X	2	1	Officials
Navenchauc	1950's	1957	2	X	4	2	Officials
		1982	+ 2				
Apaz	1962	1960	4	X	3	2	Officials
Nachig	1967	1976	2	[c]	4	2	Officials
Paste	1971	1977	2	X	2	4	Officials
Elanvo	1972	1979	2	—	2	4	Officials
Chajtoj	1967	—	0	—	0	3	Residents
Zequentic	1971	—	0	X	1	3	Residents
Jocchenom	1983	—	0	X	0	4	Residents
Joigelito	1973	—	0	X	—	2	Residents

[a]Data for columns E through H are for 1984. Notes on sources and details not in the table or text are organized by column and printed as note 7.17.
[b]X indicates Church Committee present; − indicates not present. All committees had a Head (the name of the office varied), a Secretary, and a Treasurer (except Navenchauc, which had no Treasurer).
[c]Committee established when church was built was later discontinued.

After about five years a group of people came to me and said they wanted to have Mayordomos. José de la Cruz, [the past Presidente, who was apparently Lorenzo's principal rival for leadership in Paste] objected, but the problems got worked out. The Agente of Paste agreed to the plan, and I named the first two Mayordomos.

By 1982 there was a waiting list kept by the two Sacristans of the Paste church. It was ten years long for the senior position and seven years for the junior position. Each year people came to the church during the Fiesta of Rosario to request the cargos. Candles signaling appointment were carried from the Paste church to prospective incumbents each year by the Principales—thereby replicating the procedure used in Hteklum (Cancian 1965: 130).

In hamlets close to Hteklum, the informal leaders organized many early activities that followed forms already used there. In Paste, as in Nachig, first a Church Committee was appointed to take care of the church and organize the fiesta, then Sacristans were appointed, and finally cargos and waiting lists were established. Details varied a bit from hamlet to hamlet—for example, Elanvo had no Church Committee, and had permanent Sacristans rather than the term appointments of Hteklum, and in Nachig the Church Committee was eventually discontinued. Nevertheless, the influence of Hteklum as a model was clear.

Other hamlets, especially those in the Cornfields, followed new paths. They had churches without cargos. Some developed stable, cooperative ways of organizing fiestas and flower changes in their churches (Table 7.3, column H). Zequentic stands out, for it is a large hamlet and had a church since 1971. There, according to one of the local elders, a man was appointed by a hamlet meeting to administer church funds collected from the people of the hamlet. Funds were spent for the Fiesta of Dolores (the patron's fiesta) and for flower changes several times during the year. The administrator was responsible for buying the flowers and other things needed for the ritual, but did not spend his own money.

In Joigelito, a much smaller population than Zequentic, flower changes were done every two weeks, and each time a different man was responsible for the food, flowers, and whatever else was needed, according to Robert Laughlin, who participated in a flower change in 1983. Laughlin reported that 23 local men were fed when he attended, and that total expenses were $7,000 per flower change (at a time when laborers were earning $300 to $600 per day for work in Tuxtla Gutiérrez).

The mood of the cooperative ritual occasions was different from the more formal rituals of the regular cargoholders, according to two non-Zinacanteco observers familiar with both settings. Laughlin described the Joigelito ritual as "loose" and "soft." And Padre José Luis Argüelles was enthusiastic about the community spirit in Chajtoj, where the 30 families shared a meal after Mass when he arrived to say it every month or two. In the middle 1980's, these egalitarian activities distinguished Zequentic and the smaller populations (Joigelito and Chajtoj) from Nachig, Paste, and Elanvo, where the time from the first church construction to the establishment of cargos had been less than a decade in each case. Whether this distinctiveness will last is hard to tell.[14]

Shortly after the construction of churches and the establishment of cargos by Zinacantecos, the priests serving the churches from headquarters in San Cristóbal recruited local residents in each hamlet to serve as Catechists, lay teachers of doctrine who held weekly sessions in the local churches. In keeping with Vatican Council II, the church demanded greater preparation from those receiving the sacraments and sought to provide instruction in the native language.[15]

Summary

During the 1970's, hamlets grew in importance as formal hamlet offices were established; public works projects helped mark hamlet identity. Revision of land-tenure laws and formalization of the Cornfields as a distinct unit further decentralized the political organization of the municipio. Construction of hamlet churches and the creation of hamlet cargos freed many Zinacantecos from involvement with the religious cargo system in Hteklum.

Many of these changes preceded the conflict of the late 1970's. They can be viewed as early signs of the conflict and, at the same time, as providing the institutional preconditions that promoted the political process that is the focus of Chapter 8.

8 / EVENTS AT THE CENTER

Open political conflict began in 1976, and lasted for more than ten years. During this period, routine community activities like fiestas and service in public offices reflected political divisions—and the administration of large state grants to the municipio government further focused the conflict. Though they were never of immediate importance to the majority of Zinacantecos, violence and the threat of force became much more prevalent than they had been in the immediately preceding decades.[1] In general terms, the institutional bases of interaction among Zinacantecos were constantly negotiated and changed, as were party alignments and personal alliances. The expectations of many people about how things should be were repeatedly violated and altered.

This chapter focuses on the events of the period, especially those involving civil government, party politics, and factions. Three elections for Presidente Municipal (in 1976, 1979, and 1982) marked turning points in the course of events, and I will organize the exposition around them and the local administrations they produced. My presentation and analysis depend on many different accounts by Zinacantecos and others present at the time, and relate the events to a few major themes.

I will argue that crucial events and alliances that were seen locally in political terms are better understood as competition for control of lucrative transport routes. This interpretation does not depend on subtle insight or careful observation: by the middle of the period, the largest political factions in Zinacantán were popularly labeled "Truckers" (*Camioneros*) and "Peasants" (*Campesinos*)—a clear suggestion that class interests were emerging in politics. Yet, both the Truckers and the Peasants were led by members of the transportation elite, that is, by wealthy men who had interests in trucking and/or passenger transport. Zinacantán's elite competed with each other for control of the economic resources brought by the national prosperity—rather than unifying to consolidate their positions.

The events may also be seen as a struggle to fill the power vacuum left by the demise of Mariano Hernández Zárate, who headed the ejido movement and dominated Zinacantán's politics for three decades (Chapter 6). Zárate's situation was importantly different from that of the new leaders, for his power depended on resources (land) that he distributed to individuals after he led a broad-based drive to get the land-reform laws applied to Zinacantán. In contrast, the power of the new elite of the late 1970's and early 1980's depended on wealth gathered from individual Zinacanteco passengers (after deals with the bankers who financed privately owned trucks)—and on the ability to broker distribution of government development funds.

The events of 1976 also reflect the strain between the Center and the outlying hamlets. Navenchauc had long felt a rivalry with the Center: in the 1950's and 1960's, its political leaders had opposed Mariano Hernández Zárate and had found support in the Cornfields, in part because those hamlets had a separate ejido and did not depend on Zárate as much (Chapter 6). Despite this rivalry and pressure, or perhaps because of it, the Presidentes who served between 1960 and 1976 were all from hamlets closer to the Center. Navenchauc, Apaz, and the Cornfields had been closed out of political leadership for many years.[2] The Center's control of auxiliary religious posts like Sacristan and Scribe (Chapter 6) added to the tension.

The larger context of these local events resists summary, for it extends to the national political situation, and the extraordinary importance of petroleum during these years, and from there to the international political economy of the period. Nevertheless, it is important to emphasize the local effects of the government and church programs described in detail in Chapters 3 and 7. Without the persistent intervention in Zinacantán's internal life, the enormous increases in the resources controlled by Zinacantán's politicians, and the high rate of labor migration, the history of these years would have been quite different.

The Pérez Years, 1977–1979

Most Zinacantecos traced the origins of open political conflict to the process leading to Domingo Pérez's nomination in 1976. During his administration political parties developed, and the sharp division of Zinacantán's population into parties jelled. Municipio services, the collection of taxes, and the organization of religious ritual were all modified. Tradition was repeatedly upset.

Traditional Elections

The election of 1976 was different from traditional elections in the 1950's, 1960's, and early 1970's. To mark the difference, I will describe the four major steps involved in traditional elections. First, political leaders met informally to identify appropriate candidates. During much of this period, Mariano Hernández Zárate probably dominated these small meetings. Second, at a nominating meeting in July or August, hundreds of men, including some from each hamlet, gathered in the churchyard on a Sunday, heard nominations, and indicated support or opposition. This process sometimes ended with obvious strong support for a single candidate, and sometimes involved voting to choose between two men with strong support. After the Presidente was chosen, the slate was filled out with the remaining civil officials. It was considered appropriate for a strongly supported losing candidate for Presidente to take another high position on the slate, that is, to become the candidate for Síndico or First Regidor. Third, the PRI party apparatus outside Zinacantán accepted the people named at this meeting as its official slate of candidates. Finally, at an election on the third Sunday of November, ballot boxes for all the voting districts of Zinacantán were assembled at the town hall in Hteklum, where officials marked the overwhelming majority of ballots for PRI (and a few for other parties) and put them in the ballot boxes.

This picture of traditional elections is supported by many Zinacanteco accounts. It also conforms to the account given by Pablo Ramírez of procedures used in all highland Indian municipios during the 1973 and 1976 elections, which he supervised for PRI; and it fits with my observation of activity in Hteklum during an election in the 1960's. Vogt's account of elections (1969: 290f.) is probably a better characterization of the early elections of the period; however, it does not include the last two steps, which integrate Zinacanteco actions with the PRI party apparatus and the national election system.

These procedures left plenty of room for pressure from interested parties inside and outside Zinacantán. Zinacanteco leaders had to produce candidates that could survive the sometimes stinging criticism shouted from the crowd at the nomination meeting—candidates who, after discussion and compromise in response to internal opposition, could retain the respect of the vast majority of Zinacantecos and function effectively while in office. At the same time the leaders had to find a candidate who could effectively mediate between the community and the outside government (see Dennis 1973 on the Presidente Municipal in Oaxaca).

Conflict often accompanied the selection of the candidate for Presidente and those who would serve with him; but, according to older Zinacantecos, opposition leaders did little if anything to disrupt the administration of Zinacantán's business after the election. Municipio services, construction projects, taxation, and the appointment of fiesta officials, as well as the local court system (see J. F. Collier 1973), all worked without major disruption. Even in 1960, when the Presidente (Yermo) and Mariano Hernández Zárate clashed and the Presidente was forced to resign from office, the conflict was viewed more as a clash of persons than as a clash of parties or a breakdown of the system (Vogt 1969: 286f.).[3]

The Election of 1976

All this changed in 1976. By the third Sunday in November, when the PRI candidate was elected Presidente Municipal, the traditional pattern had been decisively altered, a strong opposition group had formed, and the period of intracommunity conflict that was to last more than ten years had opened.

The election process began as usual: the public nomination meeting on August 22, 1976, named candidates for Presidente and other offices described above, and PRI accepted the candidates as its slate. But then—in an expression of the simmering dissatisfaction left from the meeting—two candidates resigned from the slate. In the weeks that followed, many candidates, including those for the three highest offices, were replaced. Domingo Pérez became the second official PRI candidate for Presidente, and eventually was elected.

The following account, from *El Caminante*, a church newsletter dated February 1977, dates and describes the major events of the summer and fall of 1976, and gives one assessment of what happened. Accounts based on the recollections of various other participants follow it.[4]

ZINACANTÁN

On August 22 Mariano Jolote, who had been a Sacristan for more than twenty years, was nominated as candidate for Presidente. His nomination was made by a majority, and in the presence of Lic. Angel Robles [the head of PRODESCH] and the local representative of PRI. That same day an official slate was drawn up. But, soon resignations were submitted by the Síndico, from Navenchauc, and by a [Civil] Regidor from Chainatic.

Navenchauc has been for some time a population in rivalry with the Center, Zinacantán [Hteklum], even to the point of discussing its desire to have the seat of municipio government moved from Zinacantán to Navenchauc. This population also has a group of leaders who enjoy government support. Navenchauc did not agree with the nomination of Mariano Jolote because he is not from there. Navenchauc hoped to have, at least, the Presidente.

On September 19th Lic. Pablo Ramírez declares that the nomination is valid, but that, because of the resignation of the Síndico and the Regidor, there must be a new election [nomination]. Therefore, Domingo Pérez was nominated, it seemed, without having a majority and with signs of imposition. It was said that there were more people there involuntarily than voluntarily [*mas acarreados que gente*]. Ramírez himself charged on this occasion that the local head of PRI had made a compromise with Navenchauc. Given this situation, Mariano Jolote officially resigned the nomination given him by the people.

The supporters of Jolote disagree with what was done and protest; but Angel Robles tells them definitively that no change is possible.

Domingo Pérez is an agricultural extension agent at PRODESCH, a friend of Robles and of Dr. Velasco Suárez [the outgoing governor], an informant for anthropologists; he speaks Spanish well and has been to the United States. Nonetheless, the people do not accept him, since he was famous for levying high fines during the period when he was a Regidor [1971–73], and soon rumors began circulating that he is to blame for mishandling funds relating to the purchase of a bell for the Navenchauc church, the construction of the church, and the reforestation of Apaz.

On November 7 there was an informal meeting at which the [incumbent] Presidente was present. Accusations against Domingo came out there. People wanted to adopt a resolution from this meeting, but the Presidente forcefully opposed doing so. The reaction of the people was to pull him down and to tear his clothes, and to try to put him in jail. A judge notified the [outside] authorities, and that night the judicial police jailed eight men from Zinacantán, and another group from Navenchauc that had asked for protection from Tuxtla. Others escaped to the woods.

On November 9 Angel Robles and the agent from the attorney general [*ministerio público*] accompanied by lawyers and soldiers representing both sides presented themselves and signed an agreement with the two parties: Domingo is the single candidate and everybody is disposed to cooperate in order to celebrate the upcoming fiesta.

The election took place November 21; and the people of Zinacantán, the supporters of Mariano Jolote, and part of Navenchauc abstained. Only a part of Navenchauc (estimated to be 50–60 men) and the hamlets beyond voted for Domingo Pérez.

Other accounts of the first nominating meeting agree that Jolote was supported by a clear majority of the crowd present. Only Robert Laughlin (see note 8.4) remembered that a clear "slice" (about 25 percent of the pie-shaped crowd that surrounded the kiosk in the churchyard) failed to raise their hands in support of Jolote. In fact, he recalls, they left the meeting in protest and regrouped at a local bar for over an hour—while the meeting's chair, the president of Zinacantán's PRI committee, José Sánchez (the Presidente for 1965–67) tried to get them to come back. These protesters were people from Navenchauc and beyond. Finally they returned, and the slate that was completed included a Síndico from Navenchauc and a First Regidor from Chainatic.

The compromise was problematic from the start. The candidates for Síndico and First Regidor protested when they were nominated. According to Yermo, the man from Chainatic, a school teacher working outside of Zinacantán, insisted he could not afford to leave his work. But the crowd insisted that he accept the nomination, because, Yermo said, service cannot be refused. While some observers felt he had put personal benefit ahead of public service, others felt he really wanted to be Presidente and did not want the lesser post.

Whatever his motives, the school teacher from Chainatic soon resigned as a candidate in a letter presented at PRODESCH. (It was no doubt presented to Pablo Ramírez, who besides being a PRI official was also an employee of PRODESCH.) The Navenchauc man who was the candidate for Síndico also resigned. Some accounts added that half a dozen or more official candidates for lower offices also resigned at this time—arguing that, while a good man, Jolote spoke too little Spanish to be an effective Presidente.

The resignations brought Pablo Ramírez to Zinacantán for the meeting of September 19. According to various accounts, including his own, Ramírez read the letters of resignation to the crowd, and said that new nominations for Síndico and First Regidor were needed. Some in the crowd insisted that, if the Síndico and the First Regidor could be replaced, so could the Presidente. According to Yermo these men were angry because they felt manipulated "like children" by the inappropriate resignations of duly nominated candidates. The meeting continued, and, after some argument, Ramírez confirmed the possibility of replacing the Presidente candidate as well, if it could all be done soon in order to meet official deadlines. In what followed, at least one man (Pedro Vázquez, who was to become Presidente six years later) successfully declined to be considered by pointing out to the crowd that he had just served as Head of the Church Committee and needed time to earn.

Domingo Pérez was nominated with the support of the majority of those present, according to most accounts. Substantial numbers were opposed, according to all accounts, including Pérez's own. Jolote formally resigned, saying he did not want to serve amid conflict. Some, including some of his supporters, felt he did not "fight like a man."

At the unofficial third meeting, on November 7, the diehard opposition, frustrated by its inability to upset Pérez's nomination, roughed up the incumbent Presidente. Some protesters were arrested, and outside police were sent to Zinacantán to protect the Presidente. The tumultuous period had begun.

PAN Forms, Conflict Spreads

The opposition formed around Marcos Pérez, the Presidente during 1971–73, who remained well connected in state political circles. Despite his contacts in PRI, or, some think, because of them, he and the protestors associated with the major national opposition party, PAN,[5] and they made an alliance with Manuel Chuchcun, leader of a long-standing internal opposition in Navenchauc.

Public conflict was renewed on January 1, 1977, the day of Domingo Pérez's installation as Presidente. The people supporting Pérez formed in front of the town hall, and the opposition gathered in the churchyard (see Vogt 1969: 158–59, 376–77). Each group broadcast its arguments with a bullhorn. Just before the ceremony, a man from Navenchauc asked the Elders to refuse to take their traditional part in it, but they decided to attend, and Pérez was sworn in in the traditional manner. By the Fiesta of San Sebastián a few weeks later, the Elders had changed their position: they did not invite Pérez to the traditional meal with them, and thus broadcast their split with him to the many hundreds of people present.[6]

There was also trouble with Pérez's immediate colleagues in the civil government. Three of the four Alcaldes Jueces (judges) elected with Pérez refused to be sworn in with him. After high state officials intervened, the three and a newly chosen fourth judge were sworn in and set up independently of Pérez in a building away from the town hall. Thus, Zinacantecos seeking settlement of disputes could choose Pérez and his people or the opposition judges. The opposition judges attended installations of religious officials, thus making each ceremony a reaffirmation of the division.

Bands at fiestas became an important symbol of the split. Traditionally the one Ladino band hired by the Fiesta Committee had been called upon to accompany various groups of officials and volunteers in many ritual processions on each day of the fiesta. But, during 1977, the opposition refused to pay taxes for the traditional band and sponsored a separate band—there was a "Presidente's band" and an opposition band at each of the major public events of the year. Suddenly, ritual activity required declarations of party affiliation—for one band or the other had to be asked to participate.

More important still, every household in Zinacantán had to declare party affiliation in order to pay its fiesta taxes. By the second year of Pérez's term, the opposing groups agreed on joint sponsorship of a single band at each major fiesta, but while the settlement provided for a joint meeting to select a single Head of the Fiesta Committee, it also fixed and formalized the collection of taxes by party. Under the agreement each party paid for half of the band, and contributions from members were gathered by party-affiliated tax collectors. People who wished to change parties told one tax collector to stop coming and the other to add them to his list. Thus, in a very short time the division became institutionalized in a way that reached every household in Zinacantán.

The Pérez years began the period of open political conflict in Zinacantán. Events redefined Zinacanteco expectations about the political process in the municipio. The new tax system, divided by party, and divisions in other government activities (like the appointment of parallel Alcaldes Jueces and Agentes, and the refusal of PAN members to contribute labor to the new town hall)[7] institutionalized the separation of the population. While issues were often defined as old political ones involving the power of the Center and the hamlets, we will see below that the leaders of both factions were also involved in a struggle for control of the transport routes in Zinacantán.

Pérez managed to restore some joint activities, but the problems continued through all three years of his term. These troubles were not an indictment of his leadership, for many Zinacantecos respected him as a courageous and effective leader. As we will soon see, succeeding Presidentes had no better luck.[8]

The Conde Years, 1980–1982

The major events of Manuel Conde's administration were directly connected to the CODECOM program (Chapter 3) under which the state government made block grants to municipios. Conde's troubles reflected both the difficulties that the block grants created in many municipios, and the special arrangements made for Zinacantán because of its political divisions. Many Presidentes Municipales in Chiapas left office before the end of the three-year term—usually because of disagreements about the handling of the block grants. Although Conde survived his term, Zinacantán became the only municipio in the state to have two Municipio Development Foundations receiving block grants—one for PRI and one for PAN.

The 1979 Election

The conflict continued in the context of two new voting practices introduced by outside government. First, in the 1979 election an opposition slate had their names printed on the ballot. Previously, major national opposition parties had had symbols on ballots in municipio elections in Zinacantán, but only PRI normally organized a formal slate of candidates. In 1979 the second slate represented PAN. Though Marcos Pérez remained the effective leader of the party, Mariano López was its candidate for Presidente Municipal.

Second, ballot boxes were located in each of Zinacantán's five election districts. While the division into election districts was not new, 1979 was the first year in which the ballot boxes were actually distributed to the official polling places.[9] Individuals (almost exclusively men) voted by marking ballots at open tables monitored by poll watchers from each party. In Nachig, according to Yermo, they then went to stand with the other members of their party. When the balloting was done, the boxes were assembled in a central place for counting.

This process elected the PRI candidate, Manuel Conde, in 1979. Domingo Pérez remembered that Conde, who was from the Cornfields, received more than 3,000 votes, while the PAN candidate, who was from the Center, had about 1,500. Thus, while the victory was clear, the opposition was large. PAN had shown great strength in Zinacantán, and Manuel Conde took over the administration of an openly divided community.

CODECOM Comes to Zinacantán

The state government provided an environment that nurtured the division. Like other new Presidentes in Chiapas, Manuel Conde soon received large block grants for public works. The CODECOM program that provided these grants was both part of a national effort to decentralize government decision making[10] and part of a state-level effort to quiet political unrest (Chapter 3). For Conde, the grants meant responsibilities never before faced by a Presidente in Zinacantán. During his term Domingo Pérez was involved with two major public works projects—the rerouting and paving of the road from San Cristóbal to Hteklum and the construction of a new town hall—but in each case the funds granted by the state were administered by state officials according to project proposals developed in advance. While Pérez promoted the projects and had to ensure the contribution of unskilled labor by Zinacantecos during construction of the town hall, he controlled no money. Workers on the road project were paid by the state.

Conde was given control of large lump sums, advised about appropriate projects, and told to account for disbursed funds before he asked for more. Between February 1980 and June 1981, he received $10 million, in blocks of $1 to $3 million. (Even with the rapid inflation a mason earned $500 per day in wages in Tuxtla at the end of the period; a microbus could be purchased for about a quarter of a million pesos in the middle of the period.)

Formally the funds were administered by a Municipio Development Foundation. According to both policy (Chiapas 1980) and practice in most municipios, the Presidente Municipal also served as Head of the Foundation; but in Zinacantán, Mariano Hernández (DD) was named to the post, along with a Paste man as Treasurer and a Vochojvo man as Secretary. By the end of Conde's first year in office, Zinacantán stood out in another way, for it was given a second Municipio Development Foundation: in order to adapt to the political split in the municipio, state officials began to make separate grants to Marcos Pérez's group.[11]

This arrangement ensured representation of each of three major power blocks. Marcos Pérez stood alone, with PAN. Within PRI there were two opposing blocks: Conde was allied with José de la Cruz of the Center, who was the head of PRI in Zinacantán (eventually, the Peasants), and Mariano Hernández (DD) represented the transportation elite of Nachig and Navenchauc (eventually, the Truckers).

CODECOM projects were oriented towards public works and public service.[12] Production-oriented programs like CODECOA were more difficult to implement, and were much smaller than CODECOM. Most of the more than 150 projects in 1980 and the first part of 1981 were done in the hamlets.[13]

The PAN Foundation, headed by Marcos Pérez, received its first grant of $500,000 in December 1980. Pérez, regarded as an effective administrator even by his political enemies, undertook projects in areas dominated by PAN members, and sometimes appeared to carry out projects the Presidente could not do. For example, in July 1981, Pérez reportedly went to the Presidente to discuss coordinating work on street improvements, and found that the Presidente had used up his budget and could not contribute until he got another grant. Thus, Pérez's projects reflected badly on Manuel Conde's administration.

Conde's worst problem began in late 1980, when there were complaints that he had not accomplished much with CODECOM money. Then, in January 1981, Conde, along with José de la Cruz of the Center and some others, purchased six Volkswagen microbuses with which they intended to connect the Center and San Cristóbal.[14] Soon afterwards rumors began to link the microbuses to CODECOM money. By May there were formal complaints and a public meeting in Nachig, at which Conde and his Foundation staff were not able to account for a large amount of the CODECOM grants—$631,000 according to a man experienced with budgets, and amounts ranging from $300,000 to more than $1 million according to others on different sides of the conflict. By June, formal reports had been demanded and the Secretary and Treasurer of the Foundation had been changed.

On June 20, at a regional meeting of thousands of people in Chamula, the governor publicly asked the Zinacantecos in attendance if they supported their Presidente, and was satisfied enough with the response to grant another $1,000,000 to Conde's Foundation (making its total $10 million) while at the same time making his third grant of $500,000 to the Foundation headed by Marcos Pérez. Conde's problems diminished somewhat in the months that followed, as did grants to Zinacantecos under the CODECOM program.

Zinacantán was unique in having two Foundations, and Conde's problems were severe, but he served to the end of his term—by itself an accomplishment, given that in the state as a whole more than a third of municipio Presidentes fell during the three-year CODECOM period. During immediately preceding periods, the resignation or removal of a Presidente was a rare event.

The Politics of Transport

PRI's dominance in Zinacantán was partially rebuilt during the second half of Manuel Conde's term. The turning point came in November 1981, when three transport groups signed an agreement to cooperate, and Marcos Pérez returned to PRI. The three were the dominant Altos de Chiapas group, the Nachig and Navenchauc truckers associated with Mariano Hernández (DD) who had remained at the core of PRI throughout, and two PAN groups: Marcos Pérez's group that ran buses out of Zinacantán Center, and José Hernández's Hortifruticultores, a smaller group based on Hernández's leadership in Apaz. They agreed to divide routes and not make trouble for each other. Hernández later reported that the troubles he had with officialdom while he was a PAN leader ended after he signed the agreement and again affiliated with PRI.

Many people followed the ex-PAN leaders, and PRI soon dominated numerically. By early summer 1982, when Zinacantecos voted in the national presidential elections that put de la Madrid in office, Nachig voted 600 for PRI to four for PAN, according to Yermo, and another man reported that he had heard PAN had less than 100 members in the whole municipio. PAN had substantial following only in Navenchauc, where it was sustained by the long-standing factionalism, and in Apaz, where its members were angered when their leader, José Hernández, joined Marcos Pérez in the switch to PRI that secured a share of transport routes. PAN's few other members were scattered around the inner hamlets, and included a good number of loyalists in Hteklum.

The agreement among members of the transport elite did not completely unify PRI, because Manuel Conde and José de la Cruz were not included.[15] The Nachig-Navenchauc transport group had cooperated with the PAN leaders because they feared that Conde and de la Cruz would become important forces in local transport. Thus, the realignment left PAN weak and PRI divided into two major factions. As Zinacantecos began to choose Manuel Conde's successor, PRI was numerically dominant, but internally divided.

The Vázquez Years, 1983–1985

In 1982, 108 of 110 municipios in Chiapas elected the PRI candidate for Presidente Municipal.[16] Zinacantán was one of the two exceptions. This happened because one of the PRI factions, frustrated when its candidate lost the nomination, supported Pedro Vázquez, the PAN candidate.

Zinacantán became more sharply divided than ever—with its elected officials on one side and large numbers of PRI leaders who had access to the PRI-dominated state government on the other. After months of internal struggles, Pedro Vázquez resigned from PAN and joined PRI. As we will see below, the change of party temporarily relieved a few problems of his administration, but it did not unify Zinacantán. By the end of Vázquez's term, four sharply defined factions had developed.

The 1982 Election

In mid-summer 1982, the stage was set for the struggle to control PRI. José de la Cruz, the head of PRI in Zinacantán, was allied with Manuel Conde, the incumbent Presidente, who could deliver votes from the Cornfields. The alliance of Navenchauc and Nachig truckers, with Manuel Garcia of Navenchauc emerging more clearly as its leader had been strengthened by many new members who had left PAN, but it remained out of power. Some Zinacantecos began to talk about three parties: the "Presidente's people" (PRI), the "Truckers" (PRI), and PAN.

In early August, as the PRI nominating meeting approached, there was talk of going back to the conciliatory practice of naming strongly supported losing candidates for Presidente to another high

Pedro Vázquez's campaign poster, 1982.

office on the slate. Localist interests were acknowledged in discussions of a proposal to choose the candidate for Presidente from each of the five election districts in turn, starting with the Center.

The battle was joined at the public meeting on August 22.[17] Party leaders presented three names to the meeting. Two, José Sanat, a dump-truck owner from the Center, who had prospered during the CODECOM period, and Juan Martínez, also from the Center, had substantial support. The third had no great support and was soon dropped. Sanat was assailed as the Trucker candidate by men who shouted that they did not want a truck owner. Both sides strongly supported their candidate. After several informal votes produced no clear majority for Sanat or Martínez, it was clear that the meeting was deadlocked, and that the losers would remain bitter if the deadlock were broken by a vote. In an effort to resolve the problem, the outside PRI officials present at the meeting proposed that two completely new candidates be named. Sanat's group agreed. While they did not like the idea, the Martínez group eventually gave in, and two other candidates were named. They were Juan Jolote, Head of the Ejido Committee for the hamlets near the Center and brother of Mariano Jolote of the 1976 election, and Juan Bromas, who apparently had connections to PAN and was an Alcalde Juez in the Conde administration. When it was seen that Bromas had no substantial support, Martínez's followers demanded that Martínez be put up against Jolote. Consensus was clearly impossible, and the outside party officials suggested a vote.

The crowd was separated into two groups. The Jolote supporters went (in trucks) to the churchyard of San Sebastián, a few hundred meters away, and the Martínez people stayed in front of the church of San Lorenzo, where the meeting had begun. When the count was over, Jolote had won, 1,367 to 1,050, according to Yermo.[18] The slate, including a First Regidor from the Cornfields for balance, was quickly completed and informally recorded, and the meeting ended at about 4 P.M. The outside PRI officials suggested that, because it was late and everyone was hungry, the formal slate be drawn up and signed by party officials the next day.

The Truckers had won the first round, the vote to nominate their candidate. Manuel Conde and José de la Cruz had lost. But, according to Yermo, the next day, de la Cruz, who was still head of PRI in Zinacantán, refused to sign the formal slate headed by Juan Jolote. He argued that people were unhappy, and that Martínez had lost the count because it was late in the day and many had left the meeting. (The Conde/de la Cruz supporters, concentrated in the distant Cornfields area, may have been the first to leave the meeting.) As head of PRI he insisted on another meeting.

The factions solidified as each struggled to get its slate registered as the official PRI slate. By September 5, when they met to confirm their support for Juan Martínez, the Conde/de la Cruz slate was being called the Peasants (*Campesinos*), and being identified as the party of the poor—those who opposed the rich Truckers (*Camioneros*).[19]

By mid-October the Truckers won again. Following meetings with state-level PRI officials, including one with the governor-to-be, the Trucker slate was confirmed as the official PRI slate. On October 17, a Paste man was chosen to replace de la Cruz as head of PRI in Zinacantán, and the slate was officially registered with his signature. Thus, de la Cruz and Conde had failed to name their candidate, and de la Cruz had lost his post as formal head of PRI in Zinacantán, after six years in office. Most important, PRI was clearly split into two camps—the Peasants were born.

Meanwhile, PAN had nominated its candidates—at leadership meetings in August, including one attended by the PAN member of the national legislature, who had been elected in July, and at a public meeting on August 29, the Sunday following the PRI public meeting. Pedro Vázquez, the candidate for Presidente, had declined to be considered at the PRI meeting that nominated Domingo Pérez in 1976. Originally from Navenchauc, Pedro Vázquez had lived in the Center since he moved there to be head of the church (Presidente del Templo) in the early 1970's. The other eight men on the PAN slate came from seven other hamlets. None was from the Cornfields, where, through Manuel Conde, PRI was dominant. This PAN slate was registered with state election officials in September, on schedule.

The leaders of the Conde/de la Cruz faction of PRI (the Peasants), decided to support the PAN candidate. Some talked of saving the unity of the party by electing no PRI candidate, others of resisting the dominance of the Truckers, who had, it was rumored, paid $50,000 to have their slate registered as the official one. In early November, the new alliance was confirmed when Navenchauc PAN people joined people from the Cornfields in a show of force against PRI Truckers who were terrorizing their opposition in Paste. Six truckloads of men gathered in Nachig, but a direct confrontation was averted.[20] In Navenchauc Peasants and PAN people stayed away when Jolote, the PRI candidate, came to campaign for their votes. Outside representatives of PAN held meetings, explained election procedures, and organized poll watchers.

TABLE 8.1

Voting by Election District, November 21, 1982

District[a]	Location	Votes			PAN plurality	PAN percent
		PRI	PAN	Total		
1	Hteklum	375	254	629	(121)	40.4%
2	Patosil	276	85	361	(191)	23.5
3	Nachig	771	821	1,592	50	51.6
4	Navenchauc	688	795	1,483	107	53.6
5	Zequentic	121	595	716	474	83.1
All districts		2,231	2,550	4,781	319	53.3%

[a]Districts include more than one hamlet. See the text on the 1979 election.

The vote, on November 21, is shown in Table 8.1. Conde's following in the Cornfields tipped the balance toward PAN, and Zinacantán entered another era of special status that paralleled its distinctive two Foundations during Conde's term as Presidente.

The Period Between the Election and Pedro Vázquez's Installation

The election result was confirmed by a recount the next Sunday, the results were declared final, and the Truckers immediately sought ways to block Vázquez from taking office. Moves and countermoves dominated early December. Rumors of bribes to officials spread among PAN loyalists, who hoped that Vázquez would take office. Some said that Jolote would be imposed by bribed officials, others organized support for Vázquez. Pablo Ramírez, who had access to information about government intentions, seemed certain that Vázquez would take office.

The national economic crisis that began in August added to the local turmoil. Jobs in public works were scarce. In early December, the de la Madrid administration announced a doubling of gasoline prices, from $10 to $20 per liter. Overnight, local transport fares doubled. The Navenchauc to San Cristóbal fare, for example, went from $35 to $70, before settling back to $55. The argument that Pedro Vázquez would fight to control fare increases charged by truck owners became important again. Though unemployment increased after the crisis began, Zinacanteco corn farmers suddenly found that they had to pay unprecedented amounts for field workers.[21] Overall, political and economic life in Zinacantán was very uncertain.

The Truckers made a show of force as the day of Pedro Vázquez's installation approached. On December 27, they assembled truck-loads of men from various hamlets, and took control of the town hall. They broke in, occupied the building, and set up a marimba to entertain themselves during the day. Manuel Conde was in Tuxtla, and Juan Bromas escaped because he was not near the town hall; but according to PAN loyalists, three other officials were roughed up and locked in one of the rooms. By nightfall the Truckers had stationed watches at various points where Pedro Vázquez, Manuel Conde, and José de la Cruz might appear, and they had blocked the road to the Center at the pass near the edge of the municipio. Vázquez, return-ing from an official visit to Tuxtla, was advised of the situation, and spent the night in Navenchauc. Other PAN officials came and went by night. Manuel Conde, it was reported, slipped out of José de la Cruz's house in the early hours of December 28, and, with armed companions, made his way to Tuxtla in a microbus by taking the rough road that connected the Center to the Pan American Highway in Nachig. After consulting PAN and state officials, he returned with advice to keep his people calm.

The next day, the Truckers publicly announced that they had taken the town hall—explaining that they had built it with their labor during Domingo Pérez's term. PAN members had refused to contribute work, and now a PAN Presidente could not use the build-ing. They meant to stop Pedro Vázquez from taking office.

A compromise was reached in Tuxtla on the last day of the year. More than 20 leaders of the two factions met with the governor and other state officials. The PAN national legislator was there with Pedro Vázquez. According to one PRI man (a Trucker) who was there, it went like this:

Governor: Pedro, what do you think?
Pedro Vázquez: I want to take office.
G: How will you get people together?
PV: People, friends, will come with me. I will respect everyone.
G: But others say that you should not use the town hall.
PV: Why?
G: Because you [PAN] didn't work on it. Your people didn't put in days.
PV: We'll do work too. How many days did they work?
José Sanat: Here's the list of days we worked. There are 3,800 days of work.
PV (and Mariano López, the Head of PAN in Zinacantán): We'll put in the days too.
G: What if your people won't work?
PV: We're in agreement. They'll work.
G: What money will you have to work with?
PV: We'll think about that.

G: O.K. If your people are in agreement we will send a document for you to sign. If your people are not in agreement, let me tell you the truth clearly, Pedro: you've got 90 days to get it resolved. Otherwise I'll remove you from office.

Then the governor urged the PRI people to turn over the civil registers so that Vázquez could provide birth certificates and other documents needed by Zinacantecos. More importantly, he declared that Vázquez could serve as Presidente without entering the town hall—that he could enter the building later, when the problems had been resolved.

The PAN Period

Vázquez was installed as Presidente on January 1, 1983, as specified by law. Soon, he and his government were bobbing like a small cork on a stormy sea of conflict. While his own decisions contributed to what happened in the months that followed, his fate was mostly a product of actions he could deflect only slightly from his official position. In this he was like Domingo Pérez and Manuel Conde before him, but as a PAN Presidente he had additional problems—those created when the opposition Truckers led by Manuel Garcia asserted themselves locally and traded on their contacts with the state government and PRI officialdom. Vázquez's resignation from PAN and request to enter PRI came in late August, after many confrontations, much uncertainty, and dissatisfaction and defections among his followers. When he changed parties the town hall was opened to him, and his old office in the Community Building was turned over to a group of police from outside Zinacantán, who took up residence in the Center. The state gave up any hope that negotiations would keep the peace in Zinacantán.

In this section I will document the turmoil between January and August, with special attention to the status of the town hall and the civil register, and to public meetings in April and July. Vázquez's resignation from PAN in August, and the situation after his change of party will be described in the following two sections, one on the control of public funds, the other on the organization of fiestas.

The Truckers' ability to withhold the town hall and the civil registers symbolized Vázquez's tenuous position, and these visible humiliations were repeatedly the focus of attention during his first three months in office.[22] In early January, Vázquez and Manuel Garcia reportedly met with the director of PRODESCH to discuss the town hall. PAN loyalists heard that it would open on January 17, just before the Fiesta of San Sebastián, but it did not. Garcia and Vázquez had another confrontation at the fiesta—over a drunk Trucker that Vázquez had jailed—and police from San Cristóbal came to restrain Garcia and his followers. In February, the civil registry was still closed, and another rumored date for the opening of the town hall passed with no change.

When I visited Zinacantán in late March, the Truckers' camp was discussing Vázquez's impending removal, after 90 days in office. On Sunday mornings, PRI officials were opening the town hall to hold party meetings and to allow the Municipio Secretary to issue documents to those who needed them. During this period, the de la Madrid administration's attempts to deal with the economic crisis were being felt in many ways in the state. Zinacantecos were having more trouble finding wage work, and students in Tuxtla were burning buses to protest increased fares. Inflation continued.

PRI tried to put its own house in order. A new head of the party for Chiapas was named in March (on March 18, PRI members from Zinacantán went to Tuxtla to celebrate his installation). One of his first acts, according to Pablo Ramírez, was an attempt to unify the party in Zinacantán. Some Zinacantecos had shifted parties since the November election, but just how the groups were aligned was not clear. Truckers said that PRI people who had voted PAN in the election were returning to "PRI." The Peasants said they were PRI all along, just as PRI as anybody else. And PAN people emphasized the split in PRI and their alliance with the Peasants. When a meeting to elect a new PRI head for Zinacantán was announced, PAN people sought PRI party credentials so that they could support the Peasant candidate.

The PAN/Peasant alliance won again at that meeting (on Sunday, April 3, 1983). Juan Bromas, the former PAN Alcalde Juez and confidant of José de la Cruz, was elected head of PRI in Zinacantán by a vote of 2,922 to 2,882.[23] Following the conciliatory practices typical of PRI nationally (and formerly standard practice in Zinacantán), José Sanat was named party secretary. Peasants and Truckers had mustered essentially equal strength again. The township remained deadlocked.

PRI efforts to unify Zinacantán continued to confront this reality in the months that followed. On July 30, for example, the major factions of PRI in Nachig came together in a meeting with a PRI representative from "PRODESCH." I attended. Before the meeting, Juan Bromas and José Sanat stood far apart in Nachig's park talking with some of their local followers. When the formal session started the two PRI leaders sat at the official table separated by the Ladino official from San Cristóbal (the "Official"). Thirty to 40 adult men sat on benches formed in a "U" facing the table or stood up immediately behind them—the ("PAN") Agentes and their followers on one side, the "PRI" Truckers on the other (with Yermo, definitely a Truckers supporter, in the middle of the middle bench). Fifteen to 20 of them eventually spoke.

There were two main issues: (1) party membership, and (2) its relation to 30 public-works jobs that were about to be created on projects in Zinacantán. The Official said that there should be a formal membership registration so that they could all reaffirm PRI membership, in keeping with the resolution on unification adopted at the April meeting.[24] He pushed for membership registration as the solution to all problems of disunity, and ignored attempts to discuss the separate tax-collection systems maintained by the Truckers and the Peasants. When he finally understood the problem, he had no solution to it.

The jobs were the big issue. Juan Bromas, who seemed to control the jobs, and his followers (the Peasants) said that they were all PRI members and should all be eligible to work. Others (from the opposition Truckers) insisted that the jobs go to real PRI people, those who had supported the party in the 1982 election, and the Official said that they might delay hiring doubtful people until after the membership-registration drive. He made it clear that these were PRI programs, of a PRI government, and that the jobs should go to PRI members (no participants showed any interest in separating his roles as a party official and a government employee). The meaning of PRI membership was discussed again and again in terms predictable from the economic interests of those who spoke.

After the Official left, the men continued their discussion. They moved towards organizing a single tax collection for the Fiesta of Rosario in October. But, in the end, the meeting reflected the first seven months of Pedro Vázquez's term: there were many disagreements, and nothing was resolved.

The PRI Period: Government Funds

A struggle for control of public funds drove much of the controversy from summer 1983 through early 1984, when Manuel Garcia and the Truckers got control of the funds. The funds came to the municipio under the federal government's decentralization program (Chapter 3, above; Rodriguez 1987). The block grants of the Conde years were replaced by a revenue-sharing program under which municipios received substantial sums in two categories: operating expenses and public works. Though the national economic crisis reduced allocations, by summer of 1983 the de la Madrid administration had begun to fund public works in Chiapas.

Pedro Vázquez's control over all these funds was first restricted by the eight-point agreement (Appendix F) he was forced to accept when he sat in the PRI office in the municipio, and signed his resignation from PAN on August 24, 1983. The Truckers demanded, and got, an increased role in the spending of public funds, and corresponding restrictions on the administrative prerogatives of the Presidente. The agreement also created an ad hoc arrangement that removed the civil registry from Vázquez's control (point eight in Appendix F). With this, the town hall was opened to Vázquez, and, as noted above, the Community Building that had served as his office was turned over to Ladino police forces stationed in Zinacantán to protect the arrangement.

The settlement did not last. Charges that Vázquez was not complying with the August agreement peaked after he delivered his public annual report at the end of the year. The Truckers brought truckloads of followers to the Center, faced down the police, and occupied the town hall. Vázquez was forced to operate out of his house. The situation was again in disarray.

New stability was established in May 1984, when Manuel Garcia and the Truckers took control of the public-works funds. An ad hoc Committee on Public Works (locally known as the "Foundation") was created, and the town hall was again opened to Vázquez. Truckers and the state government seemed to see the arrangement as a way of avoiding the complications of the Presidente's resignation. The commmittee distributed funds to hamlets in proportion to their PRI membership, and used the bulk of them to pave the churchyard in front of San Lorenzo. By summer 1984, Vázquez had the town hall and his formal responsibilities, but little power over the resources normally associated with his office.

The PRI Period: Bands

Sponsorship of bands reflected the decline of Pedro Vázquez's power and the continued splintering of the population. Opposition groups again sponsored their own bands at major fiestas: the compromise constructed by Domingo Pérez in 1977 and maintained by Manuel Conde through 1982 collapsed. By spring 1984, Pedro Vázquez had been stripped of his responsibility for fiesta arrangements, and there were three bands playing at the Fiesta of Cuarto Viernes: one from PAN, one from the Truckers, and one from remnants of both parties that remained loyal to the Presidente. By the following year, PAN had split, and there were four bands at the two most important fiestas. Traditional tax collection ground to a halt, and each splinter group operated by its own rules. The details that follow are interpreted in the last paragraph of this section.

Under Domingo Pérez's 1977 compromise with the opposition, there was a single band at each major fiesta. As noted above, a single Head of the Fiesta Committee was jointly selected, and each party collected and contributed half of the expenses from its members.[25]

This system continued for the first year of Conde's three-year term (1980–82). During the last two years, all Zinacantecos paid regular fiesta taxes into a single fund, and hard-core PAN people (led at first by Marcos Pérez) sponsored a second band at the major fiestas in January and August. While the political import of the second band was obvious, Conde's control was not directly challenged—all men paid regular taxes for the official band, and some paid voluntary additional contributions for the second band. Thus, the second band was like other adornments to fiestas (Cancian 1965: 190), and some Zinacantecos softened the confrontation by noting the increasing number of fiesta activities needing the accompaniment of a band. The tax-collection system seemed to mend itself during Conde's term.

When Pedro Vázquez was elected, the Truckers took the opposition role. They collected voluntary contributions for a second band at the Fiesta of San Sebastián following the election—thereby publicly signaling their existence. After the turbulent spring described above, there was an attempt, on Sunday, May 29, 1983, to unify the nominating meetings and to name a single Fiesta Committee Head for the Fiesta of San Lorenzo to come in August; but on the meeting day, the Truckers stayed in front of the town hall, while the Presidente's meeting took place in front of the church. A separate Truckers band was scheduled for the Fiesta of San Lorenzo, the last one before Vázquez's shift to PRI.

The total collapse of the delicately balanced taxation system began in September (1983). Pedro Vázquez tried to reestablish unified tax collection for the Fiesta of Rosario, but his unified list was late—he issued it on September 21, barely two weeks before the fiesta. The meeting to plan the fiesta was also late, hamlet representatives complained about the timing, the Head of the Fiesta Committee threatened to resign if he was not given a budget immediately, and some men insisted that the Presidente pay for the band himself with the operating funds and salary he was receiving from the government. They argued that Presidente should not be a money-making office, and Vázquez agreed to ask the state government if the funds could be used for the fiesta.[26] But the trouble subsided—most hamlets paid their shares, Vázquez supplemented them with funds from the PRI state treasury (not the state government), and there was one band at the Fiesta of Rosario. The Fiesta of San Sebastián in January 1984 also passed with a single band, though by then many PAN people refused to pay their taxes.

The definitive breakdown began in early March. Vázquez's preparations for the Fiesta of Cuarto Viernes were behind schedule, and the Senior Alcalde Viejo intervened to get him to send out requests for hamlet contributions. These requests for specific amounts arrived in the hamlets at the same time as the call for hamlet representatives to meet in Hteklum to name the committee that would recruit the band and set the budget; the budget had been set before the committee was named. This administrative lapse gave opposition leaders another reason to protest, and set the stage for further disarray.

Three bands appeared at the fiesta, and traditional taxation was almost completely replaced by party-oriented collections. The Presidente paid for one band with funds from his supporters in both PAN and PRI.[27] The Truckers sponsored another. PAN leaders in Navenchauc (representing PAN loyalists in Jechchentic and Vochojvo as well), who had been irritated by Vázquez's defection from PAN and the late invitation to the planning meeting, decided to sponsor a third band. They contributed nothing to the official (Presidente's) band, and supplemented contributions of $100 from about 250 followers with contributions of $3,000 from each of a dozen leaders. Nachig delayed paying its share while the problems were unsettled, and Juan Bromas eventually told the people of Nachig that the official band could be paid for without their contributions, that their money would be useful for embellishments on the fiesta. Hearing this, they decided to contribute nothing.

By summer 1984, the separation was well established. For example, the organizers of the Presidente's band for the Fiesta of San Lorenzo sent no request for contributions to Navenchauc. They knew that the Truckers and the PAN groups there would organize their own bands, and that the hamlet included no supporters of the Presidente.[28]

By 1985, Pedro Vázquez's last year in office, there were four clearly defined factions. PAN had split into two parts, each with some support in the PAN leadership outside Zinacantán. One was led by Manuel Chuchcun, the longstanding leader of the Navenchauc opposition; the other was led by Mariano López, the head of PAN for Zinacantán, and it included Chuchcun's PAN opponents in Navenchauc. As a result, for the major fiestas in January and August bands were sponsored by the "official" Church Committee Head, the Truckers, Chuchcun's PAN group, the other PAN people.[29]

In sum, little unity remained. It was no longer possible to see the situation as a community band plus expressions of opposition. Bands represented factions. Leaders of factions regularly contributed large amounts to supplement the smaller contributions of their followers, making the connection between wealth and political power more blatant than it has been in the traditional system. Different factions collected different amounts from regular members for the same fiestas, and, as might be expected, the amounts varied with the size of the group. Thus the size of contributions became an issue affecting leaders, members, and transfers from one group to another. Ten years before, the collection of fiesta taxes had marked a public activity in which all Zinacantecos were equal. Each hamlet had customs that honored those residents who did great public service by exempting them from taxes, and all other men (with very rare exceptions for disabled oldsters and hopeless alcoholics) paid equal shares. By the end of Pedro Vázquez's term of office, these traditions were gone—or at least clearly suspended for the foreseeable future.[30]

Summary

Open conflict dominated public life in Zinacantán during the ten years that began in 1976. Confrontations among Zinacantecos often involved processes driven by the concerns of outside government, e.g., elections and development programs. Factionalism pervaded the municipio—every household was forced to declare party loyalty, and the communal system of fiesta sponsorship was undermined.

Two broad issues structured the conflict. One was more economic: the elite who owned trucks and buses fought over the control of routes, while among the population as a whole parties of Truckers and Peasants, both led by men of the transport elite, vied for control of communal resources. The other was more political and territorial: Navenchauc and the Cornfields asserted themselves after many years of being excluded from power. The age of the sophisticated Center and the subservient hamlets ended in sharp division.

These issues, along with personal followings, long-standing animosities, and other staples of political divisions, produced major upset and institutional change that promised to last for some time.

9 / THE CARGO SYSTEM IN PUBLIC LIFE

The cargo system in Zinacantán reflected changes in the society and the larger system in which it was set. In the 1960's, it was the core institution of public life. Virtually all men participated to some degree, and a man's position in the community was closely tied to that participation. Cargoholders and their families moved from the hamlets to the Center, and often settled there for the year of cargo service. Participation defined the boundaries of the community (Chapter 6, above; Cancian 1965). In these ways Zinacantán fit Eric Wolf's characterization of the closed corporate peasant community (see Chapter 1).

Chapters 7 and 8 document the dismantling of the cargo system's institutional context during the 1970's and early 1980's. New offices, especially civil ones at the hamlet level, competed for men's time. Egalitarian taxation for fiestas and for community projects was displaced by a flood of money from government, political parties, and rich Zinacantecos. The tight political control connected to the ejido program in earlier decades was replaced by bitter, entrenched political factions. New local officials and new public buildings in the hamlets undermined the authority of the Center.

At the same time the cargo system's role in public life changed in two important ways: the number of men seeking cargos went down, and participation by the men of different hamlets began to differ substantially. These trends and the organizational and administrative changes associated with them will be described after reviewing background on two key local institutions—the Elders and the cargo waiting lists.

The Elders and the Waiting Lists

The cargo system was administered by the Elders—the two Alcaldes Viejos and the four Regidores—who occupied the higher levels of the system (Table 6.3). Led by the Senior Alcalde Viejo, they were responsible for ensuring that each cargo was filled by a competent man. In the early decades of the century, there was a shortage of men willing to serve. The Elders had to seek out and pressure potential incumbents, and they had the power to jail a man whose explanation of his reluctance to serve did not satisfy them. Then, as Zinacantecos became more numerous and more prosperous, it became easier to find men willing to serve. By the 1930's, a few men actually came forward to request cargos when they were ready to enter.

By the 1940's, waiting lists were established.[1] That is, there were so many volunteers for some cargos that the Elders began recording their names for service in the future. By the early 1950's, several cargos had half a dozen or more men waiting to serve them, and the lists continued to grow into the 1960's (Cancian 1965).

Even when most cargos were requested, the Elders had to be active in administering the cargo system. Some cargos were unpopular and rarely filled by volunteers. Some volunteers died or were taken ill before their terms began. Others, as the day of their expensive service approached, realized they were not financially ready, even after years of anticipation; they withdrew, sometimes disappearing into the lowlands to avoid social pressure and embarrassment. In these situations the Elders often had to convince a man who came to request one cargo that he should serve a different one years sooner. Or they had to use their authority to coerce acceptance from a man who was seeking no cargo at the time. As we will see, sometimes they had to scramble and compromise at the last minute in order to ensure that all cargos were filled.

The waiting lists (Figure 9.1) were kept by the Scribes associated with the Elders. Each entry included the man's name and hamlet of residence, and the year and cargo he was committed to serve. The men on the lists confirmed their intentions once each year, usually at the Fiesta of San Lorenzo in August. When new Elders took office, they began with a fresh copy of the lists, and the used copy was kept as a memento by the outgoing Senior Alcalde Viejo.

I was fortunate to get permission to copy ten of the annual lists used between 1952 and 1987.[2] Taken together they document demand for cargos over time and changes in the involvement of men

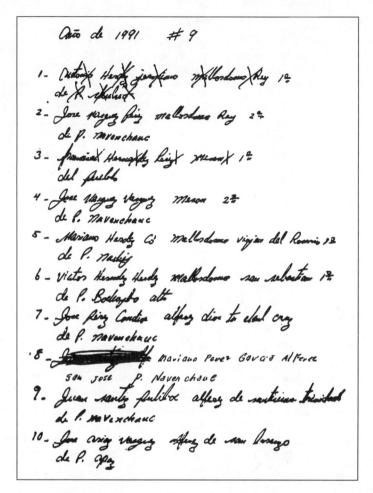

Fig. 9.1. Page from the books used by the Elders in 1983.

from the various hamlets. They provide the basis for the tables in this chapter. Detailed data are given in Appendix D (see also Cancian 1965, 1986, 1990).

Aggregate Demand for Cargos, 1952–1987

The demand for cargos increased rapidly in the 1950's and 1960's. By 1966, a man seeking to serve in the most popular cargo had to

TABLE 9.1

Requests for Cargos, 1952–1987[a]

	Cargos			
Year	Total all levels	First level	Second level	Other	Length of waiting list (years)[b]
1952	119	57	39	23	10
1958	247	138	66	43	16
1961	309	179	86	44	20
1966	346	221	80	45	22
1971	331	216	70	45	20
1975	290	196	57	37	17
1978	256	169	52	35	17
1980	222	144	50	28	16
1983	217	127	58	32	16
1987	193	94	64	35	15

[a] All levels include 41 cargos: 20 first level, 12 second level, and 9 other (see Appendix D).

[b] Calculated as the last year for which there was at least one request minus the year the list was used. For example, the last year for which there was a request on the 1952 list was 1962; on the 1987 list it was 2002.

sign up for 1988, a 22-year wait, and the Elders' lists included 347 men registered for service in later years (Table 9.1).

A few years later the backlog of requests was falling steadily (Table 9.1, Figure 9.2); i.e., not all those who served and thus were dropped from the waiting lists were replaced by new aspirants to cargo service. In this way the aggregate demand for cargo service reflected the decline, or at least the transformation, of the Zinacantán community after the 1960's.

Three features of context complicate the interpretation of the simple pattern. First, the requests tabulated in Table 9.1 do not include cargos served in the hamlets, for they are administered at the hamlet level (Chapter 7). Because many hamlet cargos were created just as requests for cargos served in the Center declined, to estimate total demand for first-level cargos, we must add data from the hamlet waiting lists. In the early 1980's the backlog on waiting lists for hamlet cargos created after 1966 totaled about 30, more than half of them in Paste.[3] Thus, they did not balance the decline of almost 100 in requests for first-level cargos between 1966 and 1983 (Table 9.1). Moreover, the decreasing demand during the 1970's for the unchanged number of second-level cargos was not subject to this complication; it is clear evidence for the decline of interest in cargo service.

Second, the number of men capable of passing cargos certainly increased during the 1970's as population and economic prosperity grew. Because I previously argued (1965) that these trends promoted increases in demand for cargos in the 1950's and early 1960's, I am particularly interested in the dramatic drop in demand in the 1970's. The contradiction does not lead me to reject the initial interpretation. Rather, as I will argue below, there are good reasons to expect that the relation of demand for cargos and prosperity will not be a simple linear or monotonic one.

Third, requests for religious cargos may have gone down because the increasing service required by the new hamlet civil offices may have diverted individuals inclined to request a religious cargo. Certainly some individuals who were subject to social pressure for lack of public service could have deflected the pressure at least temporarily by serving a civil office. On the other hand, the decline in the number of requests began before many new hamlet civil offices were created in the early 1970's.

The increases in requests for higher-level cargos after 1980 (Table 9.1) are hard to evaluate. An increase in requests for second-level cargos may reflect the extra eligible candidates produced by the new

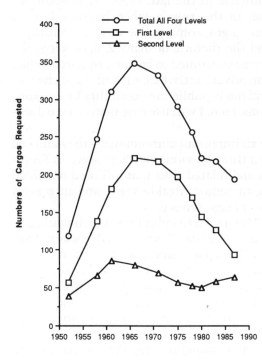

Fig. 9.2. Request for cargos, 1952–1987.

hamlet cargos, or it may signal a heightened attention to internal affairs in response to the economic crisis of 1982 (see below). The counts in Tables D.5 and D.6 show that the bulk of the increase came from the Center, Nachig, and Navenchauc. Since these hamlets share access to roads and have populations disproportionately devoted to transport and commerce, their disproportionate shares suggest increasing income differences among hamlets. Given the limited data, all these possibilities remain speculative at best.

Overall, the decline in requests for cargos all through the 1970's suggests that Zinacantecos considered other things more important; the motivations that maintained the cargo system at the center of public life cooled off.

Organizational and Administrative Changes

The administration and organization of the cargo system changed in a variety of ways during the 1970's and 1980's. When demand was falling in the 1970's, the Elders had to compromise their notions of proper procedure severely in order to fill all the cargos. When political factionalism became intense in the late 1970's, it undermined the Elders' authority. And, in the 1980's, when hamlets faced a shortage of men to fill their cargos, some cargos were discontinued. Although in the minds and the rhetoric of many Zinacantecos the obligation to do public service continued to be more important than individual desires to pursue private activities, each of these changes undercut the old norms and made public the possibility of renegotiating community obligations. Here I will use case materials to document the changes.

In 1975 the Elders made an important compromise—they allowed a man with two rather than three previous cargos to serve as Senior Alcalde Viejo. This action and related ones that followed redefined the career pattern leading to Senior Alcalde Viejo, and in general increased the negotiability of cargo service.

The events began when Manuel Hernández of Apaz fell while carrying a heavy load of corn, and died from his injuries. He was to have been First Regidor in 1976. To replace Hernández on short notice, the Elders called in Mariano Sánchez, a well-off Nachig man who had already served two expensive cargos. Sánchez had other ideas: he arrived with a bottle of liquor for the Elders (the standard gift brought by petitioners), and stated that he did not want to serve as First Regidor; he wanted Senior Alcalde Viejo, a fourth-level cargo. The Elders rejected his unconventional request and insisted that he fill the vacant First Regidor position. Sánchez left, saying that he was going home to talk with his wife about which option was better. When he returned he brought another bottle of liquor, and again insisted that he be given Senior Alcalde Viejo. After more talk, the Elders and the Scribes all agreed. Sánchez was given the cargo he wanted, for 1977—the man on the waiting list for that year had recently died and there was an opening that needed to be filled. Another man was called in to fill the First Regidor cargo, and he immediately accepted.

Lorenzo López, the Senior Alcalde Viejo in 1975, said that he and the other Elders gave in because they felt that if they were not accommodating, people would not want to take cargos. Yermo said that the Elders had checked with the Presidente, and that he had approved the appointment, saying that after it was done they could all see how people reacted. The experiment was an important one: no man I asked in the 1980's could remember an earlier Senior Alcalde Viejo with only two previous cargos.[4]

Sánchez's appointment opened the flood gates. Before his term (1977) was over the prospective incumbent for 1979 had been put off until 1983, and a man with only two previous cargos put in his place. Then, by the time lists used in 1979 were copied and turned over to the prospective Elders for 1980, a third man with only two previous cargos (Mariano Martínez) was waiting to serve in 1983. Thus, three of the seven Senior Alcalde Viejos who served between 1977 and 1983 had only two previous cargos. While the norm about proper careers had not changed, everybody could see that practice did not follow it.[5]

Mariano Martínez stretched the system a little further. His request for Senior Alcalde Viejo was made before he entered his second cargo. In August 1979, when he came to confirm his intentions at the Fiesta of San Lorenzo, he was listed for both an Alférez cargo in 1980 and Senior Alcalde Viejo in 1983. The incoming Senior Alcalde Viejo recalled that he thought it peculiar that Martínez brought two bottles of liquor, one for each of his cargos, but being new in his position, he let it pass. Thus, another new possibility was created.

Zinacantecos offered a variety of explanations for these unusual cargo careers, and a number of others during the same period (see Chapter 10). Some said the Elders no longer had to get the greatest possible service from each man because population growth had increased the supply of incumbents. Others said the increase in new jobs, especially government jobs requiring education and consistent attendance, made people less interested in cargos, whereas still others said the inflation of the late 1970's and early 1980's put off prospective cargoholders who feared they would run out of money to pay for ritual obligations. Thus, Zinacantecos saw both oversupply and undersupply as causes for the change. Whatever their explanation, they all noticed the change.

Politics further complicated the Elders' work. After the break between the Elders and Domingo Pérez, the Presidente, in early 1977 (Chapter 8), political party membership became relevant to appointments. Opposition Elders could not obligate Pérez's supporters to serve cargos. Pérez would not cooperate when the Elders wanted to put a particularly obstinate man in jail overnight. The fragility of the Elders' authority became clear to all men who wished to avoid cargo service. One knowledgeable man told me that, by the end of Pérez's term, the Elders could not even obligate members of their own party to serve.[6]

Another sign of retrenchment in the cargo system came in 1987, when two cargos in Apaz and two cargos in Elanvo were suspended. Until 1987 the religious cargo system had seen nothing but expansion for at least 50 years (Chapter 6).

Population size, politics, and economic change all contributed to the situation in Apaz. When four cargos were established there in the early 1960's, there had been debate about whether the hamlet could provide enough men to fill them, and the leaders who had advocated having only two lost (Cancian 1965: 164 n. 3).[7] In the 1980's, politics added to the demographic strain—especially when José Hernández's shift to PRI (Chapter 8) split the predominantly PAN hamlet into two almost equal parts.[8] Finally, work in construction trades (Collier and Mountjoy 1988) no doubt decreased the flexibility of many younger Apaz men who might otherwise have taken cargos.

Elanvo was the smallest population supporting two first-level cargos in the early 1980's (Table B.2).[9] Before the cargos were established in 1979, the hamlet's senior men had been conscious of a potential lack of incumbents, so they recorded a list of potential incumbents for ten years into the future. But, by 1984, some men had withdrawn their commitment, leaving only enough names to fill the cargos for two or three years. When no one entered in 1987, the cargos were suspended. Size is the most likely explanation for Elanvo's problems filling its cargos, but I do not know the details of the changes. Internal politics similar to those in Apaz may have also been a factor, for a 1987 tax list shows Elanvo divided into two parts (Table B.3, note g).

In sum, the overall decline in inclination to serve cargos documented in Table 9.1 manifested itself in organizational and administrative changes. Regional economics, municipio politics, and the idiosyncracies of personal careers and hamlet histories all contributed to the atmosphere in which Zinacantecos transformed the key institution in their public life.

Shifting Patterns of Demand by Hamlet, 1952–1987

In the 1960's, the men of all the hamlets participated in cargos in the Center at roughly similar rates. By the 1980's, differences between hamlet rates of participation reflected both the political events described in Chapter 8, and the new demands created by hamlet cargos. This section uses calculations based on the detailed data in Appendix D to document these patterns.

Tables 9.2 and 9.3 give ratios of requests for cargos served in the Center to requests expectable on the basis of population (see the note to Table 9.2). A ratio of 0.7 means the hamlet's men had requested only 70 percent of its share based on its population. Since the numbers are sometimes small, the patterns are influenced by many idiosyncratic features and need to be interpreted carefully.

Requests from the Cornfields show the clearest relation to poli-

TABLE 9.2

Cargo Requests Compared to Population Size, 1952–1987[a]

(For 20 first-level cargos)

Hamlet cluster	1952	1958	1961	1966	1971	1975	1978	1980	1983	1987
Center	0.7	0.8	0.6	0.6	0.6	0.5	0.5	0.6	0.8	1.1
Nachig	1.6	1.1	1.0	1.5	1.4	1.3	2.0	2.5	2.9	2.6
Paste	1.9	1.4	1.2	1.6	2.4	2.6	2.2	1.9	1.2	0.8
Navenchauc	1.2	1.0	1.3	1.6	1.0	1.1	1.0	1.0	1.3	1.4
Apaz	1.0*	1.6	2.0	0.6	0.9	0.9	0.8	0.7*	0.5*	0.6*
Cornfields	0.9	1.5	1.5	1.3	1.0	0.8	0.9	0.6	0.5	0.4*
Other	0.4[†]	0.1[†]	0.2*	0.1*	0.4	0.6	0.4	0.5	0.3*	0.3*

[a]The entries in the cells are ratios of the hamlet's percentage of total first-level cargo requests to the hamlet's percentage of total population. Percentages of total first-cargo requests were calculated from the data in Table D.4. For example, in 1958, 30 of 151 requests (19.9%) were from the Center. Population was determined by averaging the 1965 percentage in column C1 of Table B.4 and the 1987 percentage calculated from column G of Table B.3, in the cases where population shares were fairly constant. These were the Center (25.9% in 1965 and 25.9% in 1987), Nachig (10.1% and 10.7%: 10.4 used), Paste (11.0% and 11.2%: 11.1 used), Apaz (7.3% and 7.0%: 7.15 used), and Other (15.5% and 14.3%: 14.7 used). For Navenchauc (10.8% and 15.8%) and the Cornfields (19.5% and 15.1%), 1965 figures were used for 1952, 1958, and 1961, and estimates for years between 1965 and 1987 were made by assuming straight-line change from 1965 to 1987. For the Center in 1958, 19.9% divided by 25.9% yielded 0.8, the entry in the table.

*Cell count 5, 6, or 7.

[†]Cell count < 5.

TABLE 9.3

Cargo Requests Compared to Population Size, 1952–1987[a]

(For 12 second-level cargos)

Hamlet cluster	1952	1958	1961	1966	1971	1975	1978	1980	1983	1987
Center	0.9	0.3*	0.4	0.6	0.5	0.6	0.6	0.7	0.8	1.0
Nachig	1.3*	1.4	1.0	1.4	1.2	1.7	2.2	1.7	2.1	2.4
Paste	1.0*	1.4	1.7	1.4	1.7	2.0	1.3	1.9	0.9*	0.7*
Navenchauc	1.7	2.1	2.3	1.5	1.9	1.2	1.1	1.0*	1.2	1.7
Apaz	1.0†	1.1*	0.8*	1.5	1.4	1.2*	1.8	1.4*	1.8	1.1*
Cornfields	0.9	1.2	1.1	1.1	0.5*	0.5*	0.3†	0.2†	0.2†	0.1†
Other	0.6†	0.5*	0.5*	0.5*	0.8	0.9	1.1	1.1	0.9	0.4†

[a] The data from Table D.5 and the procedure described in Table 9.2, note *a*, were used to calculate cell entries.
*Cell count 5, 6, or 7.
†Cell count < 5.

tics. They dropped from a full share or more in proportion to population in the 1960's to about half or less of a full share after 1980 (Tables 9.2 and 9.3). Overall, the Cornfields had 88 requests (23 percent) in 1966, and 7 requests (3 percent) in 1987, and the drop was particularly strong after 1978 (Table D.3). Thus, withdrawal from the cargo system reflected the same sentiments that appeared in the political arena, and made the Cornfields the crucial voting block in the 1982 election. According to Domingo Pérez, the Cornfields' efforts to establish an ejido covering the whole area were hotly discussed in the early 1970's, were less intense during the mid-1970's while legalities were in process, and culminated with the (federal) presidential resolution establishing the new status of the area in 1981. As noted above, these moves confiscated lands in the Cornfields that some people from the Center and other hamlets had inherited, and they were the source of continuing ill will between those who lost lands and residents of the Cornfields.

Patterns of participation by Apaz men had more to do with the balance between the supply of and demand for cargos. Before the Apaz cargos were established, Apaz men were requesting much more than their share of first-level cargos. In 1961, 27 Apaz men were waiting for first-level cargos in the Center (Table D.4), twice what would be expected given Apaz' population (Table 9.2). Just what brought on this intense interest is not entirely clear, but part of it is probably explained by an extraordinary sequence of events: for three straight years (1960, 1961, 1962), the Senior Alcalde Viejo was a man from Apaz.[10] Then, shortly after four first-level cargos were established in Apaz, requests by Apaz men for cargos served in the Center dropped off. By 1966, only 11 Apaz men were waiting for such cargos. Table 9.3 shows that within a few years the many Apaz men eligible for second-level cargos in the Center were requesting more than the hamlet's share based on population.

These clear, easily interpretable patterns were not repeated in Navenchauc, Nachig, and Paste, the other hamlets with new cargos that are big enough to make analysis of the numbers a sensible project. While Paste shows a clear increase in demand before its cargos were established in 1977, the Nachig pattern is not so clear, and increased demand in Navenchauc before its new cargos were established in 1982 was small (Table 9.2). Nachig and Paste maintained very high demand for first-level cargos in the late 1970's and early 1980's, and both had an unusual number of Senior Alcaldes Viejos between 1970 and 1981 (see note 9.10). Thus, insofar as Senior Alcaldes Viejos from one's hamlet provide a local model of success, as well as easier entry into the potentially frightening world of cargo officialdom, the intensity of demand in Nachig and Paste may stem from these historical factors that are independent of demography. Navenchauc, however, does not fit this pattern (Table 9.2), though it produced four of the 12 Senior Alcaldes Viejos who served between 1970 and 1981.

The participation of Navenchauc and Nachig men seems to reflect the politics of localism in other ways. For Navenchauc, the relative lack of new requests in the late 1970's probably indicates the growing local dissatisfaction with the hamlet's relation to the Center—the same dissatisfaction that appeared in the 1976 nomination meeting for Presidente Municipal. Nachig's very high number of requests includes many from Jechchentic (eight in 1980, seven in 1983, and five in 1987). This extraordinary number, given Jechchentic's small population, probably reflects the hamlet's effort to declare its independence from Nachig and Nachig's local cargos (see Chapter 7).

In sum, the analysis of participation by hamlet shows that the Cornfields withdrew from participation in the cargo system and the Zinacantán community, and that, for most other hamlets, demand for cargos and the establishment of local cargos were linked. As noted in Chapter 7, these shifts in demand also reflected a history of competition among hamlets.

Changing Public Life in Theoretical Context

Between the 1960's and the 1980's, Zinacantán's public life was transformed. Open conflict grew, the cargo system declined, and hamlets became more important centers of activity. What we make of what happened depends on theory. Thus, I want to draw out some connections between the happenings and the theories discussed in Chapter 1.

Focus on the conflict highlights the difference between Lenin's vision broadly defined and the Wolf/Skinner interpretation of peasant communities. It also requires some attention to the size of the system analyzed and to the interests of people in different social positions. Lenin's ideas about the historical evolution of class conflicts of interest place the origins of conflict in the increasing disparities (conflicts of interest) between capitalist (capital-controlling) and proletarian (labor-selling) classes. While Lenin's vision of peasants was embedded in the historical period in which capitalists expanded and concentrated ownership of land and productive resources in Russia, for others it has become a general model for interpreting peasants.

We may see the conflict in Zinacantán originating in economic differences among Zinacantecos. Certainly many Zinacantecos enthusiastically called themselves "Peasants" and their political opponents "Truckers," and characterized the Truckers as a greedy economic elite. Because an institutional approach is taken in this part of the study, it is difficult to connect the economic positions and the political positions of individuals—i.e., to evaluate the idea that the conflicting parties are each made up of individuals who share economic interests that differ from those of members of the other party. Data on the economic rank and political affiliation of individuals presented in Chapter 11 will permit such an evaluation. In this simple extension of Lenin's approach internal processes are emphasized: Zinacantán is the principal area of directly relevant activity, and the outside world does not have an important active role.

Eric Wolf and G. William Skinner have noted that peasant communities tended to flourish when their environment was so hostile that community members withdrew from the larger world and adopted practices that clearly distinguished the community from the environment. As noted in Chapter 1, they saw the withdrawal and closing as a historical phenomenon that could be reversed by a more welcoming environment. In this framework a friendly environment diminishes community; it makes open conflict within the community more likely, because individuals may leave if things go badly for them and are thus freer to risk conflict at home.

Following Wolf and Skinner, we may see conflict in Zinacantán coming from a variety of old wellsprings newly opened by the comfortable alternatives to life in Zinacantán that appeared in the regional environment. Those alternatives increased in the 1970's, and young Zinacantecos were certainly better prepared to handle them than they had been a decade or two before. At the same time, shifts on the national political scene made the formation of an opposition party less difficult than it would have been even a few years before. Thus, we may see the origin of conflict in the environmental factors that made it possible for Zinacantecos to live more comfortably with the consequences of tension at home. With this approach the relevant arena expands greatly to include directly at least the regional political economy.

Finally, we may see the Zinacantán transport elite as, in effect, local agents of the larger capitalist system, and Zinacantán's larger proletarian and semiproletarian class as part of a national and international class system. This approach helps us understand the fact that leaders of both major factions are part of the transportation elite, but it offers less direct and simple insight into the origin of Zinacantán's particular conflicts.

I cannot tell which if any of these simple approaches is distinctly more useful in understanding the origins of conflict in Zinacantán. Each adds a dimension to my understanding, and is consistent with some distinctive details of events and trends in Zinacantán. Certainly the conflict is a very different thing—i.e., it has a very different reality in the understanding of the observer—depending on the theory through which it is seen.[11]

Focus on the decline of the cargo system highlights an even more complex set of indistinguishable theoretical alternatives. Broadly speaking, all three of the very different theoretical alternatives set out in Chapter 1 suggest that the cargo system would decline in the 1970's. Lenin, Wolf/Skinner, and modernization approaches understand the process differently, but each is at least quite consistent with the decline documented earlier in this chapter.

The three approaches differ about how people in different social positions would participate in the change. For example, it is reasonable to extend the modernization approach to predict that "modern" men would not take cargos and "traditional" men would. This is the theory implicit at the end of my study of the cargo system (Cancian 1965: 194). I would also extend Lenin's idea, through more recent Marxist thinking, to predict that the rich would take cargos (in order to consolidate their ideological dominance of the poor). These alternative "predictions" (understandings of what happened in Zinacantán) cannot be distinguished with the aggregate data on public life presented in this part of the study, but they do have different implications for the data on social stratification presented in Part III.

Finally, one aggregate pattern of participation in the cargo system does distinguish between the theories in a small way. The increases in requests for second- and higher-level cargos that began after the economic crisis of 1982 (Table 9.1) support the Wolf/Skinner idea that the local community will reassert itself, become stronger, when the outside world is more hostile. However, the many extra men eligible for second cargos because they passed one of the new first cargos established in the hamlets, and the changing career patterns leading to higher-level cargos (see Chapter 10), could also be used to explain this trend.

Focus on the florescence of the hamlets bewilders the limited theories that I have presented: despite the influences of increasing internal differentiation, improved opportunities away from home, and personal modernization, Zinacantecos changed their hamlets to make them like the municipio had once been. The new hamlets were not exactly like the municipio of old—both because they were much smaller and because some of them were split by open political conflict. But the trend was still very strong.

This movement towards replication of smaller, tighter, independent units has still other explanations. There are functional explanations that depend on a notion of optimal group size and predict the fission of groups when they become too large (Vogt 1965). The idea that "peasantness" is a cultural complex that tends to persist (see Heynig 1982) is also consistent with the reestablishment of smaller, tighter local communities in the face of increasing openness of the larger system. The notion that outside political control works more effectively on smaller units explains the government activity that provided many of the concrete resources around which the hamlets developed.

Finally, it is worth noting that, however the florescence of the hamlets is understood, it did happen. Zinacantecos were not sucked into a political world-system as individuals. Local units continued to be central to their political and social lives.

In sum, the changes in conflict, cargos, and hamlets in the two decades after the 1960's can be understood in a number of ways. Some questions that are left unresolved by the focus on public institutions and aggregate data in this part of the study will be clarified by shifting attention to social position in Part III.

PART III /

SOCIAL STRATIFICATION

> [The cargo system] is virtually the entire social structure of
> the Indian municipio. At the most general level of social integra-
> tion this structure does [for] Indians what kinship does for Afri-
> can societies, and what the social class system does for Ladino
> societies.
> (Nash [1958: 68], quoted by Cancian [1965: 2])

In 1965 this statement by Manning Nash was an apt
starting point for a study of Zinacantán's cargo system. Zinacantecos were intensely involved in their community and their cargo system. There was, as John Haviland later put it in conversation, "cargo
fever." My study done in the early 1960's showed that the cargo system reflected broad patterns of social stratification in the community: men who began careers with expensive, prestigious cargos usually continued in expensive, prestigious cargos, and those who began
with less expensive, lower-ranking cargos usually dropped out after
a single term of service. Fathers and sons tended to have similar
careers; and, most important as a sign of the wider significance of
the cargo system, the fathers of people who married tended to have
similar careers. Some men were recognized for their activities as
political leaders or curers, but, overall, the cargo system was indis-
putably the key to social position in Zinacantán.

These patterns of social stratification went along with many features that made Zinacantán much like a closed corporate peasant
community. As has been noted above, Zinacantecos had limited
contact with the external economic and political system. Most ma-
ture men were corn farmers who produced the basic foods their
families needed for subsistence. Internal politics were dominated by

a *cacique* (political boss), who was also the principal broker with outside authorities. Zinacantecos settled most of their problems through internal mechanisms—including formal proceedings in the Center, where virtually all religious cargos and civil offices were served. Schools were limited in number, usually had three grades, and were attended by boys only. Few men and almost no women spoke enough Spanish to venture comfortably very far from the area where they lived.

As Parts I and II document, the economic and political aspects of the closed corporate peasant community changed in the 1970's. New and diverse occupations brought more contact with Ladinos. Formal hamlet organization became important, parties competed in local politics, and many leaders learned to make alliances with Ladino officials. The schools expanded to include all the hamlets, and girls as well as boys. Many Zinacantecos regularly engaged in trade, wage work, and political activities far from their homes.

Part III documents changes in the patterns of social stratification within the community. While cargos were still important in the early 1980's, they were no longer the only way the majority of men established their social position. Other factors (like wealth) and other arenas (like politics) became important. Changes in the economy and the political system transformed the ways Zinacantecos constituted their public selves and established their places in the local system of social stratification. By the end of the 1970's, it was no longer possible to equate the cargo system with social stratification in Zinacantán.

Before beginning I want to mention two slippery surfaces. First, the changes in the patterns of social stratification are due less to changes in the cargo system than they are to changes in the role of the cargo system in the lives of Zinacantecos. In fact, the changes in the cargo system, especially the addition of new cargos, helped conserve rather than alter the old patterns of social stratification. They helped keep the role of the cargo system central during an era when men were developing alternative interests. This is simply to say that the cargo system was not an immutable thing. As an institution it provided continuity, but as a product of people's everyday efforts to achieve their own social goals it reflected the changes in other parts of their lives. Second, while Zinacanteco identity and Zinacantán as a political unit were at least as constant as the cargo system, the lives of many Zinacantecos became much less focused on Zinacantán. That is clear, especially from Part I. Despite these shifts, I will continue to talk about "the cargo system" and the concerns of Zinacantecos as Zinacantecos. These statements should always be understood in the context of the institutional transformation and the change in the relation of Zinacantecos to the outside world that took place between the 1960's and the 1980's.

CHANGES IN THE

MEANING OF

CARGO SERVICE

In 1960 the religious cargo system defined the Zinacantán community. Cargo service was the way most men and their families participated in public life. Service committed people who were not clear about their identification with the community, it mobilized people who were inactive, and it provided a public arena for those who sought local prominence. A few able men brought the norms of service to consciousness by challenging them, but most of the 10 percent who did not serve were lame, incompetent, or impoverished (Cancian 1965).

By the early 1980's, cargo service was no longer the universal standard by which men and their families could be socially placed. Obviously, many still took cargos: all the positions were filled each year, and the waiting lists were still long. Nevertheless, the cargo fever had passed. Although few men explicitly dismissed cargos as personal goals, many made weak affirmations of intent: they sounded and acted like American politicians who assert that an issue is certainly on their list of priorities while always finding other goals more important. The meaning of cargo service had changed.[1]

This chapter will describe and document these changes. It will show that the cargo system as a formal institution changed little while its role as the core of community social structure changed a lot. During these years nothing was absolutely unchanging, but different elements of the picture changed at different rates. I hope to use the more stable elements like the cargo roles and their ritual obligations to help understand the more rapidly changing elements—especially the social implications of cargo service.

To do this I will begin with one of the more stable elements: the relative status that came from service in different cargos, i.e., the way Zinacantecos evaluated service in one cargo as opposed to another. To give a sense for cargo careers and the complexities of interpreting them, I will look at the increasing "exceptions" to the traditional order of service as it was defined in the 1960's, then at the stable patterns shown in individual cargo careers and in the relation of fathers' service to sons' service. Statistical data on participation rates, and the relation of service, wealth, and the selection of spouses, will show how the broader social implications of cargo service changed. By the end of the chapter it will be clear that in the middle 1980's the cargo system, still vigorous in many ways, was not much like the cargo system of the 1960's.

Cargos, Social Status, and Reputation

In the 1960's, cargos were good indicators of social status. They differed from each other in cost, authority, and ritual obligations, and these differences were the keys to the analysis of social stratification in Zinacantán. For example, among men who had passed one cargo, it was clear that the man who had served as Senior Mayordomo Rey was wealthy and important, a man to be respected. The man who served as Mayordomo Santo Domingo was clearly poorer, but probably someone of consequence. The Mayordomo San Antonio was even poorer, and commanded still less respect. And finally, though they got formal credit for service at the first level, most men who passed Mayor were stigmatized by having served. These were not formal, explicit differences. They were simply recognized and used by Zinacantecos, just as many Americans use automobiles to mark social status. Since a man's record of service was public knowledge, and virtually every man participated at least once, cargo service was both important and convenient as a marker of social status in Zinacantán (Cancian 1965).

The importance of cargo service to reputation was documented by John Haviland in his *Gossip, Reputation and Knowledge in Zinacantán* (1977). His chapter "Gossip and the Cargo System" provides rich case material based on extensive interviewing about reputations and informal observations in varied settings. Haviland's general statements include:

The conversational preponderance is a symptom of the importance of the cargo system to most of the Zinacantecos with whom I gossiped. Zinacantecos, like other people, talk about what interests them; the best clue—

though not the only one—about what is on their minds is what is on their lips. (p. 91)

Gossip propagates information about people's cargo histories and performance through a huge volume of conversation about cargos and cargoholders. Complementing this conversation is correspondingly extensive knowledge about other people's cargo careers on the part of almost every Zinacanteco man. . . . In fact, it seems likely that Zinacantecos actively collect cargo histories, if for no other reason than that they can thus compare their own progress through the hierarchy with that of their fellows.

Ordinarily the most public aspect of a man's personal history will be his cargo record. People from outlying hamlets, not otherwise familiar to those outside their own areas, acquire instant names as holders of such-and-such cargo. (p. 102)

A person's cargo record is usually taken as an index of other aspects of his life and character. A distinguished cargo performance carries implications of other distinction; and failure in the religious hierarchy is taken to attest to some personal deficiency. (p. 103)

It is also true that the idiom of cargo success is, in most conversations, synonymous with virtue, diligence, and worthiness. (p. 104)

The cases Haviland displays along with these generalizations document specific ways the cargo system marks social status in Zinacantán.

In the 1960's I constructed a Cost Scale and Prestige Scale to summarize the differences among the cargos on each of the first two levels of service (1965: 80–96). The scales rank the cargos on what they cost to serve and on how much prestige a man who passes them earns (Table 10.1), and they are thus very useful for the statistical analysis of careers done in *Economics and Prestige in a Maya Community* (Cancian 1965, hereafter "1965" in this chapter) and below.

Constructing the Cost Scale was straightforward. Since each of the cargos had specified ritual duties that included events of different costs, I simply asked a number of knowledgeable men to order the various cargos on each of the first two levels by cost, and averaged the results (1965: 84).

The Cost Scale represented the meaningful differences in wealth reflected in cargo service. While the measure was not ideal (for it was based on willingness to spend, not on resources or income), average expenses for cargos were high compared to income in Zinacantán, and the differences between the extremes were very large by Zinacanteco standards. Only a few people could afford the most expensive positions, and well-off people knew that it would provoke gossip if they sought the least expensive positions. Thus, the scale promised to measure economic status effectively. As far as I can tell

TABLE 10.1

The Cost Scale (C) and the Prestige Scale (P) of Cargos

First level[a]			Second level (Alféreces)		
Ranking[b]			Ranking[b]		
(C)	(P)	Name	(C)	(P)	Name
1	1	Mayordomo Rey	2	1	San Lorenzo
2	2	Virgen del Rosario	2	2	Santísima Trinidad
7	3	Sacramento	2	3	San Antonio
3	4	Pasionero	5	4	San José
5	5	Santo Domingo	4	5	Virgen del Rosario
4	6	Santa Cruz	3	6	Natividad
8	7	Mesonero	6	7	Virgen de Soledad
6	8	San Sebastián	7	8	San Sebastián (Sr.)
9	9	San Antonio	4	9	San Jacinto
10	10	Capitán	3	10	Santa Rosa
11	11	Mayor	7	11	San Sebastián (Jr.)
			5	12	San Pedro Mártir

[a] Senior and Junior are not distinguished for the first-level cargos (see Table D.1).

[b] A letter indicating the level plus the prestige rank is used to abbreviate the cargo name while giving information about its characteristics. Thus Mayordomo Rey becomes A1 and Alférez San Jose becomes B4. See Table D.1 for a complete listing of names and abbreviations.

on the basis of anecdotal evidence, the relative cost of different cargos remained the same from the 1960's to the 1980's. The new cargos served in the hamlets were generally seen as less expensive than cargos served in the Center.

Constructing the Prestige Scale was more complex for a variety of reasons. First of all, "prestige" is a more complex concept than "cost." When I asked Zinacantecos to rank the cargos in terms of prestige, they espoused an egalitarian ideology and declared the cargos to be equal in the respect they deserved.[2] Nevertheless, many concrete cases where different cargos clearly signaled different social status convinced me that there was something like an underlying Prestige Scale (see also J. B. Haviland 1977: 106). In the end I constructed the Prestige Scale using information on the cost of each position, the authority the role carried, and a few other more idiosyncratic factors. And I confirmed the cognitive validity of the scale by showing that it structured errors Zinacantecos made in remembering cargo careers of others (Cancian 1963; 1965: 92–96).

The Prestige Scale sought to measure the more complex social motivations that went into cargo service.[3] Just how successful it was is hard to estimate. Besides the data originally used to validate the scale (1965: 94), there is at least one sign that suggests the scale was at least grossly accurate. That is the relative length of waiting lists for various cargos (Table D.2). Overall, more-prestigious cargos were requested more than less-prestigious cargos; and it seems that cargos that gave much prestige for relatively little cost (e.g., A3) were popular, and that bad bargains whose cost was high relative to prestige (e.g., A6) were much less frequently requested. The data from the waiting lists also suggest that the cargos maintained roughly the same relative prestige from the late 1950's to the late 1980's. In sum, the Prestige Scale measured something Zinacantecos cared about, and the measure apparently remained valid over three decades. That is, the relative prestige of the different cargos was important and roughly constant over the period that concerns us most.[4]

Exceptions: Changes in the Rules

Unlike the prestige associated with the different cargos, the order in which cargos were to be served in an individual's career was explicit and subject to rules in the 1960's. Zinacantecos were quite clear about what was proper. The order they expected is shown in Table D.1 by the letters A, B, C, and D in the code numbers for the first through the fourth levels—roughly speaking, the Mayordomos (A), the Alféreces (B), the Regidores (C), and the Alcaldes Viejos (D). Three of the cargos served in the Center are labeled on a different system (ADC, ASD, and ASH) and followed slightly more complex rules (1965: 31).

Later, exceptions appeared and expectations shifted. How this happened for the cargo of Senior Alcalde Viejo was described in Chapter 9. My impression on the basis of field work in the 1980's is that Zinacantecos became individually less sure, and as a group more diverse, about what to expect from the cargo system. As a result the social implications of cargo service changed.

This section will use different kinds of data about "exceptional" careers to explore different aspects of these shifts. First, the Nachig Census will be used to document the increase in exceptional careers between 1967 and 1987. Then, with case materials, I will try to give some life to the processes that created the statistics. Finally, I will look at how shifts in meaning seem to have created disagreements among anthropologists and how disagreements among anthropologists help document shifts in meaning.[5]

In 1967 there was only one exception among the 159 cargos included in the careers of the 99 Nachig men who had served in the cargo system. The other 158 fit expectations about the order of service perfectly. By 1983 there were nine exceptions in 126 careers, and by 1987 there were 12 exceptions in 134 careers.[6] How, and why, did they happen?

The individual stories make our understanding more complex. One involves Manuel BB. Three years after he married, Manuel was pressed to serve as Mayor (A11), but, he said, he preferred to help sponsor a fiesta, so he requested Capitán (A10, the least burdensome and least prestigious of the regular first-level cargos). He served the cargo in about 1970, after a six-year wait. Then, in 1977, he served his second first-level cargo, the Senior Mayordomo in Nachig. Manuel gave two accounts of how this happened. One started with an illness: he had had diarrhea for four weeks, and was facing death when the Virgin appeared to him in a dream. She told him that he would live, and that she would like him to count her rosaries, to be the Senior Mayordomo. When he went to request the cargo from the Sacristans at the Nachig church, he was so pale and weak and he staggered so much that he had to explain that he was sick, not drunk. They gave him the cargo—put him on the waiting list—and three days later he was over his sickness. In the other account, given earlier in the same interview, the events began when local people told him that the Elders in the Center were talking about naming him as an Alférez—and reminded him that the Nachig Mayordomo was also available. He talked with his wife about the options, she preferred the Nachig cargo, and he asked for it.

Many other faces may be put on Manuel's career. I believe he prospered after he learned to be a mason in the period between his cargos, and perhaps, like former Mayores who insisted on beginning again in a Mayordomo cargo,[7] he sought to begin his career anew in a more substantial cargo than Capitán. Then too, as Yermo pointed out, the Nachig Mayordomo was less expensive than an Alférez, so Manuel and his family avoided expense, periodic moves to the Center, and the efforts required to assemble the many pots and people needed to serve as Alférez. Finally, there is a political face to Manuel's case, for according to both his account and Yermo's, the Elders agreed that his service would count as his second cargo. To the local leaders who undoubtedly helped Manuel negotiate with the Elders, that agreement meant more solid recognition for the recently established Nachig cargos and more independence for Nachig.

Another case illustrates the most frequently heard explanation of exceptions: they were last-minute compromises used to fill cargos when the scheduled incumbent died or ran away.[8] According to Yermo, Mariano T. had passed A5 and requested B1 when he heard that an Apaz man who was to be A4 ran away at the last minute. Mariano told others he would like to serve A4, but feared that it would not be allowed, that he would be criticized for requesting a second first-level cargo. When his remarks were reported to the Elders, they immediately went to his house, told him it was fine, and signed him up. Later, Mariano passed B1 as planned, making his the only Nachig career with two exceptions in it.

Juan G. was recruited to serve C2 as a second cargo when the scheduled incumbent died at the last minute. The Elders could find no one else, Yermo said, so Juan was pressured to resign from the Nachig School Committee post he was about to enter and to serve the cargo.[9]

The changing meaning (social implications) of cargo service is highlighted by John Haviland's (1977: 98–102) disagreement with my earlier descriptions of the rules for and social implications of service as Junior Alcalde Viejo (1965: 31–32). Briefly put, the story goes as follows. On the basis of data from the early 1960's, I said that Zinacantecos saw Junior Alcalde Viejo (D2) as a fourth cargo, though they knew that it was not always taken as a fourth cargo; it was often an exception. My "sample" of cases (p. 208) included nine D2s, five with three previous cargos, and four with two. I said, "It is my idea that most men who have had the resources and endurance to pass three cargos will not settle for the junior post on the fourth level. Thus the cargo has few takers" (pp. 31–32); and I said that the cargo represented an honorable ending to a cargo career.

Haviland, whose work was done in the early 1970's, said:

Gossip, however, does not in most cases bear out the inference that the junior [Alcalde Viejo] represents a completely "honorable" conclusion to a cargo career. On the contrary, most men who fill the post seem to be ineffectual, weak-willed, aged failures, frequently laughingstocks. Although there seems to be no principled reason why some exceptional individual might not manage to make more out of it, the cargo seems to be something like a booby prize, forced on the vulnerable . . . even, *pace* Cancian, after only a single previous cargo. In fact, Who's Who lists show a man in Nachij who performed [Junior Alcalde Viejo] as his *only* cargo. (p. 98, emphasis original)

In the early 1980's, my impressions of Zinacantecos' attitudes toward Junior Alcaldes Viejos were closer to Haviland's description than to my conclusions in the 1960's. The Nachig Census for 1987 also supports Haviland's statements. There were three D2s, all with two previous cargos.[10]

What explains our disagreement about earlier periods? Perhaps I got it wrong in 1965, and later, with Haviland's help, got it right. Perhaps the pictures we developed varied with the status of our consultants. During much of my early work I had many low-status consultants from the Center, who probably aspired to much less than D2; and for my later work I had many high-status consultants, who would not have considered serving D2. Perhaps Haviland described the elite's view of the cargo system and I originally described the view of lower-ranking men.

Historical change may explain still more of the difference. Junior Alcalde Viejo (D2) may have been an honorable fourth cargo in the early 1960's and become something else a decade later. By the early 1980's, after the major shakeup described in Chapter 9, Yermo stated it simply: "If men pass Regidor, they don't pass Junior Alcalde Viejo anymore. Things have changed." That is, what seem like contradictory findings may be better seen as evidence for change in the way Zinacantecos perceived cargo service—change in the social implications, the meaning, of specific cargos.[11]

In sum, the number of exceptions to the traditional order of service increased in the 1970's and the 1980's. Various kinds of evidence suggest that Zinacanteco expectations about proper service shifted as exceptions increased. Expectations in the early 1980's were less firm and more diverse than those in the 1960's. The social implications of cargo service became harder to identify clearly, and they varied more within the community of Zinacantecos.

Cargo Careers and Stratification

In the early 1960's, two patterns of cargo service showed that individuals and families usually maintained their social position over time: (1) men who took prestigious and expensive first cargos took higher-ranking second cargos and reached the third and fourth levels of service more often than did men who began with less prestigious and expensive cargos, and, (2) the first cargos of men and their fathers were of similar rank. These two patterns were still present in 1967 and again in 1983: men still followed consistent careers, and fathers and their sons still had cargos of similar rank.

In this section I will document this continuity. The documentation is complex because the career and cross-generation patterns that continued over more than two decades are statistical tendencies—not behavior that followed explicit rules or met explicit expectations like the order of service discussed above.[12] A detailed description of

TABLE 10.2

Continuity in Individual and Family Cargo Service, 1962

A. Cargo Careers: First and Second Cargos

(Cargos ordered by Prestige Scale, $N = 145$)

Rank of second cargo	Rank of first cargo		Results
	High	Low	
High	48	26	$\chi^2 = 15.1$, $P < .01$
Low	22	49	67% for continuity

B. Fathers' and Sons' First Cargos Compared

(Cargos ordered by Prestige Scale, $N = 103$)

Rank of father's first cargo	Rank of son's first cargo		Results
	High	Low	
High	32	18	$\chi^2 = 7.07$, $P < .01$
Low	19	34	64% for continuity

SOURCES: Part A, Cancian 1965: 112; Part B, Cancian 1965: 115.

the analysis is given below. The final paragraph of this section summarizes the results.

In 1965 I showed the rank consistency of cargo careers mostly by cross-tabulating the first two cargos in the careers of many Zinacanteco men. Table 10.2, Part A, shows the pattern when the first and second cargos of many men were compared, and Part B shows the continuity of family position seen in the first cargos of fathers and their sons. Each part includes the chi-square statistic and the percent of cases showing continuity of position, i.e., social stratification.

My goals in that study and this one were quite different. There I was concerned with a then-dominant interpretation that saw peasant communities as distinctively homogeneous and stable because people who got wealthy were required to spend more in cargo service than poorer members of the community. It was called the leveling interpretation of the cargo system.[13] I showed that, despite the leveling consequences of the cargo system, Zinacantán was internally stratified. To do that in 1965 I distinguished between patterns like those in Table 10.2 and hypothetical random distributions that would have implied homogeneity consistent with the leveling interpretation.

For the present study, my task was to compare the non-random pattern of the early 1960's with the patterns found later to see if they are similar; i.e., the comparison was between actual distributions found at different times rather than between actual and hypothetical distributions. Once I found that the actual distributions appeared similar, I looked for systematic differences that might contradict the apparent similarity.

In manipulating the data on cargo careers, I tried to replicate the two kinds of populations used in 1965. One included all the men old enough to have had two cargos, i.e., men age 55 and older. The other included all men of any age who had passed two cargos. In 1965 the former came from censuses of two hamlets (Apaz and Hteklum), and the latter included careers recorded from a variety of sources. All my data on cargo careers for 1967 and 1983 are from the Nachig Census (Appendix C). For the comparison of fathers and their sons, I used cases from diverse sources in 1965, and cases from the Nachig Census for 1967 and 1983. Most of the early fieldwork was completed by 1962, the date put on those data here.

Because the cases in each sample were ordered by both the Prestige Scale and the Cost Scale, there was a total of six tests in 1965: four (two populations by two scales) for the hypotheses about cargo careers, and two (one population by two scales) about generations.

Many more tests were made for this study. In 1965 I satisfied myself with an antiseptic data-manipulation rule and a quiet suggestion that exploration based on ethnographic knowledge might be helpful:

All the two-by-two tables . . . are constructed by dividing the distributions in half on each variable. This system of division of the variables ensures against idiosyncratic manipulation of the data so as to support the hypotheses, but it may sometimes make too little of the patterns that can be seen in the full distribution. (p. 204)

Here I will replicate the mechanical halving of each variable and add, for each of the original six tests, two other ways of dividing the variables—ways that are based on substantive rather than methodological considerations. The additional cutting points are based on the cost ranking (1965: 84), and on global judgements that use my general knowledge of the cargo system.

The six tables from 1965 were tripled when those for 1967 and 1983 were added, and were tripled again when the two new ways to divide the variables were added. The 54 tables that resulted are summarized in Table 10.3 (36 for cargo careers and 18 for fathers and sons).[14]

TABLE 10.3

Continuity in Individual and Family Cargo Service, 1962, 1967, 1983 [a]

	Percent[a]			Cross-product ratio[a]			N
	Prestige scale						
CARGO CAREERS[a]	A	B	C	A	B	C	
Age ≥ 55							
1962	77%	80%	57%	11.0	28.6	[b]	30
1967	54	65	62	1.4	4.0	6.7	26
1983	61[c]	58	58	2.4[c]	2.8	8.8	43
Two cargos							
1962	67	84	60	4.1	17.5	10.8	145
1967	63	69	69	2.8	5.3	7.3	32
1983	60	77	70	2.2	10.7	20.9	47
	Cost scale						
	D	E	F	D	E	F	
Age ≥ 55							
1962	63[d]	57	63	3.2[d]	4.3	2.7	30
1967	81	69	65	18.3	10.3	2.9	26
1983	70	58	72	6.1	8.8	6.8	43
Two cargos							
1962	61	63	63	2.5	4.4	3.1	145
1967	72	75	72	6.5	11.3	5.6	32
1983	66	70	70	4.4	11.3	5.3	47
	Prestige scale						
FATHERS AND SONS[a]	A	B	C	A	B	C	
1962	64	61	60	3.2	2.3	1.8	103
1967	63[e]	64	73	2.9[e]	3.1	6.9	85
1983	61	60	67	2.5	2.3	4.3	108
	Cost scale						
	D	E	F	D	E	F	
1962	55	59	54	1.6	2.1	1.4	103
1967	67	67	67	4.2	3.8	4.2	85
1983	60	69	64	2.5	4.2	3.9	108

[a] The Section "Cargo Careers and Stratification" explains the origin of this table, and should be read with it. Table 10.3 reports the percent for continuity and the cross-product ratio for each of 54 2 × 2 tables. (The original tables are like those shown in Table 10.2.) Where the cells of a 2 × 2 table are WXYZ (upper left, upper right, lower left, lower right), the percent for continuity is (W + Z) / (X + Y), and the cross-product ratio is (W × Z) / (X × Y).

The Prestige Scale used for columns A, B, and C, and the Cost Scale used for columns D, E, and F, are displayed in Table 10.1. For columns A and D the distributions were divided in half on both variables, so that the marginals were as close to equal as possible (details are given in the Nachig Data Set). Other dividing points for cargo careers were: column B, A6/7 for the first cargo and B6/7 for the second cargo; column C, A6/7 and B3/4; column E, A5/8 and B3/6; column F, A6/5 and B3/6. For fathers and sons they were the same for both fathers and sons: column B, A5/6; column C, A6/7; column E, A6/5; column F, A5/8. The codes (e.g., A7) used to abbreviate cargo names are based on the Prestige Scale, and are explained in Table 10.1, note b. The dividing point A6/5 for column E for fathers and sons means that Mayordomo Santa Cruz (A6) and more expensive cargos are counted as high, and Mayordomo Santo Domingo (A5) and less expensive cargos are counted as low.

Careers that include Mayordomo Fátima Nachig, and those with Regidor as a second cargo, were dropped.
[b] Zero cell, no cross-product ratio.   [c] N = 38; five cases on the cutting point dropped.
[d] The four cases dropped in Cancian (1965: 112, table 17, test 2) are included here.
[e] N = 78; seven cases on the cutting point dropped.

The greatly increased number of tables has been balanced somewhat by reduced detail. For each of the 54 tables, Table 10.3 includes two summary measures: the percent supporting the hypothesis of stratification (to compare with the 1962 results shown in column A), and the cross-product ratio (Fienberg 1980). The cross-product ratio (described in Table 10.3, note *a*) is more appropriate than the chi-square statistic for tables with unequal marginals like those that resulted from the new, ethnographically motivated divisions of the variables. The results from Table 10.2 are included in Table 10.3—in column A in the fourth row from the top and the sixth row from the bottom. Appendix B in Cancian (1965) and the Nachig Data Set provide the complete data from which other results shown here may be reconstructed, and from which alternative formulations may be explored.

My conclusion that the three periods are similar is based on the overall pattern of results in Table 10.3. Consistent cargo careers and intergenerational similarity continued from 1962 to 1967 to 1983. The turmoil surrounding the few exceptions to the traditional order of service was not reflected in everyday behavior within the cargo system. As we will see immediately below, this internal continuity of the cargo system does not mean that its role in the community remained unchanged.

Cargos in Zinacantán Society

After the early 1960's the cargo system declined as a marker of community boundaries and the measure of social status within them. This was apparent in at least three ways: the proportion of men taking cargos went down, the tendency for young people to find marriage partners in families with similar records of cargo service seemed to disappear, and the association of cargo service with wealth weakened. Evidence for each of these trends is reviewed below. The new diversity of the hamlets (Chapter 9) limits some of the conclusions—especially because the source of most of my data, Nachig, is far from the municipio average.

The proportion of men taking cargos depends directly on the balance of cargo positions and population. If population grows faster than the number of positions in the cargo system, more and more men, whatever their inclinations, will find no positions available to them. When the proportion of men who serve goes down, the cargo system must lose its role as the universal marker of community membership.

TABLE 10.4

Participation in the Cargo System,
1961, 1967, 1983

(Percent participating by age group)
(At least one cargo)

Age (years)	Paste 1961[a] (N = 241)	Nachig 1967 (N = 208)	Nachig 1983 (N = 315)
25–29	7	2	4
30–34	12	31	22
35–39	23	29	28
40–44	29	70	22
45–49	71	84	58
50–54	85	100	66
55–59	71	91	94
60–64	88	100	85
> 64	96	100	100

[a] The Paste data are from Cancian (1965: 127, table 23).

This happened in Zinacantán. The specter of lower participation was already present in 1965: population growth had produced more adult men than the cargo system could accommodate, and the imbalance was reflected in very long waiting lists (Chapter 9). At that time I estimated that the imbalance would increase by 1980—that the age at which men took their first cargo would go up a lot as the waiting lists grew longer, and/or that a much higher percentage of men would not serve at all (1965: 161–73). It turned out that I slightly underestimated the expansion of the cargo system, and greatly underestimated the population growth: population actually doubled, while first-level cargos increased by about 30 percent.[15] Thus, high rates of participation became even more difficult to maintain. The models constructed in 1965 for the municipio as a whole underestimated the overall imbalance in 1980.

The predicted trends appear in the data on Nachig. Table 10.4 shows that men in their forties and early fifties in 1983 had participated less than men of comparable ages about 15 years before in 1967. Because the numbers are small and the estimates of age not very reliable, the decrease may actually be slight, but even a slight dip in Nachig participation would be impressive, for Nachig was not a typical hamlet. Nachig men asked for much more than their share of cargos in the Center (Table 9.2), and, counting the new cargos served in Nachig, between 1967 and 1983 they actually took more than 125 percent of their share of desirable mayordomo-type cargos[16]—and thereby left even fewer for men from other hamlets.

Men from other hamlets participated correspondingly less. While I have no survey data on their participation, Table 9.2 suggests the distribution of the imbalance. The Cornfields, where there were no local cargos of the traditional type to replace service in the Center, had the lowest rate of participation. This withdrawal is consistent with the political events discussed in Chapter 8.

In sum, as had been predicted in 1965, participation declined from the 1960's to the early 1980's. Nachig men occupied more than their share of the cargos available, but, because population grew more than cargos, proportionately fewer of them served cargos in the 1980's than in the 1960's. In addition, as noted in Chapter 9, the essentially equal participation by men from different parts of the municipio in the early 1960's gave way to a geographical imbalance that reflected political trends.

The relation of cargo service to spouse selection also changed—making cargo service a poorer index of general social position in Zinacantán. In Apaz in 1961, married people were likely to have

TABLE 10.5

*Cargos by Amount of Corn Seeded
and Economic Rank, Nachig, 1967 and 1983*

	Cross-product ratios	
	1967 $(N = 54)^b$	1983 $(N = 83)^b$
Old measure of cargos[a]		
Corn seeded[c]	9.5	2.1
Economic rank[d]	20.8	2.3
New measure of cargos[a]		
Corn seeded[e]	12.8	3.5
Economic rank	21.3	5.5

[a]High cargo service went with high wealth in the limited 1961 data from Paste (Cancian 1965: 100). The "old" measure used here replicates the procedure used on the Paste data (Cancian 1965: 104n.): cargo-service cutting points for ages 45–54 were A9/A10; for 55–64, B3/B4; for 65 and older, C4/B1. For the "new" measure, all ages are divided at A10/A11. For 1983, Mayordomo Fátima Nachig was counted as high.

[b]For 1967 all men 45 and older are included. Because of uncertain age estimates, the data for 1983 were made to include the same proportion of the census total as the data for 1967. They include men 51 and older in 1983.

[c]Corn seeded: 2 almudes or less is "Low." The year 1967 includes lowland fields only; 1983 includes small highland fields as well.

[d]Economic rank: the lower half of the rank rating equals "Low." See Appendix C.

fathers with similar records of cargo service (1965: 117); but data from Nachig for three later periods (the 1967 census, the 1983 census, and the "sample" of later marriages created by dropping men present in both 1967 and 1983 from the 1983 census) failed to reproduce that pattern. Perhaps the difference between the earlier Apaz data and the later Nachig data is due to differences between the hamlets, but I think it also reflects the decline of the cargo system as the principal marker of social position in Zinacantán.

Wealth differences did remain important in the selection of spouses. Although cargo careers of the fathers of married couples were not similar, as they had been in the 1960's, in the 1980's the rich still tended to marry the rich and the poor to marry the poor.[17]

Finally, as you might anticipate given the findings just reported, the relation of cargo service to wealth weakened between the 1960's and 1980's. Table 10.5 displays various measures that show that the relation was strong in 1967, and that it became much less impressive by 1983. This does not mean that wealthier Zinacantecos came to disdain cargo service. We will see in Chapter 11 that the fundamental change was in the relation of age and wealth. Cargos continued to be served by older men, but these older men were no longer the rich; the relative impoverishment of older men destroyed the old statistical relation between wealth and cargo service.

In sum, in the early 1960's, community membership and cargo service were virtually synonymous. Marriage usually joined families with similar records of cargo service. The wealthy were older, and the older took cargos. By the 1980's the proportion of men who participated had decreased. Wealth remained important, but its tie to age was broken, and thus its tie to cargo service was loosened. People from wealthy families continued to marry each other, but family status was no longer so clearly signaled by cargo service. Overall, it was no longer possible to see cargo service as the single most important marker of a man's and a family's position in the local system of social stratification. The meaning of cargo service had changed.

11 /   NEW INEQUALITY

No single institution replaced the cargo system in Zinacantán's public life. Inequality
in the 1980's reflected the new economic diversity, political divisions, and connections to the outside world. The kingpins of the
1960's—seniority, corn, and cargos—fell. This chapter will show
that, while the clear path to social position through the cargo system became a maze of alternative routes, economic position continued to be central to social position and public life inside Zinacantán.
The brief account of a neighborhood ceremony presented immediately below suggests some of the ways social behavior in Zinacantán reflected internal economic and political differentiation in
the 1980's. In later sections, statistical data on age, wealth, occupation, public roles, and politics give a broader picture of the new patterns of inequality.

A Ceremony

Each year in early May small groups of Zinacantecos gathered to
pray at sacred places in their neighborhoods. Responsibility for organizing and sponsoring the ceremonies rotated among the adult
males (households) who owned land in traditionally defined areas of
the hamlets. (Before piped water they were waterhole groups; see
Vogt 1969: 446–54.) In 1984 the responsibility for one area in Nachig fell to Yermo, and he invited me to the ceremony. I anticipated
a chance to meet some Nachig men in a small group, good eating
and drinking, and a break from formal fieldwork.

We gathered about 3 A.M. at Yermo's house, and ate a bit before
leaving the women and setting out on our rounds. First we went to

the church, where the Sacristan was roused and the doors were un-
locked. Yermo and the curer prayed while most of the rest of us sat
around talking. Then we went across the Pan American Highway to
the land where we would make our circuit. It sloped away from the
center of Nachig, and none of the men lived on it; it was good for
gathering wood, for corn, and increasingly, for fruit trees. After
slowly negotiating steep paths in the dark, we stopped briefly at
each of two crosses, where the musicians played, the curer prayed,
drinks were poured, and rockets shot off. At the first signs of dawn
we arrived at the main cross, set at a very wide place in the path
near a dirt overhang known as "The Cave." There, about 6 A.M.,
Yermo's nephew ambled in to join us, making the party an even
dozen.

We arranged ourselves in the open space and began to dance. Actually only five danced. Three non-owners, who had been induced
to come from the neighboring hamlet of Patosil, sat nearby on the
bank from which the path had been cut, and played the music. The
curer, who had recently bought land in the area, prayed at the cross.
An unmarried man from the neighborhood shot off the rockets, and
the man who had been in Yermo's role the year before shot off the
miniature cannon used to mark transitions in the ritual (Cancian
1965: 47–48). Yermo's older son, Francisco HH, had gone off to see
about a landowner who had been jailed because he failed to pay his
share in support of the ceremony.

I danced with Yermo, his two nephews (Mariano DD and his
brother, José), and their brother-in-law. A little excitement was
added to the mellow scene when Francisco returned and reported
that he had arranged a settlement: the jailed man was released after
he agreed to pay his full share ($460) plus a $500 penalty that the
group could use to buy a case of Pepsi. Francisco went off again to
arrange the details, and we continued to sing, dance, and joke.

This was no average group of Nachig men. The curer, a man who
had just passed a high-ranking second cargo (B2) and spoke no Spanish, owned a truck and was the Coca-Cola distributor for Zinacantán. The dancers, arranged in order of seniority to his right, began
with Yermo, a wealthy, powerful farmer and mason from the older
generation. The anthropologist, almost 50 and at least as entertain-
ing as the free case of Pepsi, was followed by Mariano DD, who
owned two vehicles, then his younger brother, who owned seven
(more than any other Zinacanteco) and the municipio-wide Pepsi
distributorship, and finally their brother-in-law, who had two trucks,
including the one that made a scheduled run early every Monday to

take Nachig men to construction work in Tuxtla. Together they owned almost half the vehicles in Nachig. Later I looked at the census done less than a year before and discovered the obvious: six of the seven married Nachig men present were in the top quartile of the wealth ranking. I had attended an elite party.

The dancing and the praying ended in full daylight. By 11 A.M. we had breakfasted on the trail, stopped to pray two more times, returned to Yermo's house for a final meal, and dispersed.

Who was not at the ceremony was also interesting. Later Yermo told me that the eight other men who owned land in the area had contributed shares—some gave the full $460 (about a day's pay for a construction laborer) to supplement the $10,000 Yermo spent, but most, who had small pieces of land on which they had not lived for years, gave just $100. Like those who came to the ceremony, all these men lived elsewhere and had obligations to other ceremonies in those areas as well. And, like Yermo's younger son, Juan KK (who was not obligated to participate because he lived in a joint household with Yermo), they may have been away working in Tuxtla. Had they come, it would have been a different party in at least one way, for five of the six for whom I had wealth rankings were in the lower half of the wealth distribution (the other was in the top quartile).[1] There were political differences as well. Six of the seven who attended were supporters of the Truckers party discussed in Chapter 8, while seven of the eight who did not attend supported the Peasants party.[2] If this pleasant occasion is any indication, associations in Nachig were segregated along economic and political lines.

Statistical Analysis: Data, Measures, and Framework

I do not know if what I saw in May 1984 was new, or typical. Perhaps it was a chance collection of people; perhaps it represented a long-standing tendency to separation along economic and political lines. Such neighborhood ceremonies were rare compared to other formal occasions, like curing ceremonies, that were organized along kinship lines. My limited experience with them does not provide enough data to assess patterns of social inequality and their change.

The Nachig Censuses for 1967, 1983, and 1987 (Appendix C) do permit such an assessment. Although there are few direct data on associations like those in the ceremony described above, the censuses provide information on all adult men in Nachig before and after the events of the 1970's. Because they incorporate the cargo history of many men and their fathers, we can ask about continuity in

TABLE II.I

Wealth by Age, Nachig, 1967 and 1983

	Count		Residual		Adjusted residual	
	Old[a]	Young[a]	Old	Young	Old	Young
1967, N = 208						
Wealth by quartile[b]						
1. (Richer)	29	31	6.8	− 6.8	2.2	− 2.2
2.	25	20	8.3	− 8.3	2.9	− 2.9
3.	9	36	− 7.7	7.7	− 2.7	2.7
4. (Poorer)	14	44	− 7.5	7.5	− 2.4	2.4
1983, N = 315						
Wealth by quartile[b]						
1. (Richer)	40	35	1.0	− 1.0	0.3	− 0.3
2.	39	36	0.0	0.0	0.0	0.0
3.	39	42	− 3.2	3.2	− 0.8	0.8
4. (Poorer)	46	38	2.3	− 2.3	0.6	− 0.6

[a]The age cutting point (25−39 = young) was chosen to separate men in the 1983 census who came of age in the 1970's from older men (see Chapter 5), and was also used on the 1967 census data.
[b]The wealth variable is divided into quartiles to make the pattern clear. Means on the original eight-rank wealth variable (see Appendix C) were old/young/overall: 5.3/4.1/4.6 in 1967 and 4.4/4.4/4.4 in 1983.

social position. Because the 1983 census includes the new occupational diversity and the new political diversity, we can ask about the relation of social position to these new features of Zinacanteco life.

The tables reporting the results of statistical analysis are crucial to the exposition that follows. Most of them include an unusual statistic, the adjusted residual, which is helpful here because it makes it easy to compare across subpopulations of different sizes. I will first use Tables 11.1 and 11.2 to describe the statistic and its relation to more familiar ones, then concentrate on interpreting the substance of the tables.

Table 11.1 includes an eight-cell table (four categories of wealth by two categories of age) for 1967 and a comparable one for 1983. There are three measures for each cell: the count, the residual, and the adjusted residual. The count is the number of cases in the cell. That is, there were 29 Nachig men 40 or older who fell into the top wealth quartile in 1967.

The residual is the count (the observed) minus the cases expected in the cell on the basis of the marginals and the assumption that the variables are not related. Note that the 29 men just referred to are more than expected (the residual is + 6.8). That is, in 1967, older men tended to be in the top quartile more than younger men. Residuals are familiar to many as the "observed minus expected" used

TABLE 11.2

Occupation By Age and Wealth, Nachig, 1983

Occupation	N	Mean		Adjusted residual	
		Age (years)	Wealth (rank)[a]	Age (older)	Wealth (richer)
Corn farmer	91	49	5.3	6.4	3.7
Semiproletarian	54	40	3.2	0.6	− 5.3
Wage worker	41	39	2.0	− 2.5	− 5.9
Trader	36	39	4.3	− 1.3	0.3
Truck owner	20	36	7.3	− 3.0	4.8
Other[b]	73	41	4.9	− 2.7	2.5
Total N	315			164	150
Overall mean		42	4.4		

[a] There are eight wealth ranks (see Appendix C).
[b] Government workers, masons, and truck drivers are lumped in with the "other" category in this table and those that follow because they include too few cases, and expected values are often less than 5.

in calculating the chi-square statistic. They vary with both the strength of the relationship and the number of cases being analyzed. When the variables are not much related, the residuals approach zero; when the variables are related, the residuals are larger. And, when the number of cases being analyzed is large, the residuals may be large numbers even if the relationship is not very substantial. The first of these characteristics, response to the strength of the relationship, is of course, desirable. The second, response to population or sample size, is undesirable—especially when comparing across a variety of measures involving categories of different sizes.[3]

Adjusted residuals, which are also shown in Table 11.1, have four desirable characteristics: (1) they vary with the strength of the relationship; (2) they compensate for the number of cases, making the size of the statistic less dependent on the number of cases involved; (3) they compensate for chance variation that may be introduced when a small number of cases with high variance is involved; and (4) they provide a rule of thumb that can be used to interpret results—specifically, a value of 2 or more for the adjusted residual suggests the relationship is worth thinking about as a substantive one.[4] By this standard, Table 11.1 shows that in 1967 the old tended to be richer than the young, and that by 1983 there was no wealth difference between the old and the young.

Because adjusted residuals for dichotomous variables sum to zero and the age and wealth variables used are dichotomous, Table 11.2 gives only one adjusted residual value per variable. Had I chosen to report the relation of occupation to being younger and poorer (rather than older and richer as is done in Table 11.2), all the values would have been the same but all the signs would have been reversed. The table shows that corn farmers are older than average and that men of other occupations are of average age or younger. The negative scores for semiproletarians and wage workers on the wealth variable reflect the very low wealth ranks of these men—while all the other occupations listed are average or above average in wealth.[5]

In sum, using the adjusted residual permits easy comparison of the patterns described in this chapter. Since this use of the adjusted residual is unusual, at least in sociocultural anthropology, and since some readers will prefer to do other kinds of analysis, the counts on which all the tables are based are available in the Nachig Data Set.

This analysis will focus on four basic variables: age, wealth (rank),[6] occupation, and public roles. Age and wealth are important in most systems of inequality; in Zinacantán they are especially important because their roles in local relationships and their relationship to each other changed between the 1960's and the 1980's. The other two variables are more embedded in local history: in economic life (Part I) and in local public institutions (Part II).[7] A fifth concern, the size of the economic and political world relevant to Zinacantecos, is part of the context for the analysis in this chapter. It will be of direct concern in Chapter 12.

Age, Wealth, and Occupation

The statistical analysis shows how social stratification in Zinacantán was transformed. Young men became much richer than they had been, thereby breaking the tie between wealth and age that existed in 1967; by 1983 there was no systematic relation between age and wealth (Table 11.1). This happened when older men remained corn farmers while younger men took up the new occupations (Table 11.2; see also Chapter 5). In the new order, the richest (truck owners) and the poorest (wage workers) were young men in occupations created by the economic transformation. The results shown in the tables lead to three questions.

First, how can we understand the new economic power of the young? Was it still growing in 1983? Had Zinacantán (at least Nachig) become (or become part of) a society in which young people were best equipped to dominate economic activities? That is, had things changed such that future generations of young men would be as wealthy as their elders? Or, had there been an historical change in which the particular cohort of men who came of age in the 1970's fell into a good thing and would consolidate their power against new generations of youth? Or, finally, did age simply become less relevant to economic rank? In sum, did the young get richer; did a particular generation get richer; or did seniority become as unimportant as it appears to be under the new economic structure seen from the cross-sectional point of view?

These questions cannot be fully addressed with the limited time perspective of this study—but any answer is apt to mix the alternatives mentioned above, at least the last two. As George Collier (1989) has shown, historical periods in Zinacantán have had an important influence on the economic fortunes of the men who came of age during them. And worldwide trends suggest that the occupational diversity and employment in the world outside of Zinacantán will lead to less age differentiation in income—in part because fathers will have less control over their sons.

Second, has wealth inequality among Zinacantecos grown? Because my measure of wealth is relative rank (see note 11.6), I cannot answer this basic question with the data used in this chapter. I have

TABLE 11.3

Economic Position Over Generations,
Nachig, 1983

	Father's wealth, 1967[a]	
	Mean rank[b]	Adjusted residual
Wealth, 1983		
Richer	6.4	4.1
Poorer	4.6	− 4.1
Occupation, 1983		
Corn farmer	6.3	1.7
Semiproletarian	5.4	0.0
Wage worker	3.9	− 2.8
Trader	4.8	− 3.0
Truck owner	6.7	2.0
Other	5.8	1.6
Overall mean	5.5	

[a]For the 131 men in the 1982 census whose father's wealth rank in 1967 is known. Probably because rich men had more sons who survived, and because they lived longer themselves, rich men are overrepresented: 94 of the 131 fathers are in the top half of the wealth rank, and their mean wealth of 5.5 is much higher than the overall 1967 mean (N = 208) of 4.6.
[b]See Table 11.2, note *a*.

no other systematic measures of absolute wealth distribution over the period covered in this study. The best systematic longitudinal measure is the amount of corn seeded, and inequality in the amount of corn seeded grew substantially between 1966 and 1973 (Chapter 2), but it is hard to know how much that changed wealth distribution. Overall, impressionistically, wealth inequality became greater (Chapter 5).

Third, what is the relation of men's economic ranks in 1983 to the economic ranks of their families of origin? Did the economic transformation mix up old wealth relationships, or did the new rich and the new poor simply continue in the ranks of their fathers? Comparing fathers' wealth in 1967 with sons' wealth in 1983 strongly suggests that the new rich are the sons of the old rich, and the new poor are the sons of the old poor (Table 11.3).

Overall, these data on age, wealth, and occupation suggest that substantial wealth differences among Zinacantecos remained. Age no longer varied with them, but occupation clearly did.[8] Amid the newness, wealth remained in the hands of the same old families.

Public Life: The Consequences of New Institutions

The institutional change described in Part II was reflected in the public lives of individuals. Men, especially young men, were pressed to fill the new civil offices in the hamlets, and all men had to affiliate with a political party. Thus, the way individuals used public roles to construct their social positions changed—civil offices and politics were much more central to public life in the 1980's than they had been in the 1960's. While cargo service was still respected, it remained largely the preserve of older men.

The relation of these new patterns of public service to wealth and occupation, as well as to age, is shown in Table 11.4. It is no surprise that, in 1983, older men/corn farmers were concentrated in religious cargos and younger men had taken a disproportionate number of the new civil offices.[9] Younger men were pressed into service in the new civil offices for at least three reasons: (1) fewer of them had passed religious cargos that entitled them to rest, (2) older men considered the new offices less important and used their power to avoid them, and (3) some of the new offices required Spanish reading and writing skills that were more common among the young.

The rich served more than the poor. Even among the young, who served mostly in civil positions, the rich occupations like truck owners (and government workers and truck drivers not shown in the

TABLE 11.4

Public Service by Age, Wealth, and Occupation, Nachig, 1983[a]

(Percent taking cargos)

	No cargos	Civil offices only	Religious cargos only	Both	N
Age					
Older	17% *[b]	21% **	46% **	17% **	163
Younger	31*	49**	17**	6*	151
Wealth					
Richer	11**	37	37*	16*	150
Poorer	35**	32	26*	7*	164
Occupation					
Corn farmer	11**	10**	59**	20**	91
Semiproletarian	34*	34	23	9	53
Wage worker	44**	42	12*	2[c]	41
Trader	28	44	19	8[c]	36
Truck owner	5*[c]	70**	10*[c]	15[c]	20
Other	22	47	23	8	73
Overall percent	23%	34%*	31%	12%	
N	73	108	93	36	314[d]

[a] Data on service from the 1987 census are used in order to include more years of performance.
[b] For entries with no asterisk, the adjusted residual is between 1.9 and −1.9; * = 2.0 to 2.9 or −2.0 to −2.9; ** = more than 2.9 or less than −2.9.
[c] The expected value for this cell is less than 5.
[d] Data for one case are missing.

table) served more than the poor occupations like wage workers. In sum, service in new civil offices, like service in religious cargos, was concentrated among the rich.

These new civil offices also required considerable sacrifice from the incumbent, especially if he was a wage worker. Thus, by serving in them, many young men reaffirmed their commitment to their community. The distinctive thing was that the community they served, the community that recognized their sacrifice, was most often their hamlet, not the municipio of Zinacantán.

Overall, service in public positions may be seen as a conservative force. Religious cargo service, especially, was stabilized as an institution by the "investments" of dispersed individuals who, as they sacrificed for the community, acquired an interest in the continuity that assured them their local social rewards. Civil offices involved less expense and were sometimes mixed with politics, but they still represented individual service to the community—an earning of social position.

Manuel Pérez, wearing the costume he used when he passed
Mayordomo in Nachig, with his
truck, 1988.

Political affiliations were quite different from service in public positions. Groups ("parties") shifted as leaders reinterpreted the mood
of their followers and the demands of and opportunities offered by
the government; the possibility of change created power for groups
and individuals.

Table 11.5 records shifting party membership during the period of
intense politics described in Chapter 8.[10] Though the PRI/Truckers
grew in the 1980's, the majority of Nachig men still remained in the
Peasant group in 1987. The Peasants began as the members of PRI
who voted for Pedro Vázquez in the 1982 municipio election, and
they had various leaders—including Antonio López, the corn trader
whose son was, in the early 1980's, the first Zinacanteco law student
in San Cristóbal (see Antonio JJ, note 4.14). Peasant group members
reaffirmed PRI ties in August 1983, probably because of Pedro Vázquez's shift to PRI and hopes of jobs for official PRI members (Chapter 8); thus they count as PRI/Truckers for 1984 in Table 11.5. The
group backed an unsuccessful candidate for Presidente Municipal in
the PRI nominating process of fall 1984 and, according to Yermo, did
not vote in the elections that followed.

The PRI/Truckers maintained connections to the official party ap-

TABLE 11.5

Political Affiliation, Nachig, 1982–1988[a]

(Counts)

	1982	1983	1984	1987
PRI/Truckers[b]	75	97	280	133
Peasants	229[c]	214[c]	—	158
PAN			33	12
TOTAL[d]	304	311	313	303

[a]From the Nachig Census. For 1982, report of votes in the election of the Presidente Municipal; for other years, from reports of party affiliation (tax-paying).

[b]There was party loyalty among core PRI/Peasants. Of 75 PRI voters in 1982, 11 were PAN/Peasants in 1983; 6 were PAN in 1984; 12 were Peasant and none were PAN in 1987. Two had died by 1987.

[c]Peasants and PAN were lumped during this period.

[d]In 1982, 11 men who were absent or legally resident elsewhere did not vote in Nachig. In 1983, 1984, and 1987, four, two, and two cases, respectively, lacked information needed to classify them.

paratus when they and the Peasants separated in fall 1982. According to one member of the Peasants, the PRI/Truckers had four leaders in Nachig—the four men with whom I danced at the ceremony described above. The Truckers had strong connections to Truckers in Navenchauc, while the Peasants were connected to leaders of the transportation elite in the Center.

Core PAN members were persistent, but their numbers remained very small. In the summer 1987 Census, and in July 1988 when I observed PAN members lined up behind their leader Antonio Pérez Ocotz to vote in the federal elections, there were about a dozen of them. They were largely concentrated in Jechchentic, and strain between some of them and people in Nachig went back many decades (see Chapter 7)—that is, PAN reflected and made more explicit very old divisions in Nachig.

The patterns illustrated in the ceremony described above are repeated in the quantitative data. Table 11.6 shows that the rich consistently supported the PRI/Truckers, as did the truck owners. The truck owners formed the clearest political block among all the occupations, but the labels put on the parties during the political conflict described in Chapter 8 were only partly descriptive of actual political affiliations in Nachig. While the Truckers label was particularly apt, the corn farmers—the obvious candidates for the Peasants label adopted by the opposition—were also relatively heavy supporters of the Truckers at the outset in 1982. At that point, party affiliation appeared to be more tied to wealth than to occupation.

As the economic crisis became more important in the middle

1980's, occupation emerged more clearly from among the complex forces that determined political affiliation. Wage workers and semi-proletarians, who were the most dependent on the government construction jobs tied to PRI membership during the latter part of the period (Chapter 8), shifted towards the PRI/Truckers. As overall support for the PRI/Truckers increased, those least dependent on government employment, the corn farmers, changed little. As Table 11.6 shows, by 1987 they were underrepresented in PRI.

The consistent opposition of the traders and the government workers (not shown in the table) to the PRI/Truckers was not so simple. As far as I can tell, it was based on personal ties, their independence from construction work, and their concern to control prices of the transport on which they depended heavily.

What is clear in these patterns of political affiliation in Nachig is that transport was the arena of competition of the Zinacantán elite. Just how to interpret the behavior of Nachig truck owners in this arena is less clear. Were they PRI because they were rich and wanted

TABLE 11.6

Political Affiliation by Age, Wealth, and Occupation,
Nachig, 1982, 1983, 1987[a]

	Percent for PRI/Truckers			For PRI/Truckers (adjusted residual)		
	1982	1983	1987	1982	1983	1987
Age, 1983						
40 and older	20%	30%	42%	− 2.1	− 0.6	− 0.7
25 to 39	30	33	46	2.1	0.6	0.7
Wealth, 1983						
Richer	35	35	51	3.9	1.5	2.3
Poorer	15	27	38	− 3.9	− 1.5	− 2.3
Occupation, 1983						
Corn farmer	32	33	37	1.8	0.4	− 1.8
Semiproletarian	15	26	43	− 1.8	− 0.9	− 0.4
Wage worker	22	26	55	− 0.5	− 0.8	1.2
Trader	11	17	25	− 1.9	− 2.0	− 2.3
Truck owner	70	75	95	4.9[b]	4.4	4.5
Other	18	31	47	− 1.4	0.0	0.3
Overall percent for PRI/Truckers	25%	31%	45%			
N	304	311	279–303[c]			

[a] From the Nachig Census. For 1982, report of votes in the election of the Presidente Municipal; for other years, reports of party affiliation.
[b] The expected value for this cell is less than 5.
[c] Some new men in the 1987 census lacked wealth and occupation information.

to protect the status quo? Were they PRI because their occupation demanded good connections with the bureaucrats who issued their licenses and processed their traffic infractions? Or were they PRI because their connections to PRI leaders pre-dated the political divisions and helped them in internal competition among truckers? The last interpretation gets some support from the fact that the original leaders of the opposition were rich, well-connected members of the transportation elite in the Center.

Changing Social Inequality in Theoretical Context

Between the 1960's and the 1980's, Zinacantecos changed the way they established social position in their community. New public roles were created, and the meaning of old ones changed. Many of the young became wealthy by entering new occupations, and new political parties reflected the diverse interests of men with different occupations. As the paths to social position became more complex, the meaning of cargo service changed and its central importance declined. However, both the positions of families relative to each other and the relation of wealth to public service persisted. Overall, the degree of inequality increased; i.e., differences of position became more important in the everyday public social life of individuals.

Here I want to address general questions to which the data on individual public careers speak. Most of these questions stem from the frameworks that oriented the fieldwork and the analysis. Some were also raised at the ends of Chapters 5 and 9.

How are we to think about semiproletarians in the local setting? Their economic role in the larger political economy, as labor for which reproduction costs need not be fully borne by capitalists who employ them, is clear in the widely accepted Marxist functionalist interpretation of political economy at the national level; but the meaning of their economic position for their social roles in their local communities is not clear. Simply put, the question is: Is their local social behavior like farmers, like wage workers (the component parts of their economic roles), or like a third unique type?

The answer is quite clear in the tables presented in this chapter: semiproletarians are poor (Table 11.2), serve few cargos (Table 11.4), and (perhaps) affiliate politically with the party of the poor (Table 11.6). On each of the measures they are close to the wage workers. In terms of their local social and political behavior, they are not farmers (peasants) who are increasing their incomes with wage work, they are wage workers who also do some farming. In these data the differences between wage workers and semiproletarians are not large enough or consistent enough, compared to their differences from corn farmers, to justify creation of a third unique type.[11]

What are the implications of modernization theory for the public behavior of individuals with different economic and social positions? As suggested at the end of Chapter 9, modernization theory leads us to predict that "modern" men would not take cargos and "traditional" men would take them—that, for example, people in the new occupations would not take cargos while corn farmers would. This is the theory that is implicit at the end of my study of the cargo system, where, by suggesting that men who bought trucks and men who spent an equal amount of money in the cargo system would have little to say to each other, I left no room for truck owners to take cargos or for cargoholders to buy trucks (Cancian 1965: 194).

The results displayed above (Table 11.4) do not support this vision. Given their age, truck owners and government employees (not shown in the table), the core of the new economic elite, took their share of religious cargos (the numbers are small). And they took much more than their share of civil cargos (Mariano DD). Their high rate of service, not any tendency to avoid service, is what needs to be explained.

Both modernization and Marxist approaches offer clear explanations. On the one hand, the extraordinary service of truck owners and government employees in civil offices may be seen as a preference consistent with their more modern orientation. On the other hand, it is tempting to interpret their service as service in religious cargos is often interpreted—as a social investment to insure against negative reactions to their deviant (counter-normative) roles, especially their great wealth. These two explanations are not exclusive alternatives, of course. My intuition, given experience with a number of younger men who did public service, is that the latter is more enlightening, but I see no clear way to reject the former.

The implications of Marxist approaches for the public behavior of individuals with different social and economic positions are vastly more complex than those of modernization theory, because contemporary Marxist approaches are many and diverse. The conceptual thicket is too dense to yield a coherent vision simple enough to use in this context.[12] It is clear that Zinacantecos became (1) more dependent on distant economic forces and (2) more diverse in their economic adaptations. More of them became proletarians; many of them controlled capital and depended on relations with the regional and national economic and bureaucratic system. It is important to recognize that Lenin's ideas about the transformation of the countryside are generally relevant to Zinacantán and many other third-world populations (Cancian 1989). Class as economic coercion involving connections to the larger system became more directly relevant to daily interaction in Zinacantán, but local connections and local public roles were also crucial to the ways Zinacantecos related to each other.

One issue related to class analysis is directly important to this study: where are we to bound the conceptual arena in which classes interact? Are the political tensions between, say, truckers and traders, or truckers and most other occupations in Nachig, appropriately seen in class terms? Or is it more appropriate to focus on the truckers and, say, the wage workers as parts of classes in the national political economy?[13] In my judgment, given what has been described above, there is something to be lost and little to be gained by favoring one of these approaches to the exclusion of the other. Both should be maintained as part of the several frameworks used to interpret Zinacantán.

In sum, I believe it is possible to be clear about what happened in Zinacantán, and not so clear about how to interpret it. The changes described in the first paragraph of this section are relevant within different frameworks, and interpretation of them gets insight from different frameworks that are sometimes thought to be contradictory.

12 / CONCLUSION

Community declined in Zinacantán between the early 1960's and the early 1980's. This is obvious from what has been reported above. It is true in different ways, within different frameworks, in terms of different definitions of community.

During this period there were four principal substantive changes: (1) men's economic activity diversified; (2) public life decentralized to the hamlets; (3) open, sometimes violent, conflict among local groups emerged; and (4) multiple criteria for assessing the social position of individuals were established.

This ordering roughly represents my idea of causal primacy. Of course, the interactions among the changes were complex, and not always unidirectional. Nevertheless, I believe that changes in the larger economy led to the transformation of the local economy, and that outside government (and church) action fostered formal organization in the hamlets. The conflict in public life and the new patterns of internal social stratification were in large part consequences of the changes that originated outside the community. In addition, population growth created internal pressure for the increase of public positions and the fission of hamlets.

Given these substantive conclusions, I want to use this chapter to discuss some of the conceptual issues encountered in the effort to describe and understand this period in Zinacantán's history as a community.

First I want to review the study's conclusions in terms of the economic and social systems that were central to Zinacanteco life and the analysis made of it. The decline in the strength of the municipio of Zinacantán as a community involved multiple changes in these systems. Zinacantán became more open in the 1970's, as many Zina-cantecos depended more directly on the larger economy. At the same time the decentralization of public roles to the hamlets made the municipio less important and the hamlets more important in the social lives of Zinacantecos. Put another way, the municipio's boundaries were eroded from both sides—from above in economic relations and from below in social relations. Increasingly, Zinacantecos lived in multiple systems of different sizes. While the conceptual manipulations involved in this vision of what happened seem quite straightforward, it is worth acknowledging them and repeating the assertion that they refer to substantive historical events.

The principal conceptual issue is the relation of the local system and the larger system in our understanding of community life, especially life in rural third-world communities. Others have written well on the difficulties of understanding events in such communities in terms of global structural generalizations, even when such generalizations are framed in historical terms. They have argued the need to consider local history and the need to give local people active roles in creating local events (Comaroff 1982; Roseberry 1988; Smith 1984). Given these statements as context, I have emphasized the distinction between the economic and social aspects of local life,[1] and the advantages of studying them in terms of systems of different sizes (Chapter 1, above; Cancian 1985). I have argued that some aspects of life, specifically those I have labeled "social," are better understood as smaller systems.

In sum, I have made two assertions: (1) that outside economic change had a major causal role in the transformation of life, including social life, in Zinacantán; and (2) that a major part of the dynamics of Zinacantán's social life was local. These statements are contradictory only if we think in absolutes, i.e., if we think that "cause" means "determine in every important detail," and that "local" means "completely isolated." If we are willing to see degrees of causal influence and degrees of isolation, it becomes possible to say that the causal effects of the national and international systems are greater in economic life and less in social life, and that the importance of the local system is greater in social life and less in economic life. This is what I have done.[2]

During the period covered by this study, the system most relevant to the economic life of Zinacantecos was very large. The emergence of occupational diversity in the 1970's and the retrenchment that began in 1982 had less to do with the particular history or local situation of Zinacantecos and more to do with variations in the world market for petroleum.

During the same period the system most relevant to social life remained small. There was much change in the public roles through which men established social position, but for most Zinacantecos the decentralization of public life to the hamlets made the relevant community smaller, not larger, than it had been. Social localism flourished in the midst of important connections to the international economic order.

Thus, it seems to me, it is worth distinguishing economic and social systems for the purpose of analysis. Doing so highlights the important ways in which they are substantively independent. The fact that they are virtually never entirely independent poses no problem unless we insist that the world conform to simple models.

EPILOGUE

This study was done during a period of great epistemological ferment in anthropology. In the last decade the idea of ethnographic description has been dismantled and only partially reassembled.[1] Thus I want to discuss what I have done and how I think about it. This is a personal statement that combines various well-known positions, not an effort to make an original scholarly contribution.[2]

As an ethnographer I want to describe. I want to see and hear about what others do, and record it. Though I know better, I have insisted on doing that in the body of this study. That is, for the most part I have treated description as unproblematic.

There are two problems with this stance. They are both classics that need little introduction. First, there are always alternative descriptions. Second, descriptions always reflect the describer.

The problem of alternative descriptions has at least two sources. From a simple realist point of view, the world is too detailed to be encompassed by any description. Thus every description is selective and limited by the fact that alternative selections are always possible. From a simple idealist point of view that gives the conceptual framework (theory) a role in the reality perceived, different frameworks lead to different realities. Every description is selective and limited by the conceptual framework used to make it; alternative frameworks are always possible. Thus both approaches lead to the conclusion that all descriptions are partial, i.e., not total.

The problem created by the contribution of the describer to the description may be seen as a subtype of the idealist point of view just stated, but the alternative frameworks involved are not simply abstract alternatives—they depend on characteristics of the describer. Currently, the idea that description (knowledge in general) reflects the social position and the efforts at social positioning of the describer (knower) is the most popular. The contribution of the knower's culture is logically similar to it. Some scholars have been concerned about the contribution of the personality and detailed personal history of knowers. Thus all descriptions are partial in another sense; that is, they are biased.

Both the selectivity of all descriptions and the contribution of the describer to all descriptions are important problems. They put those who seek total and absolutely valid descriptions in a difficult position. To proceed they would have to ignore the insights of cultural relativism, deny their personal experience of solving a problem, whether practical or intellectual, by reconceptualizing it (I assume they have this experience), and repudiate the lessons of the history and sociology of science. The more sensible alternative is to conclude that the process of knowing, including the process of knowing about the process of knowing, is always limited in known ways and possibly in unknown ways.

Given this situation, what are we to do? I find the caricatured extremes equally unattractive. Positivists/naive realists deny the conclusion just reached—and pursue objective facts often with hard, complex techniques that seem about as useful as a stainless steel powder puff. Postmodernists/deconstructionists revel in the conclusion—and it seems sometimes that they could examine the dust created by engraving the head of a pin and find in it the key to the engraver's class position and social positioning.

To break out of the impasses created by these caricatured positions, the positivist and the postmodernist, it is necessary to confront them on two important characteristics that they share: they each emphasize method over subject matter, and each is obsessed with absolute truth (in one case through attention to the impossibility of reaching it). Espousing an emphasis on subject matter over method will bring criticism from both sides, for the constitution of subject matter is unsystematic from one point of view and arbitrary from the other. Likewise, abandoning absolute truth and total relativism for a middle road will sully the product in diverse ways.

I have taken the middle road in this study; i.e., I have insisted on proceeding, and have produced partial and imperfect knowledge. Thus I want to review some ways to put the imperfection in perspective, moderate the partiality, and share the risk of building or acting on knowledge that cannot be bolstered by association with absolutes.

It seems clear that the compromises I made are universal. Everyone seems to make them in some form; for example, it is commonly observed that positivists choose subject matter in unsystematic ways and that postmodernists write traditional ethnographies. The fact that we all compromise in ethnographic practice suggests, at minimum, that we should explore different ways of comparing epistemological positions with each other and with practice. We must balance, in practice, the obvious benefits of constant self-consciousness and social criticism and the paralytic effects of the quest for perfection.[3]

An approach that sees knowledge as a social product offers ways to improve that product. First, it is possible to share the risk and diminish the selectivity inherent in the choice of framework. In this book I have tried to share the risk with a diverse set of recognized scholars. Those mentioned in Chapter 1 and at the end of each part are at least disparate enough to range across much of the contemporary political spectrum. A pessimist could point out that the focus is nevertheless narrow, that many perspectives are not represented, and that some of those not represented are radically incommensurable with those that are represented. I prefer to note that, despite their differences, these scholars tend to be interested in many similar things, and to see many similar patterns. I believe that their joint vision is no arbitrary concoction. It is broadly embedded in contemporary society—they have identified substantive issues of importance to many students of society and many people who think along with them. In social terms, theirs is useful knowledge. That many alternative visions exist is part of the process, not a flaw in the result. That alternative institutional settings, different politics of knowledge, yield different results is reason to open the process, to shift its center, and to engage with alternative visions, not reason to abandon the effort.

Second, the partiality can be moderated and the risk shared by making the process public (social) in at least two other ways. That is, observations that could easily be made by others are preferable to those that, even in principle, are difficult to replicate; and reports and analyses that can reach a broad audience are preferable to those written in esoteric language. Given the technical nature of this study I must emphasize that these principles should be applied with judgment and within social context. Complex societies will have specialists, and specialists will have esoteric practices. Within this context it is important to value public procedures and clear communication—for they make possible the review and criticism that moderate the partiality inherent in the process of knowing.

Finally, the risk may be shared with the user—the reader. Many discussions of ethnographic authority emphasize ways authors manipulate readers. But readers are responsible for themselves. They are not passive knowers. They participate in the use of ethnography as much as its writers. They can believe it or not. That is the risk they take. That is how they contribute to making the knowledge social.

APPENDIXES

A /   FIELDWORK

The relation of the fieldwork to the Harvard Chiapas Project and practices regarding the confidentiality of personal statements are described in the Preface.

When I visited Zinacantán for seven weeks in summer 1981 to begin this study, I did "formal interviews,"[1] visited and attended public events in Zinacantán, and talked with Ladino officials in San Cristóbal. About half my formal interviews were with Guillermo Pérez Nuh (Yermo) and José Hernández (Chep Apaz), who had been principal assistants on my corn-farming study in 1967. I also interviewed five young men whom I had known as kin of friends and consultants during previous visits and four new consultants (including two Ladino government officials). Working mostly with Yermo, I updated the 1967 Nachig Census. George Collier visited for about ten days to update the Apaz Census (Cancian 1972: 165).

In summer 1982, I renewed old friendships and made new contacts. Many of my interviews were with Mariano Martínez, another principal assistant from the corn study, who was about to become Senior Alcalde Viejo for 1983. I also visited the Fiesta of San Lorenzo in August, where Mariano's group of Elders confirmed many of the names that were on the waiting lists they had received in late June (Chapter 9).

On Sunday, August 8, as I began visits to say good-bye to friends who would be away as migrant laborers when I left at midweek, I learned that many men had been laid off from construction jobs in Tuxtla the previous day. They were told that the President of the Republic wanted them to return to farming, that there would be no more work until the next year

1. Formal interviews were two-to-eight-hour sessions for which Zinacantecos were paid the prevailing wage for the days they lost from alternative employment. The sessions were usually scheduled a day or more in advance. During summer 1981 and spring and summer 1984 (when family members were with me part of the time) I interviewed in a rented house in San Cristóbal. On other trips I stayed in a hotel in San Cristóbal that became familiar to me and to the people who worked there with me. Parts of some interviews were done in Zinacantán.

(when the new administration would enter). About ten days later, Jesús Silva Herzog, Mexico's Minister of Finance, visited Washington to say that his country would not meet its debt payments (Wyman 1983a: 1). The economic crisis had struck. What had begun as a fairly straightforward study of internal conflict as Zinacantán became more connected to the larger system, suddenly had a new twist. The ideas of Eric Wolf and G. William Skinner that I had explored in a theoretical paper (see Chapter 1) became relevant to Zinacantán; the environment had become more hostile.

I returned in December 1982 to check on the effects of the economic crisis, but by then the internal political crisis created by the election of Pedro Vázquez as Presidente Municipal (Chapter 8) seemed more important than the limited employment opportunities. That was again true when I visited in March 1983 and in summer 1983, when I returned to complete the Nachig Census and to work with Mariano Martínez on the activities of the Elders.

The major fieldwork was done in 1984. Though planned for April through August, it began fortuitously in February and March, when I was asked to replace Robert Wasserstrom (who had other commitments) on a World Bank team evaluating a multifaceted proposal for agricultural and roads loans for many parts of Chiapas. Though virtually all my time was spent in contact with Mexican officials in Mexico City and the lowlands of Chiapas, and in Washington writing reports, the work gave me valuable perspectives on the "other" side of government programs. Then, from late April to early August 1984, I spent most of the time in the field. I collected the life histories that make up Chapter 4, and had the interviews with Pablo Ramírez that helped orient me for the work in Chapter 3 and parts of Chapter 8.

I made brief follow-up visits in the summers of 1985, 1987, and 1988.

On most trips I did some library work—in the libraries of CIES and Na Bolom in San Cristóbal, and in the state congress and state university libraries in Tuxtla Gutiérrez.

While many days were spent doing errands and library work, socializing with individuals and families, visiting at public events like fiestas and political meetings, asking and doing favors, the improved transportation system and the burgeoning of contacts that came as the work developed made the pace rather intense. Sometimes I went to the Center, Nachig, or Navenchauc to visit and/or make arrangements before and after a day of interviewing. By 1988 I had done more than 80 formal interviews with 33 people, including 32 men and one woman, 27 Zinacantecos, four Ladinos, and two anthropologists. I also had the help of some men who wrote texts and collected other material when I was not in the field.[2]

2. All these people are called "consultants" rather than "informants." That label seems more appropriate given the work they did.

B /   POPULATION AND PLACES, 1940 – 1987

This appendix is based on data from official censuses and documents. Interviews and anthropological publications also helped me to understand official materials and fill in gaps. I have two purposes in what follows. First, I want to produce good estimates of population size and distribution within Zinacantán—ones that can be used for analysis of social and political change, especially of shifting patterns of participation in the cargo system between the 1950's and the 1980's. Second, I want to record the information on places and population in its extensive form and display the detail that supports the simplifying assumptions in the analyses.

The appendix has three sections. The first presents the place names needed to understand the population data. The second presents data from censuses done by national government agencies. The third describes and discusses the data available from summaries of tax lists kept by local government, i.e., by Zinacanteco officials.

Places

An inventory of place names is needed to handle the data and history relevant to estimating population size, distribution, and change over recent decades. Government censuses and tax-collection lists that used the hamlet as an official unit (see Chapter 6) were not always uniform and consistent among themselves. The cargo waiting lists (Chapter 9) that I wanted to compare to the population distributions sometimes used still other place names. And, between 1950 and 1987, many factors, including population movements and political considerations, led to changes in the way Zinacantecos used place names. Thus, the official hamlet designations in use at any one time are not detailed enough to support description of recent history in Zinacantán.

Table B.1 displays all the names of socially defined, geographically localized collections of people relevant for this study. The table also includes detailed information on location and alternative renderings of the names. The spellings in column A are used in this study.

Data from Censuses

Table B.2 displays data from two types of censuses maintained by national agencies: the official national census done every ten years, and some of the censuses done by the government's malaria eradication program (CNEP) annually.

The national census for 1980 did not publish data for the localities within Zinacantán. Work on the 1980 census encountered many problems at the national level, and the census is probably not as trustworthy as other recent national censuses. For Zinacantán it showed a population of 13,006, a total that seems much too low.

While many local officials think the CNEP censuses are the best available, the CNEP figures have problems too. For example, they show a consistency of population increase rates that suggests that between 1972 and 1982 the figures were updated by simple multiplication rather than actual house-to-house census work.[1] In addition, observers who were in Zinacanteco homes when the CNEP teams passed have reported that the teams are routinely given incorrect information that would lead to undercounting. Nonetheless, the totals in the CNEP censuses are much higher than those given in national censuses.

Table B.2 also includes information on the classification of the places listed in the various national censuses, and on their appearance on the tax and cargo lists discussed below and in Appendix D.

Data from Zinacanteco Tax Lists

The tax system is described in Chapter 6. Tax lists compiled by Zinacantecos for local government and communal activities are the most interesting, and I think the most accurate, source of information on changing population size and distribution. These lists are likely to be distorted in ways that reflect political interests within Zinacantán, just as the national and CNEP censuses are likely to be distorted in ways that reflect priorities and interests of external agencies.

Table B.3 uses data from tax lists to give an overview of the official places that existed during the period 1962 to 1987. Columns A, B, D, and E are from fiesta tax lists and column C is from a public-construction tax list. The actual lists give tax amounts rather than a count of taxpayers, and are used here only to document the official status of places. The lists used for columns F and G included the counts of taxpayers shown in the table. Column F includes data on the number of Agentes Municipales (AM) and Representantes (R) in each of the places at that time. Notes to the table give details on the lists.

1. Calculations using figures in Table A.2 for the 34 places with a 1982 population of more than 100 show that, for 22 places, the ratio of 1982 to 1972 population is 1.57/1 and, for ten of the remaining 12, it is 1.56/1 or 1.58/1.

Table B.4 displays percentages of taxpayers attached to each place for each of the 13 lists included in Table B.3.

Given that my main purpose is to estimate population size and distribution relevant to cargo service, it would be best if hamlet tax shares were based on a strict and complete count of adult males. The actual lists are less than ideal for two reasons related to their role in the Zinacanteco political system. First, while the lists show tax shares calculated on the basis of the number of taxpayers in each hamlet, not all adult men were taxpayers. At all times some men were free from tax obligations, and thus not counted when the hamlet share was calculated (Chapter 6). Second, the numbers reported to authorities in the ceremonial center (Hteklum) were sometimes deliberately distorted by hamlet officials for political reasons. For example, I believe that part of the growth of Navenchauc relative to Nachig and Paste shown in the table can be explained in this way.

Despite these problems, I believe the figures in Table B.4 are the most accurate of those displayed in this appendix. Because they originate with Zinacanteco officials, they are also the most appropriate for comparison with the cargo lists that also originate with Zinacanteco officials.

TABLE B.I

Place Names

Common rendering[a]	Tzotzil (location)[d]	As in censuses[j]
	ʔAhteʔtik	1. Actetic
Elanvo	ʔElan Voʔ	2. Ambo El
Apaz	ʔApas	3. Apaz El
Vochojvo[b]	Vo'ch'oh Voʔ	4. Bocholbo
	K'ak'et Teʔ	5. Caquete
Zequentic	Sek'emtik	6. Cequentic
	k'on lum (550)	7. Comlum
Chainatic	Chaynatik	8. Chainatic
Chajtoj	chak toh (891)	9. Chajtoj
Chiquinibalvo	Chikinibal Voʔ	10. Chiquinivalho
Jocchenom	Hok' Ch'enom	11. La Granadilla[k]
	[e]	12. Icalum
Joigel	Hoyihel	13. Joigel
Joigelito	bik'it hoyihel (642)	14. Joigelito
Masan[c]	Masan	15. Mazan
Nachig	Na Chih	16. Nachij
Navenchauc	Navenchauc	17. Navenchauc
Paste	Pasteʔ	18. Paste
Patosil	Pat ʔOsil	19. Patosil
Petztoj	pets toh (488)	20. Pestoj
Piedra Parada	va'al ton (663)	21. Piedra Parada
Potovtic	Potovtik	22. Potojtic
	[f]	23. El Prospero
Pig	P'ih	24. Refugio Pig El
Salinas	Ats'am (Salinas)	25. Salinas Las[l]
	san-antonyo (970)	26. San Antonio
San Nicolás	san-mikulash (23)	27. San Nicolás
	[f]	28. Santa Rita Ajil
	[f]	29. Santa Teresa
Shucun	shʔukun (935)	30. Shacum[m]
Shulvo	shul voʔ (347)	31. Shulbo
Tierra Blanca	sak-lum (847)	32. Tierra Blanca[l]
	tsoh lum (874)	33. Tierra Colorada
	ts'ub (483)	34. Tzum El
Yalentay	Yaleb Taiv	35. Yalentay
	ya'al shulem (496)	36. Yashulen
	Ya'al Ts'iʔ	37. Yaltzi
Hteklum	Hteklum	38. Zinacantán (Pueblo)
	san-sigro (976)	San Isidro
	[f]	San José Bocemtenelte
	[f]	Escuela Vocacional
Avanchen	ʔavan ch'en (221)	
Bomchen	vom ch'en (353)	
Jechtoch	hech toch' (202)	
Jechchentic	[g]	
Jocotal	[g]	
Ivestic[c]	ʔibestik (986)	
La Selva	[g]	
Muctajoc[c]	muk'ta hok'[h]	
Propriedad SPM[c]	[i]	
Santa Rosa	[g]	
Tojtiquilbo[c]	tohtikil voʔ (447)	
Tsahalnab	ts'ahal nab (135)	

NOTES TO TABLE B.1

*a*These spellings of place names were commonly used. Many are from the 1983 Fiesta of Rosario tax list (see Figure 6.1 and Table B.3, note *a*). Others appear elsewhere on tax or cargo lists. I have tried to pick a common rendering that will not be confusing to readers and other researchers. Minor variations in written form were frequent, especially in the use of "b" and "v" or "s" and "z" as alternatives. Three of the variations shown in the table could lead to misidentification: (1) the various spellings of Zequentic, (2) the two commonly used alternative names for Jocchenom, and (3) the three commonly used alternative names for the political/ceremonial center (*cabecera*): "Pueblo," "Hteklum," "Zinacantán." Tzotzil names are pronounced with primary stress on the last syllable.

*b*By the 1980's, Vochojvo was divided into two hamlets: Vochojvo Alto and Vochojvo Bajo. See Table B.3.

*c*These five names appear only on cargo lists.

*d*Capitalized names with no number following them are as they are found on map 5 of Vogt (1969: 156). (Of the place names on Vogt's map, only Pahal Chiste is not found on tax, cargo, or census lists.) Most of the place names not found on Vogt's map are found in the atlas in Laughlin (1975). In column B these are followed by the number Laughlin assigned to them on his maps. Their locations are as follows:

550—place in Navenchauc; 891—NE of Elanvo; 642—N of Joigel; 488—W of Salinas; 663— near Zequentic; 970—S of Paste; 23—in E part of Vochojvo; 935—S of Elanvo; 347—between Nachig and Paste (see Vogt 1969: 172–76); 847—NW of Salinas; 483—W of Salinas; 496—SW of Salinas; 976—a place S of Apaz; 202—E of Nachig; 447—part of Pig; 353—near Paste, toward Pahal Chiste (see Vogt 1969: 172–76); 221—NE of Paste on the road to Elanvo; 986—S of Apaz, near Ivestic; 135—part of Vochojvo Alto.

*e*I could not identify Icalum. A place by that name near Navenchauc's microwave tower had no people. None of the several places with similar names (ʔikʼal lumtik) listed by Laughlin could be identified as the censused population.

*f*El Prospero was a place in the Salinas area (Edel 1962); Santa Rita Ajil and Tierra Colorada were both near Salinas (Vogt 1969: 28). Santa Teresa was near the Church of San Sebastián in Hteklum (Vogt 1969: 376). San José Bocemtenelte was east of Nachig, and may have become officially part of the municipio of San Cristóbal de las Casas. I cannot tell whether Escuela Vocacional referred to the boarding school at Santa Teresa or the one at San José Bocemtenelte.

*g*Jechchentic, Jocotal, La Selva, and Santa Rosa were established after Vogt and Laughlin did their work. Jechchentic was the western part of Nachig. Jocotal (El Ocotal), an ejido colony, was in the extreme western part of Zinacantán, near Muctajoc. La Selva was part of the Ladino-owned land near San Nicolás, see Vogt (1969: 28). Santa Rosa was an ejido colony in the lowlands.

*h*Muctajoc was a settlement of Zinacantecos who lived in the municipio of Ixtapa at the extreme western border of Zinacantán (Price and Price 1970).

*i*Propriedad San Pedro Mártir was in Vochojvo Bajo.

*j*The numbers shown are those used in the censuses done by the government's malaria eradication program (CNEP). The censuses (Relaciones de Localidades Existentes) for 1972 to 1977, 1980, and 1982 were available at the CIES library in San Cristóbal de las Casas. (I am grateful to María Elena Fernández Galán M. for her help with these and other documents.) The spellings for those numbered 1 to 38 are those used in the 1980 (mostly) and 1974 (when 1980 included an obvious typo) CNEP censuses, except for "Pueblo" (38), which is from the national census. San Isidro, San José Bocemtenelte, and Escuela Vocacional appear only in the national censuses.

*k*La Granadilla was an alternative name for Jocchenom.

*l*Salinas and Tierra Blanca were sometimes listed as "Salinas-Tierra Blanca" in national censuses.

*m*Shucun was sometimes written "Guadalupe Shucum."

TABLE B.2

Population of Places in Zinacantán, 1940–1982

Codes for public listings [a]	Place [b]	National censuses [c]				CNEP censuses [d]			
		1940	1950	1960	1970	1972	1975	1980	1982
– – I – –	Actetic					146	170	218	229
TC P C C C	Elanvo	182	371	400	402	592	688	885	931
TC P C C C	Apaz	375	480	704	722	721	837	1,076	1,132
TC – – P I	Vochojvo			914	316	659	766	985	1,036
– I – – –	Caquete					125	144	185	195
TC P C C C	Zequentic	661	872	672	977	724	842	1,084	1,140
– I – – –	Comlum					72	84	107	113
TC – – P I	Chainatic			121	274	137	160	206	217
T – I – –	Chajtoh					22	25	31	32
TC P P P I	Chiquinibalvo	215	66	*	258	244	284	365	385
TC P C C E	Jocchenom	217	404	300	331	245	285	367	386
– I – – –	Icalum					97	112	144	152
TC – – – I	Joigel					178	206	265	279
TC – – – I	Joigelito				194	113	131	168	177
– C – – –	Masan					72	84	107	113
TC P C C C	Nachig	269	415	915	974	1,414	1,642	2,111	2,221
TC P C C C	Navenchauc	819	1,145	1,227	1,706	688	831	1,067	1,122
TC P C C C	Paste	273	607	1,225	1,500	1,332	1,548	1,990	2,093
TC P C C C	Patosil	285	272	347	593	731	849	1,091	1,148
TC – – – –	Petztoj					169	197	253	266
T – – – I	Piedra Parada					88	103	132	139
TC – – – I	Potovtic				280	140	162	208	219
– I R R R	Prospero El	12	13	*		8	8	8	8
TC R E E –	Pig	37	54	*		154	179	230	242
TC P C C C	Salinas	239	344	433 [e]	568 [e]	453	527	678	713
T – R – –	San Antonio	36				92	107	137	144
T – R R R	San Nicolás	60	108	*	149	195	226	291	306
– I R – –	Santa Rita Ajil	20		*		338	371	476	501

Codes for public listings[a]	Place[b]	National censuses[c]				CNEP censuses[d]			
		1940	1950	1960	1970	1972	1975	1980	1982
- - R R -	Santa Teresa		11	*		51	60	72	76
T- R R R -	Shacun	31	42	*		121	140	180	189
TC - - I -	Shulvo				288	234	269	346	364
T- - - e e	Tierra Blanca			e	e	169	197	253	266
- - R R -	Tierra Colorada	3	5	*		115	134	172	181
- - I -	Tzum El					64	74	94	99
TC F E E E	Yalentay	23	87	*	287	229	266	341	359
- - I -	Yashulen					101	117	150	158
- - I -	Yaltzi					113	131	168	177
TC X X X X	Zinacantán	664	1,000	392	1,609	1,443	1,677	2,157	2,269
- R - E -	San Isidro	15		*					
- - R R -	San José								
	Bocemtenelte		16						
- - G - - -	Escuela Vocacional	73							
	TOTAL	4,509	6,312	7,650	11,428	12,589	14,633	18,798	19,777

[a] Columns to the left of the Place column contain information on where the place name has been used (the first two columns) and on the official classification of the place (the four columns to the right). In column 1, T means this place appears on the tax lists at least once. (Piedra Parada and Tierra Blanca appear only on the 1987 tax list.) In column 2, C means this place appears on the cargo lists at least once. Columns 3, 4, 5, and 6 indicate the listing of the places in the 1940, 1950, 1960, and 1970 censuses, respectively. The letter codes indicate the following categories used in the censuses: C = Congregación; E = Ejido; F = Finca; G = Granja; I = Insuf. Especif. (not specified); P = Paraje; R = Rancho; and X = Pueblo.

[b] Place names are ordered as in CNEP censuses (see Table B.1, column 3). Names are spelled as in Table B.1, column 1.

[c] Place names are listed without any population count in the published 1960 census. The census notes that San José Bocomtenelte is registered without inhabitants. The other nine places marked * in the 1960 column are "censused with others"; i.e., they are small populations whose numbers are lumped with other places listed in the census. (Vogt 1969: 162 suggests how some of them are lumped.)

[d] I have CNEP census counts for 1973, 1974, 1976, and 1977 also.

[e] In the national censuses for 1960 and 1970, "Salinas-Tierra Blanca" is listed as a single Congregación.

TABLE B.3

Hamlet Status on Official Lists, 1962–1987 [a]

Hamlet [b]	1960's			1973	1983			1987
	A	B	C	D	E	F	F'	G
Hteklum	T	T	X	T	X	X 2R	136	151
Vochojvo	T	T	X	T	−	− −	−	−
Vochojvo Bajo	−	−	−	−	XT	X 3R	183	182
Vochojvo Alto	−	−	−	−	XT	X 2R	127	135 [f]
San Nicolás	−	−	X	T	X	X 1R	36	34
La Selva	−	−	−	−	XT	X 1R	15	16
Patosil	X	X	X	X	X	X 2R	136	132
Salinas	X	X	X	X	e	X 1R	25	20
Petztoj	−	−	−	−	e	X 2R	59	53
Tierra Blanca	−	−	−	−	−	− −	−	20
Nachig	X	X	X	X	X	X 1AM	210	223
Jechtoch	−	−	−	XT	−	X 1R	27	25
Jechchentic	−	−	−	−	XT	X 1R	29	21
Chajtoj	−	−	−	T	X	X 1AM	18	20
Elanvo	X	X	X	X	X	X 1R + 1AM	62	57 [g]
Abanchen	−	−	−	−	XT	− −	−	5
Paste	X	X	X	X	X	X 1AM	219	257
Bomchen	−	−	−	−	XT	X 1R	40	23
Shulvo	−	−	−	XT	X	X 1R	67	45
Yalentay	X	X	X	X	X	X 1R	30	31
Pig	−	X	X	X	X	X 2R	32	30
Navenchauc	X	X	X	X	X	X 2AM	434	397
Apaz	X	X	X	X	X	X 2AM	190	175
Chainatic	X	X	X	X	X	X 1AM	54	20
Joigel	X	X	X	X	X	X 1R	15	15
Zequentic	X	X	X	X	X	X 1AM	165	165 [h]
Joigelito	−	−	−	XT	X	X 1AM	32	27
Jocchenom	X	X	X	X	X	X 1AM	120	116 [i]
Potovtic	−	X	X	X	X	X 1AM	40	35
Jocotal	−	−	−	−	XT	X 1R	26	25
Shucun	T	X	X	X	X	c	8	13
San Antonio	T	d	d	X	X	c	5	−
Santa Rosa	−	−	−	−	−	−	−	40
TOTAL							2,540	2,508

NOTES TO TABLE B.3

NOTE: X, present; −, absent; T, see discussion in Chapters 6 and 7; R, AM, see below, note *a*, column F.

*a*I collected 11 tax lists and two lists of the number of taxpayers (household heads) in each hamlet. Those that showed exactly the same place names are lumped here, yielding the seven categories that are the basis for columns A to G in the table. The sources for the columns were (1) Mariano Anselmo Pérez, who was a Treasurer for many Fiesta Committees during the 1960's (for A to C); (2) Antonio Conde Vázquez, who was Treasurer for many Fiesta Committees and the Church Reconstruction Committee that operated during the 1970's (for D); (3) Pedro Vázquez Sánchez, who was Presidente from 1983 to 1985 (for E, F, and F'); and (4) Antonio de la Torre López, who was the Junior Scribe in 1987 (for G).

Some detail on the fiesta calendar is found in Cancian (1965: 216–22).

Details on the 11 tax lists providing the basis for columns A through E are as follows. For the period 1962 to 1966, I have band tax lists for the following fiestas (the lists were dated): column A1—Cuarto Viernes, 1962 (March 25, 1962); A2—Cuarto Viernes, 1964 (February 23, 1964); A3—San Sebastián, 1965 (December 6, 1964); B1—Cuarto Viernes, 1965 (May 23, 1965); B2—Sagrado Corazón de Jesús, 1965 (May 23, 1965); B3—San Lorenzo, 1965 (June 27, 1965); and B4—Cuarto Viernes, 1966 (February 1, 1966).

For 1965 I have two construction tax lists: C1—whitewashing the church (August 25, 1965) and C2—building a bridge (December 1, 1965).

For 1973 I have a single band tax list: D—San Sebastián (estimated December 1972).

For 1983 I have a single band tax list: E—Virgen de Rosario (September 21, 1983). See also note *e* below.

Columns F and F': I was able to make notes on a typed list of officials (column F: R = Representante; AM = Agente Municipal) from each hamlet that included numbers of household heads added to the list by hand (apparently by some official). Column F' provides the numbers. Because of the complications of Zinacantán's political groupings in 1983, some hamlets had divided populations, and there were different sorts of official arrangements. Places with more than one official probably had more than one party. Navenchauc, for example, had two Agentes Municipales, and its household heads were listed as 220 + 214.

Column G: This list was used by the Elders for the collection they take to pay for Mass and skyrockets at major fiestas. It may be the most accurate, for the Elders are less involved in politics than the Presidente.

*b*The order of places Zinacantecos used is followed in this list. It reflects geographical location, status/size, and history. The list starts with Hteklum and Vochojvo, and continues through Patosil, Nachig, Paste, Navenchauc, and the distant western hamlets. Shucun and San Antonio, being of a different status, were usually at the end, though their location would put them in the middle of the list. New places, like Abanchen and Bomchen in 1983, were often at the end.

*c*Shucun and San Antonio were not on the typed list of representatives (column F). They were added by hand with the numbers.

*d*San Antonio was missing from one of the four band tax lists used for column B (that for Fiesta of Cuarto Viernes 1966, dated February 1, 1966), and the bridge tax list (dated December 1, 1965), suggesting that it may have had a temporary change of status.

*e*Salinas and Petztoj were not on list E, probably because the fiesta is held there. I also have a list for the Fiesta of Cuarto Viernes. Probably written in early 1983, it is undated and very sloppy, and includes three or four generations of annotations and additions. These problems make it unsuitable to use in comparison with the well-ordered lists that are the basis for this table. It is useful as a supplement to list E because it includes the hamlets of Salinas and Petztoj, confirming the hypothesis that they are not listed on E because of their special status for that fiesta.

*f*Including 12 from Tsahalnab.

*g*Including 18 from Elanvo Alto and 39 from Elanvo Bajo.

*h*Including 10 from Piedra Parada.

*i*Including 36 from Chiquinibalvo.

TABLE B.4: *Hamlet Tax Shares, 1962–1987* (Percent of total taxpayers)

Hamlet	A1[a] 1962	A2 1964	A3 1965	B1 1965	B2 1965	B3 1965	B4 1966
Hteklum							
Vochojvo							
Vochojvo Bajo							
Vochojvo Alto							
San Nicolás							
La Selva							
Patosil	8.6%	9.7%	8.9%	9.1%	8.9%	9.1%	8.9%
Salinas	6.5	6.0	6.7	7.1	7.0	6.4	6.9
Petztoj							
Tierra Blanca							
Nachig	13.7	14.7	13.6	12.7	12.4	12.4	12.4
Jechtoch							
Jechchentic							
Chajtoj							
Elanvo	8.6	8.0	8.9	8.7	8.5	9.1	8.5
Abanchen							
Paste	13.7	14.8	13.6	14.2	13.9	13.5	14.0
Bomchen							
Shulvo							
Yalentay	1.3	0.6	1.3	0.5	1.2	1.3	1.3
Pig				1.3	2.8	1.3	2.8
Navenchauc	13.7	14.8	13.6	13.8	13.5	13.3	13.6
Apaz	8.6	8.0	8.9	8.7	8.5	9.1	8.5
Chainatic	0.3	1.5	1.2	0.7	0.7	1.2	0.7
Joigel	2.5	1.5	1.2	0.5	0.7	1.2	0.7
Zequentic	10.8	9.0	11.1	11.4	11.1	11.1	11.2
Joigelito							
Jocchenom	9.9	10.3	10.2	5.1	5.0	5.2	5.0
Potovtic				5.1	5.0	5.2	5.0
Jocotal							
Shucun	0.9	0.5	0.4	0.7	0.5	0.4	0.5
San Antonio	0.7	0.4	0.3	0.5	0.5		0.3
Santa Rosa							
TOTAL	99.8%	99.8%	99.9%	100.1%	100.2%	100.1%	100.0%
Pesos							
(rounded)	$1,150	$1,194	$2,137	$1,179	$1,207	$1,942	$1,254

[a] The lists are identified in Table B.3, NOTES.
[b] Table B.3 gives the numbers of men on which these columns are based.

Hamlet	C1 [a] 1965	C2 1965	D 1973	E 1983	F' 1983	G 1987
Hteklum	7.3%	7.2%		4.5%	5.4%	6.0%
Vochojvo	11.0	11.0				
Vochojvo Bajo				7.1	7.2	7.3
Vochojvo Alto				4.5	5.0	5.4
San Nicolás	0.3	0.7		1.2	1.4	1.4
La Selva				0.5	0.6	0.6
Patosil	7.3	7.2	8.5	5.3	5.4	5.3
Salinas	5.3	5.3	8.5	0.0	1.0	0.8
Petztoj				0.0	2.3	2.1
Tierra Blanca						0.8
Nachig	10.1	10.0	12.7	9.9	8.3	8.9
Jechtoch				1.2	1.1	1.0
Jechchentic				1.1	1.1	0.8
Chajtoj				1.0	0.7	0.8
Elanvo	7.3	7.2	6.5	3.3	2.4	2.3
Abanchen				0.2	0.0	0.2
Paste	11.0	11.0	10.5	11.1	8.6	10.2
Bomchen				1.5	1.6	0.9
Shulvo			3.5	2.5	2.6	1.8
Yalentay	1.1	1.2	2.5	1.1	1.2	1.2
Pig	1.2	1.2	2.5	1.0	1.3	1.2
Navenchauc	10.8	10.8	14.0	17.0	17.1	15.8
Apaz	7.3	7.2	8.5	7.6	7.5	7.0
Chainatic	1.1	1.1	0.4	2.0	2.1	0.8
Joigel	1.1	1.1	0.8	0.6	0.6	0.6
Zequentic	8.9	8.8	11.0	5.9	6.5	6.6
Joigelito				1.1	1.3	1.1
Jocchenom	4.2	4.4	4.9	4.5	4.7	4.6
Potovtic	4.2	4.2	4.4	2.3	1.6	1.4
Jocotal				1.0	1.0	1.0
Shucun	0.3	0.4	0.4	0.6	0.3	0.5
San Antonio	0.3		0.4	0.2		0.2
Santa Rosa						0.6
TOTAL	100.1%	100.0%	100.0%	99.8%	100.1%	99.0%
Pesos (rounded)	$2,678	$2,774	$2,360	$ 58,678	[b]	[b]

C / THE NACHIG CENSUS, 1967, 1983, AND 1987

The Nachig Census was done as part of a study of men and men's activities. It includes two kinds of information: (1) basic genealogical information for all married men and women in the hamlet; and (2) the results of a survey of the adult men in 1967, extensive interviewing about each of the adult men as of 1983, and additional details on adult men as of 1987. What follows describes the data gathered, and then discusses some issues involved in delimiting the population of men appropriate for analysis.

The Genealogical, Survey, and Interview Data

The genealogical work was first done in 1966–67 as background for the survey of Zinacanteco corn farmers that is analyzed in *Change and Uncertainty in a Peasant Economy* (Cancian 1972). At that time Yermo and his brother José Hernández Nuh were the main sources of information. They asked others in Nachig for details they did not know themselves, and we were once joined in a formal interview situation by Pedro Pérez con Dios, an old man who was at the time the political leader of Nachig. He helped trace relationships among older people and deceased generations.

For the purposes of the genealogical work, every adult Nachig resident who was ever married was included, and each couple was treated as a unit. Each person's parents were recorded, and genealogical connections were then traced backwards in time as far as consultants could remember. Unmarried children were not recorded; thus the use of the term "census" is not entirely appropriate.

Using this procedure, the work in 1966–67 yielded 283 units, 258 that included a living married male, 22 where the male had died ("widows"), and three units that were difficult to classify (including one formed by two older women who had never married). Residence was treated separately. It was typically in nuclear households, or in joint parent-child households that included recently married people from the children's generation or widowed people from the parental generation.

A survey of adult men was done in spring 1967. Of the 245 married males identified in genealogical work before the survey, 232 were interviewed about their economic activity (Cancian 1972) and their beliefs (Francesca Cancian 1975). These 232, minus the 24 of them who were less than 25 years old in 1967, are the 208 individuals in the 1967 survey (Cancian 1972: 165–68).

In the summers of 1981, 1982, and 1983, I worked with Yermo again to update the genealogical work we did in 1966–67. By this time Yermo was in his late sixties, and his son Francisco (age 28) was our main helper. Yermo again asked others in the community for details he did not know, and we once worked with his wife and daughters-in-law to get details on recent marriages. Though I worked on genealogical details and added some information on all the men during spring and summer 1984 and again in summer 1987 (see Tables C.1 and C.4, below), the population that is used for most of the analysis here was "frozen" as of summer 1983 (and excluded two adult men—ages 32 and 35—who were discovered by cross-checking procedures used in 1984). By summer 1983 there were 475 units recorded in the census. Of these, 96 were dropped from the 1983 list of married males for whom data were collected, leaving 379. Of the 96 cases dropped, 66 were men who died between 1967 and 1983 (65 of these had been among the 258 noted in 1967), 22 were the widows mentioned above, and eight were special cases (including the difficult-to-classify units mentioned above).

No direct survey of Nachig men parallel to that done in 1967 was done in the 1980's. Rather I gathered data on a variety of variables directly from Yermo, Francisco, and sources they were able to consult. For each of the 379 men, they provided information on economic activity (mostly on occupations), cargo service, wealth ranking, political party affiliation, and a variety of other variables which are listed in Table C.1.

Because these survey-like data collected in interviews with consultants are central to the analysis of social relations in Nachig, I want to say something about their quality. In evaluating them, my main concerns were: Did my main consultants stretch their knowledge too far? Were they systematically biased in some way? For example, to take one of the most difficult variables we covered, how able were they to estimate the landholdings of every household in Nachig? When does observation shade over to impression in these matters? Francisco had recently been involved in the Ejido Committee in the hamlet for three years, and Yermo had been involved in the purchases that groups of Nachig people had made from nearby Ladino ranchers some years before, so their estimates on these parcels of standard size were apt to be based on direct observation. House plots and other communal land, because of their continual transformation through inheritance and sale, are much more difficult to keep track of.[1] In some cases, Yermo and Francisco's estimates were probably based on limited knowledge. My main concern with regard to systematic bias was that their elite status would lead them to be ignorant of details of the young and poor in Nachig.

1. Information on land holdings was not used in this study.

TABLE C.I

Information in the Nachig Census, 1967, 1983, 1987[a]

(For each man)

	1967	1983	1987
Age	X	X	—
Where resides	X	X	—
Where pays taxes	—	X	—
Size and type of land holdings	—	X	—
Relative wealth[b]	X	X	—
Political party and voting record	—	X	X
Amount of corn seeded	S	X	—
Location of lowland fields	S	—	—
Corn-marketing practices	S	—	—
Whether hires workers in cornfields	S	—	—
Works for others in cornfields	S	—	—
Types of non-agricultural work done	—	X	X
Relative income from occupations	—	X	—
Religious cargos passed or requested by the man, his father, and his wife's father	S	X	X
Civil cargos passed	—	X	X
Spanish-speaking ability	—	X	—
Whether a curer, a musician, an alcoholic, or physically disabled	—	X	—
Whether has a television set	—	X	—

NOTE: X, yes, from consultant; S, yes, from survey; —, no.

[a] Some of the categories of information listed—for example, the religious cargos passed—are represented by several variables.

[b] The relative wealth measures were constructed by averaging ranks from pile sorts (three in 1967, three in 1983) done by Yermo (and/or his brother José in 1967) with the help of others in some cases, and then dividing the resulting continua into octiles.

Besides my work reviewing the data and informally testing the reliability of the work of my main consultants, I have three reasons to think the data are generally accurate. First, most of the information recorded is based on knowledge that is public for any resident of Nachig. My doubts about the information I got from consultants stem from the possibility that few people would care enough to attend to so many details about their neighbors, not from the privacy or delicacy of the information.

Second, my consultants were exceptional people. Yermo and Francisco, especially Yermo, were very involved in the affairs of the community. Yermo is a man of rare intelligence and maturity; he is a respected elder of Nachig, a man with countless *compadres* and godchildren, and a man who has served in a number of leadership posts over the years (see Chapter 7). It's hard to imagine a more knowledgeable person of his age. Since Nachig is growing, and many of the important younger people are in Yermo's children's generation, Francisco's participation in much of the recent census work helped greatly with details about younger people. My confidence in the work of my main consultants was increased by the fact that they frequently, when they could not retrieve some answer from their collective memory, deferred their response until they could investigate the details.

Third, during the 1981-to-1984 period I had many formal interviews (see Appendix A) with other Nachig residents, attended a number of fiestas and public meetings in Nachig, and I made countless trips to the hamlet to socialize and to recruit consultants to work in formal interview situations. All these activities gave me many opportunities to confirm the accuracy of the information provided by the main consultants. While I occasionally discovered errors they had made, their reports were confirmed in the overwhelming majority of the many opportunities I had to make independent checks.

In sum, all things considered, I believe the information on the variables listed in Table C.1 is generally very accurate. Yermo and Francisco Pérez were neither greatly overtaxed, nor systematically biased in any important way. Given the problems of doing house-to-house survey work in Zinacantán (or any community where the population is subjugated to the paper-wielding classes), what I collected from principal consultants is certainly more accurate than comparable information based on direct-interview survey techniques would have been.

The Boundaries of Nachig

As a place of residence Nachig can be defined spatially. It was also the place of origin for people who resided elsewhere. And, not so obviously, it was a political entity to which adult males had tax and other obligations.[2] While most men associated with Nachig were born and raised there, resided there, and paid taxes there, those few with mixed status need to be discussed. The details of their situations raise questions about the boundaries of the community that are relevant for this study, and illuminate the strength and nature of ties to one's hamlet of origin. Thus, what follows has two purposes. I want to record some ethnographic detail relevant to hamlet organization, and I want to expose the choices I made in selecting the populations of men analyzed as "Nachig married men."

Men of mixed status came to my attention in the course of collecting the data described in the first section of this appendix. Each data-collection procedure produced a slightly different population. First, in 1966–67, a rough genealogical census was done from the memory of principal consultants who knew the hamlet. More people were discovered in spring 1967, when assistants were asked to recruit any and all married men from Nachig as interview respondents. More were added in the early 1980's, when data on every previously included person were reviewed with principal consultants, newly married sons and male siblings of each man were sought out, unrelated newly arrived and newly married people were added, and lists of Nachig people engaged in local or municipio offices were checked against the

2. Taxes were usually paid out of household funds, and thus affected both men and women, but only men were formally taxed; i.e., unmarried young men paid taxes, but widows and unmarried women did not.

TABLE C.2

Where Men in the Nachig Census Resided and Paid Taxes, 1983

| | Paid taxes | | | |
Resided	Nachig	Other hamlet in Zinacantán	Not in Zinacantán	Total
Nachig	331	9	—	340
Other Hamlet in Zinacantán	9	20	—	29
Not in Zinacantán	—	—	10	10
TOTAL	340	29	10	379

census. Residence was routinely recorded at each step just mentioned, and, during the 1984 interviewing, tax-paying status for 1983 was recorded for each individual in the census.

In Zinacantán, tax obligations do not change automatically with residence (see Chapter 6). They are embedded in a complex of obligations to one's hamlet, and they change somewhat as citizenship might change among Western nations. The adult male pays taxes for both hamlet and municipio purposes through the officials in his hamlet. He is also obligated to attend semiannual hamlet meetings, and to serve in hamlet offices when appointed to them. While some people change the hamlet to which they have these obligations, and some people abandon them altogether, such changes are not taken lightly.

Residence is another matter. While most Zinacantecos seem to stick to their hamlets all their lives, marriage, divorce, land pressure, and social conflicts lead a good number to move. Some go to another hamlet, especially to a wife's hamlet, and a few leave Zinacantán on a permanent basis. Such a change makes them different from the typical Zinacanteco, whose only shifts are likely to be from one house plot to another within his or her hamlet.[3]

Table C.2 shows that the vast majority of adult males in the Nachig census (331 of 379) resided in Nachig and paid taxes there in 1983. The exceptions to this pattern are discussed below. They reveal the principal reasons for movement across hamlet lines and their relation to taxpaying and other civic obligations.[4]

3. This characterization is historically limited. It applies to the present adult generations of Nachig. As Wasserstrom (1983) has pointed out, there have been important migrations of Zinacantecos to some hamlets in the past. Desire for quick access to main roads has brought some people into Nachig recently (Mariano EE), and this trend, as well as others yet to come, may make these generalizations inapplicable some years from now.

4. Although the process of data gathering I used was intended to include all currently living married males of Nachig origin, the census process probably missed some who left Zinacantán permanently when they were young—even if their relatives remained in Nachig.

Of the nine men (Table C.2) who resided in Nachig and paid taxes in another hamlet, eight moved to Nachig from adjoining hamlets, and the ninth was the recently married son of one of these. Eight of the nine were married to Nachig women, while the exception was married to a woman from Paste, his home hamlet. Many of these cases seem to be straightforward uxorilocal residence motivated by the wife's landholdings.

All of the nine men who resided in another hamlet and paid taxes in Nachig were children of Nachig parents (including one Chamula orphan raised by a Nachig couple). Seven had wives from another hamlet. Among the two couples where both partners were of Nachig origin, one left Nachig to join the wife's family (who had previously left—see the "talking saint" case below), and the other went to an adjoining hamlet because of the wife's (reason unknown to me) desire to live there.

Two conclusions follow from these 18 cases. First, men who leave their hamlets of origin for residence in another hamlet in Zinacantán usually move to a hamlet where their wives have connections. Second, tax obligations to their hamlet of origin continue after they leave. Since four of the men who reside in Nachig and pay taxes elsewhere have been in Nachig since the 1967 census (the others are too young to have been included), it is clear that these obligations to hamlet of origin do not fade rapidly.

Ten men of Nachig origin resided outside of Zinacantán and paid no taxes in Nachig. One murdered a *compadre*, apparently while having an affair with his *comadre* (the *compadre*'s wife), and went to jail in San Cristóbal. Another, a Protestant, was banished because of his religion, and was not allowed to visit his land in Nachig. Still another, a mute, left Nachig years ago, before he was married, and was rumored to be in the lowlands where he drove a cart. Two were soldiers in Tuxtla Gutiérrez, the state capital. Each of them had a wife from another hamlet, who, upon being abandoned, returned home. Another, an alcoholic in his late twenties who had many debts in Nachig, had recently abandoned his Nachig-born wife, who moved in with her widowed mother. He too was in Tuxtla, and apparently paid taxes in Nachig on the rare occasions when he was both present and sober. Two very poor men with very little land in Nachig were among the original members of the opposition political party (PAN). They left in the early 1980's, when they tried to suspend their taxpaying and were jailed by Nachig authorities. Two others have lived and worked away from Nachig for years—one as a bus driver in Tuxtla and the other as a school teacher in Mexico City. Both of these last two married Tuxtla women.

The twenty who resided and paid taxes in other hamlets of Zinacantán fall into four types.

1. Four were resident in Nachig in 1967, and were in the 1967 census and survey. All four came from Paste, and three were married to Paste women. By 1983, two had returned to Paste, one had moved on to Zinacantán Center, and the fourth, who was married to an Elanvo woman, had moved to Elanvo. Six others were included in the census as sons or brothers of these

four men. None of the six was married to a Nachig woman, or resided in Nachig, in 1983.

2. Three others who were in the 1967 census (but not in the survey) had also left Nachig. Two left their wives, who were of Nachig origin, and returned to the hamlets from which they came. The third, a native of the nearby Tzotzil-speaking settlement of San Felipe, moved on to Paste, his wife's hamlet of origin.

3. Three of the remaining seven are men of Nachig origin who were in the 1967 census and survey. Two had since moved to their wives' hamlet of origin, and are distinguished from others who made similar moves because they have changed the place where they paid taxes. One sold all the land he had in Nachig, and the other still held land at the very edges of the hamlet. The third of these men left Nachig under pressure, for local authorities were concerned about the "talking saint" he maintained in his house. He moved to a hamlet between Nachig and his wife's hamlet of origin, sold his land in Nachig, and stopped paying taxes in Nachig. In effect, the first two of these men changed their citizenship. The third was forced into exile, and then broke ties with Nachig.

4. The four remaining cases are from the adjoining hamlet of Patosil, and it is not certain that they were ever full Nachig residents. One, the only one who was in the 1967 census and survey, was married to a Nachig woman, and may have been in Nachig living on his wife's land at the time of the survey. He had long since resided in Patosil. Another was his son. The final two were brothers. They lived in Patosil at the border of Nachig, and apparently originated from there, although their deceased parents were Nachig people. The first was married to a Patosil woman, the other (whom I classified among these 20 even though my consultants were not sure where he paid taxes) was married to a Nachig woman and lived on her land in Nachig for a time.

In the statistical analysis of the 1983 male population in the body of this study, I have eliminated those who neither pay taxes nor reside in Nachig (making $N = 349$). I have kept all 18 of the men who either reside or pay taxes in Nachig (though such a practice, if extended to all hamlets, would lead to double counting) because the cases are few in number, and it is hard to decide which of the two groups is more appropriately included.

Economic Independence

Many young couples in Zinacantán live in the house of the husband's parents. The women cook on the same fire, and the couples merge their finances under the control of the father. This is often a short-term arrangement (Juan KK). It may last only as long as it takes the new couple to build a house of their own nearby, usually on land provided by the husband's parents. For others it is a longer-term arrangement—especially for those cases in which the son has agreed to stay with his parents until they die and leave to him their house and other possessions (Vogt 1969: 130). The cases reviewed below illustrate these variations.

TABLE C.3

*Age and Economic Independence of
Married Men, 1983 [a]*

Joint with parents?	Age		Total
	≥25	<25	
No	315	9	324
Yes	10	15	25
TOTAL	325	24	349

[a] I do not have enough confidence in the age estimates supplied by my principal consultants in 1967 and 1983 to speculate about the apparent increase in men over 24 who are living jointly with their parents. Because Francisco Pérez was 28 when we did the work in 1983, most of the estimates around age 25 should be quite accurate, but, of course, there is reason to believe that the marital status and economic independence of the individuals involved might influence the age estimate provided.

In my earlier study based on the 1967 survey and census material, I wanted to work exclusively with men who were economically independent of their fathers. In order to approximate economic independence I dropped men younger than 25, and those 25 or older who remained in joint households with their parents (1972: 166–67). In the 1967 data, 24 of 232 Nachig married men interviewed were younger than 25. None of those 25 or older still worked and lived jointly. (In Apaz, the other hamlet involved in the 1967 study, there were two men 25 or older who maintained joint finances with their fathers.)

Table C.3 shows comparable figures for the 1983 census. A review of the 34 cases involving men who were younger than 25 and/or lived jointly reveals some clear patterns. The majority (15 of 24) of all married men younger than 25 were living jointly. Among the nine who were not living jointly, the father was dead in two cases, and the couple had moved in with the wife's parents in another. In each of the other six cases, the father with whom they were not living was relatively young—younger than 53 (born in 1930 or later). This suggests that the father's household may have included a younger son who was expected to stay at home and care for his parents. Among the 15 who were living jointly, only seven of the fathers were younger than 53; and those seven cases included all three married men younger than 20, and one young man who moved back home after his wife died. I conclude that the young men living with relatively old fathers are probably youngest sons—those who typically fill the stay-at-home role for the family.

A look at those 25 and older who were living jointly when the census was done in 1983 (summer) shows that the stay-at-home role is not a permanent status. There were ten such men (Table C.3). Two had moved out by the time the 1984 census work was done, 12 months later. The fathers of two others died in early 1984. Another of those classified as living jointly was

TABLE C.4

Census and Study Populations: 1967, 1983, 1987

	1967	1983	1987[a]
Total married men in the census	258	349	329
Men 25 years old or older	229	325	313
Men economically independent and with complete data	208	315	305

[a]The 1987 population included 24 men not in the 1983 ($N = 315$) population. Sixteen of the 24 were present in $N = 349$ but too young to be included in $N = 315$. Many of those present in $N = 315$ and not present in $N = 305$ died between 1983 and 1987.

living with his parents because his wife had died; and another was in an unusual arrangement, for he had a younger brother who was married and lived independently in 1983.

In handling these data I followed the same rules I used in 1967. Men who lived jointly with their parents, and men younger than 25 were dropped from the analysis where economic independence was relevant. Dropping these 34 cases made $N = 315$. Since these 315 cases were selected by the same criteria used to get the 208 cases that form the core of the 1967 survey and census, I took these two populations to be comparable for many purposes in my analysis of Nachig. Table C.4 summarizes the different populations referred to in the text here and in tables in the body of this study.

D /   CARGO WAITING LISTS, 1952 – 1987

The cargo waiting lists are described in Chapter 9. This appendix records some of the basic data from the ten lists I was able to copy (see Chapter 9). Table D.1 gives the names of the 41 cargos served in the Center and administered by the Elders, and the 16 cargos served in the hamlets during the early 1980's.

Table D.2 displays the 2,873 entries from the ten lists by cargo requested,[1] and Table D.3 presents the same requests by hamlet of residence of the requester. Tables D.4, D.5, and D.6 show requests for the 20 first-level cargos (Mayor is not requested), the 12 Alféreces served at the second level, and the nine cargos served at higher levels (see Table D.1), classified by the hamlet clusters used in the analysis in Chapter 9.[2]

These records are from lists copied after they were used by the Elders, and include both the men who entered and the men who requested cargos during the year of use.[3] The figures in Table 9.1 reconstitute the "fresh" lists by dropping the men who entered during the year of use.

1. The lists include three other entries, one in 1961, one in 1966, and one in 1971. They all represent one man from Muctajoc, a hamlet of Zinacantecos in the municipio of Ixtapa, who was waiting to enter as A5S in 1973.

2. The 77 cases for which the hamlet is not known (Table D.3) are dropped from these tables. Most lists have very few cases where the hamlet of residence is illegible. The high number for 1980 is the result of my error in photographing the lists. I know the cargos requested in 1980 from a tabulation made before making the photographs.

3. The Elders actually receive the fresh copy of the lists they will use on June 24 (the Fiesta of San Juan) during the year before they enter. For the remainder of that calendar year, the incoming Elders use the fresh lists to record new requests and to plan for the administration of the system beginning on January 1, when they enter. At the same time the incumbent Elders use the old lists to administer the system.

TABLE D.I

A Complete List of Cargos Served, 1952–1987

Cargos Administered by the Elders

FIRST LEVEL[a]

Mayordomos		Others	
A8S-A8J	San Sebastián	A7S-A7J	Mesonero
A9S-A9J	San Antonio	A1S-A1J	Mayordomo Rey
A2S-A2J	Virgen de Rosario	A4S-A4J	Pasionero
A6S-A6J	Santa Cruz	A10S-A10J	Capitán
A5S-A5J	Santo Domingo	A11	Mayor
A3S-A3J	Sacramento		

SECOND LEVEL[b]

Senior Alféreces		Junior Alféreces	
B8	San Sebastián	B11	San Sebastián
B6	Virgen de Natividad	B10	Santa Rosa
B5	Virgen del Rosario	B9	San Jacinto
B4	San José	B12	San Pedro Mártir
B2	Santísima Trinidad	B3	San Antonio
ADC	Divina Cruz	B7	Virgen de Soledad
ASD	Santo Domingo	B1	San Lorenzo

THIRD LEVEL

		OTHER	
C4	Regidor Cuarto	D2	Alcalde Viejo Segundo
C3	Regidor Tercero	D1	Alcalde Viejo Primero
C2	Regidor Segundo	ASH	Alcalde Juez (Shuves)
C1	Regidor Primero		

Cargos Served in the Hamlets

In Apaz		In Navenchauc	
MReyAS-		MGNS-	
MReyAJ	Mayordomo Rey	MGNJ	Mayordomo Guadalupe
		MSCS-	
MAS-MAJ	Mesonero	MSCJ	Mayordomo Santa Cruz
In Elanvo		**In Paste**	
MSSS-MSSJ	San Sebastián	MRPS-MRPJ	Mayordomo Rosario
In Nachig		**In Salinas**	
MFNS-MFNJ	Mayordomo Fátima	MRSal	Mayordomo Rosario
		MYSal	Mayor de Salinas

SOURCE: After Cancian (1965: 30, table 2) for cargos administered by the elders.

[a]On the first level, all cargos are served in pairs—one senior (S) and one junior (J)—except Mayor, which is different from the other cargos in many ways (for details, see Chapter 6). This table orders the cargos by the order in which they walk during rituals (Cancian 1965: 33).

[b]ADC and ASD are usually served on higher levels (see Chapter 10).

TABLE D.2
Entries on Ten Cargo Waiting Lists, *1952–1987*
(By cargo)

Cargo					Year list used						Total
	1952	1958	1961	1966	1971	1975	1978	1980	1983	1987	
A1S	8	16	20	23	20	18	16	16	16	15	168
A2S		13	17	19	18	16	15	13	11	10	132
A3S	10	16	17	19	15	14	12	10	10	8	131
A4S	8	10	10	12	14	10	8	8	9	9	98
A5S	8	12	15	13	11	14	12	11	8	6	110
A6S	4	6	8	10	8	7	8	8	5	6	70
A7S	1	9	14	14	14	13	13	14	12	8	112
A8S		6	7	14	13	13	10	10	10	6	89
A9S	1	7	13	15	14	13	10	6	6	3	88
A10S	2	3	4	7	11	11	10	9	6	5	68
A1J	3	15	18	21	20	17	15	13	14	11	147
A2J		3	11	16	16	14	11	8	7	5	91
A3J	10	13	9	13	13	11	8	7	4	2	90
A4J	7	8	8	9	10	7	6	5	6	6	72
A5J	4	6	3	5	4	3	4	3	3	1	36
A6J			7	8	6	4	3	1	2	2	33
A7J	1	7	8	10	10	11	12	10	9	6	84
A8J		1	3	4	5	2	4	3	1	1	24
A9J			1	5	4	6	4	3	3	1	27
A10J	2	1	1	3	10	11	8	6	5	3	50

Entries on Ten Cargo Waiting Lists, 1952–1987

(By cargo)

Cargo	Year list used										Total
	1952	1958	1961	1966	1971	1975	1978	1980	1983	1987	
B1	10	16	15	14	15	13	13	10	14	15	135
B2	11	13	15	13	12	10	9	10	12	12	117
B3	7	11	11	10	11	8	9	10	8	9	94
B4	8	10	10	9	10	10	9	8	9	6	89
B5	4	8	11	12	8	6	3	1	6	5	64
B6	2	4	9	5	4	2	4	3	2	7	42
B7	2	6	5	4	4	4	3	5	3	5	41
B8		5	10	13	8	8	7	8	8	7	74
B9			1	1		1	1	1	1	2	8
B10								1		1	6
B11		2	2	2		1	1	2	2	4	15
B12		1	4	8	7	5	4	1	4	3	39
ADC	8	13	15	17	14	17	17	17	16	15	149
ASD	2	7	10	9	7	3	3		3	6	50
C1	7	8	7	8	11	9	8	6	5	4	73
C2	7	7	7	4	8	6	6	3	3	2	53
C3		4	2	3	1	1			1	1	13
C4		1				1			2	1	5
D1		5	7	8	7	5	4	5	3	6	50
D2			1	2	2	1			2	4	12
ASH				2	3	3	3	2	6	5	24
TOTAL	137	273	336	384	368	330	294	259	258	234	2,873

TABLE D.3

Entries on Ten Cargo Waiting Lists, 1952–1987[a]

(By hamlet)

Hamlet	Year list used										Total
	1952	1958	1961	1966	1971	1975	1978	1980	1983	1987	
Hteklum	14	18	15	13	8	9	9	10	16	21	133
Vochojvo	5	13	21	27	23	19	19	8	9	4	148
Vochojvo Alto									10	9	19
Vochojvo Bajo									8	11	19
Patosil	7	10	13	18	21	17	15	12	12	12	137
Salinas	6	5	3	3	4	4	4	2	1	2	34
Petztoj								1	2	3	6
Tierra Blanca										1	1
Nachig	21	37	36	59	51	48	49	32	55	51	439
Jechtoch							1	2	5	4	12
Jechchentic							7	10	7	7	31
Paste	22	42	48	65	93	85	56	36	25	19	491
Bomchen							2	4	5	2	13
Shulvo		1	2	4	4	14	11	8	6	5	55
Elanvo	3	2	3	5	9	6	2	2	1		33
Avanchen							1	1	3	1	6

TABLE D.3 (continued)

Entries on Ten Cargo Waiting Lists, 1952–1987[a]

(By hamlet)

Hamlet	Year list used										Total
	1952	1958	1961	1966	1971	1975	1978	1980	1983	1987	
Yalentay	1	1	1	2	4	3	3	3	3	3	24
Pig	2	2	7	4	4	5	4	2	2	1	33
Navenchauc	21	42	61	71	58	53	48	38	53	57	502
Apaz	10	29	40	25	29	24	23	13	17	14	224
Zequentic	13	37	43	53	33	30	28	13	12	5	267
Jocchenom	8	17	25	19	10	4	4	1			88
Joigel		6	9	7	5	1			1	1	30
Chainatic	3	5	5	7	5	3	1	1	3	1	34
Potovtic				2	2	1					5
Joigelito					2	3	3	1			9
Chiquinibalvo		1				1	1				3
Not known	1	5	4		3		3	59	2		77
TOTAL	137	273	336	384	368	330	294	259	258	234	2,873

[a]Because there are sometimes gaps between years for which requests are recorded, the most distant entry may be farther away than the number of entries suggests (see Cancian 1965: 178). For the 10 years in the table, the dates of the last requests for the most popular cargos are as follows: 1962, 1974, 1981, 1988, 1991, 1992, 1995, 1996, 1999, and 2002.

The entries are not independent of each other. A request for a cargo far in the future appears on the lists each year until the cargo is served. For example, the three requests from Masan noted in the next paragraph (1966, 1971, 1975) represent only one man, who requested Alférez Trinidad for 1976. His name was on the 1966 lists when the Elders received a fresh copy from the Scribes in June 1965, and presumably stayed there through 1976 when he entered his cargo.

Vochojvo includes one request in 1983 and four in 1987; all five recorded as the hamlet of Tsahalnab, and Vochojvo Bajo one in 1983 recorded as Propriedad San Pedro Mártir; Pig includes one in 1961 as Tojtiquilbo; Navenchauc includes one in 1952 as Ivestic; and Potovtic includes one in 1966, one in 1971, and one in 1975 as Masan.

TABLE D.4
Requests for First-Level Cargos, 1952–1987
(By hamlet clusters)

Hamlet Cluster[a]	Year list used										Total
	1952	1958	1961	1966	1971	1975	1978	1980	1983	1987	
Center	13	30	32	40	35	29	25	18	31	31	284
Nachig	11	17	20	37	35	29	40	33	43	31	296
Paste	14	23	26	44	62	62	45	27	19	10	332
Navenchauc	9	17	27	43	29	32	25	18	28	26	254
Apaz	5	17	27	11	15	14	11	6	5	5	116
Cornfields	12	44	55	60	43	30	30	13	12	6	304
Other	4	3	5	5	15	19	12	10	7	5	86
TOTAL	68	151	192	240	234	215	188	125	145	114	1,672

[a] See Chapter 6 for a discussion of hamlet clusters. Here, the clusters are based on Table D.3 and its note: Center includes Hteklum through Patosil; Cornfields includes Zequentic through Chiquinibalvo. Other hamlets not listed are included in the cluster named for the hamlet just above them in Table D.3. Salinas, Shulvo, Elanvo, Yalentay and Pig are included in Other.

TABLE D.5

Requests for Second-Level Cargos, 1952–1987

(By hamlet clusters)

Hamlet cluster[a]	Year list used										Total
	1952	1958	1961	1966	1971	1975	1978	1980	1983	1987	
Center	10	5	10	13	11	10	9	9	15	20	112
Nachig	6	11	9	13	10	12	14	9	15	19	118
Paste	5	12	17	14	15	15	9	11	7	6	111
Navenchauc	8	17	23	15	18	11	9	7	13	20	141
Apaz	3	6	5	10	8	6	8	5	9	6	66
Cornfields	8	18	20	19	7	6	3	2	2	1	86
Other	4	6	7	7	9	9	10	8	9	4	73
TOTAL	44	75	91	91	78	69	62	51	70	76	707

[a] See Table D.4, note *a*, for explanation of hamlet clusters.

TABLE D.6

Requests for Higher-Level Cargos, 1952–1987

(By hamlet clusters)

Hamlet cluster[a]	Year list used										Total
	1952	1958	1961	1966	1971	1975	1978	1980	1983	1987	
Center	3	6	7	5	6	6	9	3	9	6	60
Nachig	4	9	7	9	6	7	3	2	9	12	68
Paste	3	7	5	7	16	8	4	2	4	5	61
Navenchauc	4	8	11	13	11	10	14	13	12	11	107
Apaz	2	6	8	4	6	4	4	2	3	3	42
Cornfields	4	4	8	9	7	7	4	1	2		46
Other	4	2	3	6	1	4	3	1	2	7	33
TOTAL	24	42	49	53	53	46	41	24	41	44	417

[a] See Table D.4, note *a*, for explanation of hamlet clusters.

ADDITIONAL TABLES

TABLE E.I

Cargo Service, Wealth, and Spouse Selection, Nachig, 1967 and 1983

(Mean of husbands' wealth rank octile)[a]

| | First cargo of husband's father | | |
First cargo of wife's father	High A1–6	Middle A7–10	Low All–none
1967 census (N = 103)			
High	5.9	3.0 *	4.7
Middle	5.8 *	5.1 *	5.4 *
Low	5.9	4.5 †	2.9
1983 census (N = 175)			
High	5.7	4.6	4.0
Middle	6.0 *	4.3 *	3.6 *
Low	5.0	4.8 *	3.2
1983 "new" marriages (N = 94)[b]			
High	5.5	5.1 *	3.2
Middle	6.6 *	3.5 †	3.0 †
Low	4.6	5.5 †	2.9 *

[a] Calculation of the eight wealth ranks is described in Table C.1, note *b*. Lowest octile = 1.
[b] The 175 marriages in the 1983 census with complete information, minus the 81 cases that were also in the 1967 census.
* Cell count 5–10.
† Cell count < 5.
Other cells 11–55.

TABLE E.2

Classification of Occupations

Category	Alone	With corn	With other	Total
Corn farmer	75	[a]	16	91
Semiproletarian	54	[a]	[a]	54
Laborer	27	12	2	41
Trader	24	11	1	36
Vehicle owner	12	—	8	20
Government employee	12	—	3	15
Mason	8	3	1	12
Vehicle driver	10	—	—	10
Other	[a]	[a]	[a]	36
TOTAL				315

[a] See note 11.5.

F / THE EIGHT POINTS

1. The Presidente publicly confirms his application to enter PRI and recognizes the good work realized by the group directed by José Hernández Hernández [Sanat], Secretary of the Municipio Committee of PRI for the benefit of Zinacantán.

2. All agreements of the municipio will be made solely in the town hall. No meetings concerning municipio affairs will take place with private persons or groups.

3. The following are recognized and respected as members of the general assembly of the municipio for making agreements:

    I. The Municipio Government
    II. The Agentes of Zinacantán
    III. The Municipio Committee of PRI
    IV. Ejido and Communal Authorities
    V. The Education Committees
    VI. The Municipio Judges

4. There will be monthly meetings so that the Municipio Government can inform the PRI, the Agentes, the Ejido authorities, and the citizens about funds received under revenue sharing, income, and expenditures of the municipio government.

5. Any member of the Municipio Government who fails in his obligation, carries out his functions badly, or puts the municipio in danger will be removed from the town council.

6. No money from revenue sharing will be given to any private person or groups unless authorized by law.

7. Special meetings shall be held when urgent problems need to be discussed and resolved—with the participation of the municipio government, PRI, the Agentes, the Alcaldes Jueces, and the Ejido or Communal authorities.

8. The civil register is the direct responsibility of the General Secretariat of the Chiapas state government.

REFERENCE MATTER

NOTES

Notes to Chapter 1

1.1. I believe this currently popular characterization of the past. As Silverman (1979) has pointed out, Steward and his students, especially Wolf and Mintz, began to employ an alternative vision in the 1950's. See also Geertz (1962).

1.2. Carol Smith (1984), William Roseberry (1988, 1989), and many others take similar positions.

1.3. Cancian (1989) reviews some of them in detail.

1.4. Marxist approaches have been elaborated in a vast literature on Latin American peasants. See Heynig (1982), Hewitt de Alcántara (1984), and Deere (1987) for reviews of these discussions. I am interested in Lenin's simple idea that change leads to groups with conflicting interests—even when their emergence as classes is only partial (Cancian 1989).

1.5. Though they are very different, both of these primordialist schemes are relatives of the rural-urban continuum and various other Gemeinschaft-Gesellschaft conceptualizations of change. Thomas Bender (1978) characterizes the evolutionary, ahistorical nature of modernization theory and its relation to such schemes (and also provides the best discussion of "community" versus "society" that I have found). Lenin's scheme is different from modernization theory because it predicts that differentiation will lead to class conflict rather than functional integration.

1.6. Many anthropologists—I can vouch for one—used the first half of Wolf's paper without adopting the historical perspective suggested in the second half. Wolf, too, reflected the times, for in 1957 he led with his now-famous ideal type, and tacked on the historical argument, while in recent years (see 1986: 325) he has been emphatic about his historical intent. Wolf's message has been consistent (not static) for three decades; the radical shift in style of anthropological work is reflected in the opening paragraphs of two of his great contributions (1957: 1; 1982: 1).

1.7. In 1960, when assessing the chances that Mexico would maintain its economic growth and distribute the benefits so that it would "absorb the Indian population not only economically, but socially and culturally as well" (1960: 6), Wolf was pessimistic because he saw most of the benefits going to the cities and non-Indian areas in the north. The energy extraction that drew attention to remote Indian areas like the state of Chiapas had not yet begun.

1.8. Skinner separated normative, economic, and coercive opening and closure, and suggested that, when opening, communities first relax the coercive aspects, then the economic, and finally the normative; that when closing they do the opposite, first emphasizing local normative standards ("particularized subculture," 1971: 278), then withdrawing from regional trade towards subsistence farming and economic boundaries like those set by ceremonial systems, and finally expelling outsiders and forming local militias.

1.9. When my father plastered houses during the building boom after World War II, anxious owners often asked about how the work would come out. Many times I heard him explain that he worked very carefully and with good materials, but that he guaranteed there would be some cracks in the walls (due to the drying of green lumber and the settling of foundations). Despite the certainty that results would be flawed, people valued his work and kept him very busy. I think the parallels to scientific work are direct. The inevitability of cracks need not prevent construction. Rather, it should influence how the results are used. On these issues, anthropologists who emphasize social rather than cultural analysis may find the "debate" between Erik Olin Wright (1987) and Michael Buraway (1987) more relevant than the many statements by anthropologists.

Notes to Chapter 2

2.1. Corn (maize) was the principal product of most Zinacanteco men. Most of them also interplanted beans and squash whenever the soil was appropriate—that is, they were milpa farmers. Women's work was also transformed after 1960 (see L. K. M. Haviland 1978).

2.2. George Collier (1975) and Robert Wasserstrom (1983) each discuss work patterns and their relation to the regional political economy since the Spanish Conquest. Collier's historical work is a small part of a study of regional ecology and ethnicity, and Wasserstrom's is the major part of a study of class relations in the region. They differ from each other on some important issues, and should be read by those interested in the interpretation of Zinacantán and its environment before the recent period that is the focus of this study.

2.3. Mariano EE's account of his working life is in Chapter 4. He refers to the struggle of mule drivers during his early childhood. When an account included in Chapter 4 is relevant to points being discussed, I will give the man's name in parentheses ( ), as I have done here.

2.4. My *Change and Uncertainty in a Peasant Economy: The Maya Corn Farmers of Zinacantán* (1972) gives an overview of work patterns in the 1960's. It is based on fieldwork done in 1966–67. Surveys of adult males from Nachig and one other hamlet (Apaz) done in spring 1967 covered their farming activity for crops seeded from 1957 to 1966 (1972: appendix A). My study focused on the dramatic changes in economic practices during the decade before 1967, and treated the years before 1957 as a period of "traditional" practices. The works of G. A. Collier (1975) and Wasserstrom (1983) correct this simplistic picture.

2.5. Those who were not corn farmers (e.g., full-time corn traders) were suspicious to many farmers. Details about Nachig men who had no lowland fields in 1966 support the normative dominance of corn farming; that is, they are mostly exceptions that prove the rule. Only two of the 78 men 35–44 years old had no fields. Five of 54 older men had no lowland fields. Three appeared to be retired. They were over 70 and had fields in the highlands near their homes—suggesting that they could no longer stand the rigors of trips to the lowlands.

Eight of 76 younger men (25–34 years old) had no fields. They present a variety of interesting and unusual stories, especially when the 1983 census (Appendix C) is used to put their 1966 behavior in the context of their later lives. By 1983 two had died, one at age 35, the other at age 44. Two others were among the relatively few Nachig men who no longer lived in Zinacantán: one stayed in San Cristóbal after finishing a jail term served for killing another Zinacanteco; the other lived and worked in Tuxtla, the state capital. Both were among the small number of men who permanently left Nachig and no longer paid taxes there (Appendix C). Three others were in Zinacantán, but were not corn farmers in 1983: one owned and operated two trucks, another worked for the government reforestation program, and the third moved to his wife's hamlet of origin and was engaged in full-time flower production. The remaining man, who in 1966 was the somewhat unsteady son of an important political leader in Nachig, had become the only representative of the old norm. In 1983 he was working exclusively on farming in the lowlands. The high proportion of unusual personal and residential histories among those without cornfields in 1966 suggests that corn farming was the social norm as well as a statistical norm at that time.

On the other hand, the cross-sectional data suggested a life-cycle pattern—from labor as a youth to corn farming at maturity—that was historically limited. By the time the youth of the late 1960's had reached maturity in 1983 (roughly the 40-to-50-year-olds), a number of them had left corn farming.

2.6. I am using the word "occupation" to designate the ways Zinacantecos make a living. This usage is a matter of convenience, for "economic activity," "economic pursuit," and "productive activity" are awkward, and terms like "job" are less appropriate. I mean to describe conveniently what is going on—without taking a position on the complexities involved in distinguishing farmers' work from that of industrial workers and peasants, and "jobs" from other "occupations." Perhaps the descriptions provided here will be useful to those who focus on those issues. See Coughenour (1984) and de Janvry and Vandeman (1987).

2.7. The household, not the male household head, is the economic unit in Zinacantán (see especially L. K. M. Haviland 1978: 189), and in some cases attention to the individual occupation may distort the relationship of the household to the outside world. This distortion is not great, however, for there are few joint households (in Nachig at least) that last many years. The most powerful joint economic units emerge at the point in the family cycle when teenage sons contribute significantly to the household (Manuel BB, contrasted with Antonio AA), and sometimes when the youngest son marries and takes up joint residence with the father (Juan KK). The data I use here exclude a few younger men living in this arrangement (Appendix C).

Notes to Chapter 3

3.1. The township of Chamula had the highest density, with $358/km^2$. This is five times the density of neighboring Zinacantán (1970 census figures cited in PRODESCH 1977: 10). Chamulas had, for many decades, regularly migrated to coffee plantations in the Soconusco region on the Pacific coast of Chiapas (Wasserstrom 1983).

3.2. To facilitate description of its resources, potentials, and problems, the state was usually divided into six to nine regions (e.g., see Velasco Suárez 1976: 41).

3.3. In constant pesos, spending increased 46.4 percent during the Díaz Ordaz years, and 122.2 percent during the Echeverría years. Based on population figures for 1965, 1971, and 1977 from World Bank (1983), corresponding population increases were 21.5 and 20.5 percent.

3.4. Statistical summaries vary somewhat, but the overall pattern is consistent. It seems that projected figures sometimes got into preliminary reports and were later carried forward into overviews and summaries. And government agencies, like other organizations, sometimes become overenthusiastic in describing their products.

In his final annual report, Velasco Suárez (1976: 65, 155) lists 3,579.5 km of roads existing in 1970, and says that 5,358.1 km were constructed from 1971 to 1976, including 3,315.6 km on labor-intensive projects designed to create jobs.

3.5. CFE planned for compensation of displaced persons around Angostura (Velasco Suárez 1971: 71–79). There sometimes was great conflict between CFE and displaced peasants (see the Tuxtla Gutiérrez newspaper *Numero Uno* for July 28, and August 5 and 11, 1981, concerning settlements at Chicoasén and problems at Itzantún).

3.6. Some Zinacantecos had been displaced in the late 1960's, when a Nestlé plant built in Chiapa de Corso, combined with extension of an all-weather road to the Angostura area, led some landowners to turn to milk production on land formerly rented to Zinacantecos (see Cancian 1972: 34–37). While the dam was filling, some Zinacantecos petitioned for and received permission to farm government land scheduled for flooding. Some did well; some lost their crops to flooding.

3.7. SPP (1981: 104) put petroleum production and natural gas production in Chiapas in 1980 at 311,751 bbl/day (16.0 percent of national production) and about 17 million m³/day (16.9 percent of national production) from 69 wells. The estimate in Chiapas (1982a: 182), which may be for 1981, is much lower for petroleum (123,000 bbl/day, equal to 4 percent of national production), and somewhat lower for gas (about 11 million m³/day, equal to 12 percent of national production) from 11 wells.

3.8. By the early 1980's, the problems of rapid expansion of energy extraction were drawing attention in official documents. The strain put on the local economy and social services by the many high-salaried outsiders associated with CFE and PEMEX, the unrest and litigation caused by PEMEX's failure to satisfy peasants displaced by its activities, and the ecological costs of development were mentioned in an official statement that questioned the overall desirability of energy development (Chiapas 1982a: 182–84). PEMEX's treatment of peasants was generally regarded as worse than CFE's. Sara Scheer (1983) has written on the agriculture-petroleum conflict in Tabasco.

3.9. When PRODESCH began, most of the residents of most of the townships in its area were monolingual speakers of Mayan languages. PRODESCH incorporated the state Department of Indian Affairs, and undertook activities that were intentionally different from those in areas with little or no ethnically Indian population. Summaries of the formal arrangements and other issues discussed below are found in Velasco Suárez (1971: 45–48), PRODESCH (1975, 1977, 1979), SP (1975: 63–64), and Velasco S. and Matus Pacheco (1976: 180–84). The distinction between the highlands development program and others in the state is marked in SP (1975) and Velasco Suárez (1976: chapter 4). PRODESCH was the only program with United Nations participation. The PIDER rural development program (see Cernea 1983) operated away from the core Indian areas in the central highlands, though even during the Velasco Suárez administration it overlapped with PRODESCH in some lowland municipalities (Velasco Suárez 1976: chapter 4).

3.10. Twenty-six municipios were in the PRODESCH region. Those listed below with an A were among 21 original municipios, comprising 5,600 km² and 280,000 inhabitants (Velasco Suárez 1971: 46–47). Those with a B were added to make the 26 listed in PRODESCH (1975: 6), comprising 7,443 km² and 335,000 people. Those with an N or an S were designated as in the northern or southern part of the PRODESCH area in PRODESCH (1979: 26). Those with a C were in the central zone. Those with an E were at the edge of the area; i.e., area boundaries and their municipio boundaries coincided in part (see Velasco S. and Matus Pacheco 1976: map). Those with an I were surrounded by others in the PRODESCH region. The municipio of Nicolás Ruiz was surrounded by PRODESCH municipios, but was not part of the program area. The municipios and their characteristics: Tenejapa ACI, Mitontic ACI, Chenalho ACI, Larráinzar ACE, El Bosque ANE, Chalchihuitán ACI, Simojovel ANE, Huitiupán ANE, Tumbalá BNE, Tila BNE, Sabanilla BCE, Yajalón ACI, Chilón ANE, Sitalá ANI, Pantelhó ACI, Ocosingo ANE, Oxchuc ACE, Chanal ASE, Amatenango del Valle ACE, Venustiano Carranza BSE, Teopisca ASE, Huistán ACI, San Cristóbal de las Casas ACE, Chamula ACI, Zinacantán ACE, and Ixtapa BCE.

3.11. In March 1979, a superordinate regional committee, COPRODE, was created, and PIDER, which had been operating in the rest of the state, was spread into the PRODESCH area. PRODESCH's "pioneering" role was acknowledged, its operations critiqued, and its power slashed (PRODESCH 1979: 27–32).

3.12. El Bosque, Chilón, Huitiupán, Ocosingo, Simojovel, Sitalá, Tila, and Tumbalá were given 57.4 percent of the 1978 appropriation, and Chanal, Teopisca, and Venustiano Carranza 23.8 percent, while the core highlands received only 18.8 percent. "It is appropriate to note that in previous years this last zone received the major part of investment" (PRODESCH 1979: 26).

3.13. When Plan Chiapas (the major programmatic document for the de la Madrid years) was printed in May 1983, three state secretariats were listed: Urban Development and Public Works (SDUOP), Indian Affairs (SAI), and Economic Development (SDE).

3.14. Different reports of the same budget categories sometimes vary, e.g., Velasco Suárez (1975: 160, table 29) and Velasco Suárez (1976: 108) on details of sector budgets for 1975. Most variations are small, and apparently due to lumping actual and budgeted expenditures at different points in a budget cycle. Annual reports in the Velasco Suárez years often gave both the reports by sector (plus some breakdowns within sectors) and a crosscutting listing of expenditures by government agency; e.g., Velasco Suárez (1975: 160) gives PRODESCH expense by government agency.

3.15. The descriptions are based on field interviews done in 1981–84 about recent and then-current programs. References to "PRODESCH" follow usage current among Zinacantecos; the offices involved had other formal labels at the time.

3.16. Commercial flower production and sale were already well established in Zinacantán when the greenhouse program began (Bunnin 1966). Much of the production was concentrated in Navenchauc, where the climate was favorable. Zinacanteco involvement ranged from small-scale, part-time production and sale to virtually full-time specialization in production or distribution and sales. By the 1980's several specialized merchants traveled in Zinacanteco-owned trucks to Mexico City (usually weekly) to purchase flowers not produced locally, and distributed them widely in Chiapas upon their return (J. B. Haviland n.d.).

3.17. Most of eight other loans for a total of $197,000 required payment of a lump sum within six months to a year. They were for seeds, fertilizers, insecticides and fungicides, pumps, and various other needs of the enterprise. SDR also provided technical advice on production and marketing, and on trucks (e.g., for the occasional transport of soil or flowers) and drivers that could be borrowed in exchange for vehicle-operating expenses and (unofficial) gifts to the drivers. The standard greenhouse was 10 × 50 m and included six long beds.

3.18. The program paralleled and extended CUC, the López Portillo administration's decentralization from the federal to the state level (Rodriguez 1987).

3.19. I was fortunate to interview Patricia Armendáriz shortly after she left a term as interim director of PRODESCH in July 1981. She gave me an overview of state actions. I believe that the Chiapas program described here provided a testing ground for the national programs described in Rodriguez (1987).

3.20. These figures come from Chiapas (1982c). Chiapas (1982b) lists $13 million as the state contribution. Since one knowledgeable Zinacanteco told me in June 1982 that the mayor had so far received $10 million in grants and that an alternative committee run by the political opposition (see Chapter 8) had received three grants of $500,000 each, it is likely that the $13 million figure represents total grants to both committees, and $11 million the total to the mayor (Presidente Municipal) alone.

3.21. I was fortunate to interview Manual Hernández Pérez in July 1981, shortly after he was replaced as secretary of the Zinacantán committee for CODECOM. He gave me an overview of activity in Zinacantán. His records show about $8 million of expenditures through June 1981, and he said there were five grants totaling $8 million between February 1980 and May 12, 1981. Reports filed at PRODESCH show the first four grants (of $1, $1, $2, and $3 million, respectively) were made in February, July, August, and December 1980.

3.22. For the major reconstruction and paving of the road to Hteklum done during Domingo Pérez's administration (a $10 million project), the private contractor hired by the state paid any Zinacantecos hired on the project. The $1 million spent reconstructing the town hall also went directly from the state to a private contractor, and Zinacantecos (at least the members of PRI) each contributed three days' labor to the project.

Notes to Chapter 4

4.1. With these criteria in mind, I selected names from the Nachig census. A few were dropped after discussions with Yermo revealed that they did not fit my criteria. Then we sought out men on the remaining list opportunistically. Some were not at home, and a couple put off immediate acceptance and were never followed up, but most readily accepted the idea of talking for a day about work and changes in work during their lifetimes.

This procedure produced five men: AA, CC, GG, II, and JJ. II introduced me to his brother, FF (whom I had also selected from the census), and I met BB, DD (I had known his deceased father well), and EE in public places and recruited them. HH and KK, Yermo's sons, were added because I saw them frequently and they happened to be free when I was. The formal interviews lasted two to four hours, and were done in San Cristóbal, usually one or more days after we had discussed the work and made an appointment.

The three oldest men were in the 1967 census ($N = 208$). The others were too young to be included. All but the two youngest were in the 1983 census ($N = 315$). (Antonio JJ, who was 25 in 1984 when he was interviewed, was 24 in 1983 when the census was done.)

The six younger men knew their exact birthdays. The older ones did not, so their ages are estimates.

The economic ranks (see Appendix C) of the nine older men (with a value of 4 equal to high) were AA 2, BB 2, CC 1, DD 4, EE 3, FF 4, GG 2, HH 4, and II 3.

Because I am not able to interview in Tzotzil, I selected men who spoke Spanish well. Of the nine included in the census (the two youngest were not), eight were rated as good Spanish speakers (see Appendix C). Good Spanish speakers were 38 percent of the entire censused population (N = 315). For the reasons mentioned in the text I concentrated on younger men and those in newer occupations—subpopulations with more good Spanish speakers (e.g., 63 percent for those under age 35, and 67 percent for those who farmed no corn and did no unskilled wage labor).

4.2. Porvenir, etc., are ranches in the Grijalva Valley. See Cancian (1972: 35) for a photo of Yermo (left) and Antonio, at Porvenir in December 1966.

4.3. *On working in Tuxtla.* After his disastrous crop in 1968, Antonio went to Tuxtla to find work. For the first three years, including a year or more with the state road agency, he earned well.

Then Antonio found a foreman who was pushy. He made the laborers work from 6 A.M. to 6 P.M., or he gave work quotas that took until 5 P.M. or longer—and docked workers a half-day's pay if they did not finish the quotas. There was no union to protect them. After he worked for this foreman a while, Antonio got sick. He lost his appetite, got a stomach ache, and felt faint. He was sent to the government health services, where he was given many pills, but it did not help. Finally, a friend told him to go to a private doctor. The private doctor said: "Look, you think you have a good job because you are earning what seems to you a lot [$25/day]. But it is ruining your health. Get an easier job, even if it pays less money."

Antonio was feeling very weak, and had no money, when he heard that there was a popsicle factory where they might give him a cart from which to sell popsicles. He went and asked, and was given a cart, and someone to show him how to do the work. The first day he earned $13—and that didn't seem so bad. During the three months he sold popsicles, he earned $18 and as much as $25 per day. Then, one day the owner asked him if he wanted a regular job in the factory—a job delivering orders, going to buy fruit, and making popsicles. He accepted, and worked there for 14 years.

The owner of the popsicle factory is a good guy, says Antonio. He invited Antonio to eat or have coffee at his house above the factory, and when he noticed that Antonio had no appetite, asked him about it. He sent him to a doctor, and paid for all the vitamins and shots Antonio got, and that is how Antonio got better. Over the years the owner came to Antonio's house to look for him if he missed work, and has visited after Antonio left the job this year. That is why Antonio stayed so long in the job. He believes he can go back to the job if he wants to do so.

He left the job because it paid too little. Things have gotten expensive in Tuxtla: though he earned enough to support himself, there was not enough to support his family. Now, living at home, he has fewer expenses.

When he first worked in the popsicle factory, Antonio rented a room in Tuxtla [when working on construction, he had slept in the tool shed on the job]. Then the owner offered him a place to sleep in the house/factory. He stayed there five or six years. It was bad because he could not go to sleep until all the peddlers had returned and checked in for the night. He got sick of that and again rented a place to sleep in Tuxtla. While most Zinacanteco construction workers went to Tuxtla Monday morning and returned Saturday afternoon, Antonio was on a different schedule during many of his years in Tuxtla: he got one Wednesday or Thursday off about three times each month.

4.4. Manuel suffered during the economic crisis because he was unemployed as a mason for the first nine months of 1983, and thus had to borrow $30,000 in cash to pay workers to help with his corn, especially for the weeding done in June and July. Though he found mason's work in mid-October, he had to sell a substantial part of his harvest to pay the $45,000 owed by December.

4.5. "I learned mason work when [Governor] Velasco Suárez [1970–76] entered. . . . When the Nachig project started I asked Yermo [who was in charge] if he couldn't give me mason's work—for I knew a bit about measures and things like that." Yermo arranged it, Manuel said, and lent him a trowel at the beginning. After Manuel worked a week in Nachig, he was called to Hteklum to work on the park, doing mostly stonework. There he learned more. The foreman was very good. He told them to take their time and do the work right; he told them to learn. Then Manuel went to San Andrés to work. He stayed a year, and learned more about laying bricks. Then he went to Tenejapa [for a few months, it seems] with Yermo, to finish up that project.

Later, when he was working at San Nicolás, Juan Gómez said, "Come with me to Chicoasén." Juan had been there, but didn't know mason work well, and wanted Manuel along to give him guidance. Manuel went, and they got work there when there were few people. Manuel stayed a long time. When he started, masons earned $60 per day; when he left they earned $150 per day. Then he went to a housing development in Tuxtla. He began in May and finished out the year there. He started there at $150 per day. Then he went to another development in Tuxtla, and finished another year there. The next year there was a different job. It was when Sabines entered as governor (1980).

That's how he learned. Now he can do a whole house alone.

In recent years [it seems] he has worked in San Cristóbal and Tuxtla, for various foremen, for short periods. He presently works with a regular mason partner. Now they both have permission to take a break from their regular job—to do milpa work.

4.6. Of the 11 men interviewed, Juan was the only one with moderate rather than good Spanish, according to Yermo (see Appendix C).

4.7. Mariano served as Mayordomo in Nachig (see Chapter 7), as did Manuel BB and José II.

4.8. José did trading for a short while, but he did not like it. He likes the regular income from construction, and concentrates on this work.

On Monday morning José rides the Nachig group truck to Tuxtla. The fare is $200. On Saturday he returns separately. Buses are better in the rainy season, and sometimes less expensive. He lives on the job, camping in one of the unfinished houses. This way, he says, he has plenty of time to cook his meals even if he works late. He brings food from home for the first couple of days of the week, then buys food in Tuxtla and cooks it. It seems that he rarely goes to the restaurants near the construction site.

He has about half a hectare of land in Nachig, away from his house. He plants a bit of corn for corn on the cob, vegetables, and flowers. The morning of the first Sunday I interviewed him (June 1984) he and his family had gone to San Cristóbal to the market. He took flowers and chard from his land and sold them in the market for a total of $400, twice the round-trip fare for him and his wife.

When he works continuously he says they pile up as much as $15–20,000. The only other capital goods they seem to have are about 30 chickens, including 12 laying hens. They get about eight or nine eggs per day. They don't buy eggs, and they don't sell chickens.

4.9. Corn: José bought 54 almudes in December 1983 at $2,500 for nine almudes, delivered to his house (roughly 85 percent of the June 1984 San Cristóbal market price). Though they feed some chickens, he hopes it will last all year. The sacks piled against the wall in his house give something of the feeling of security normal for a corn farmer's house.

Wood: He just bought four cords from a man in Elanvo at $800 each. He will pay a trucker to bring them to his house, and do the loading himself. He and his wife also carry loads of wood home from his land. These two sources provide for the year. When the population was less dense in the 1960's, women were often able to get firewood from reasonably near family and communal land, but in recent years more and more families have had to buy wood and/or pay for its transport.

Curing: He had one big ceremony for his wife this year, with a curer (Vogt 1969: 421ff.) and a trip to Hteklum.

4.10. When I interviewed him, Francisco had just sold off the fourth batch of chicks he bought for fattening. He had had consultations from a veterinarian (from PRODESCH), who advised him to get them sold off before disease set in. He got a man from San Cristóbal to come and weigh them and take them all—for a total of $38,000. The vet said that he should clean and air out the chicken house for two months to get rid of disease before starting a new batch of chicks.

He also applied for a credit of $70,000 to expand the operation, and he planned to work expanding the coop as the vet suggested—after he finished the corn and beans in his highland fields, i.e., a few weeks later. Apparently the credit request and the official organization includes five people, Francisco and four of his friends. Francisco was the only one who had money involved in the operation. As far as I could tell, the friends signed only to meet the requirement that there be an organization with various members. He planned to go to PRODESCH in a few days to see if the credit of $70,000 for expansion of the operation came through. If it did not, he planned to put his own $30,000 or more back in.

Until this point Francisco had done all the chicken operation, four batches, with his own capital. He received only technical assistance from PRODESCH. Francisco talked of the complicated technology of raising chickens. He said he learned from a book he got at the vet store, and in April 1984 he took a one-week course at PRODESCH. The 20 people who took it were given room and board for the week.

At the time of his interview Francisco also had half a hectare of squash seeded on his land in Pig. He figured to get a $40,000 crop that he could bring to the road at Pig with his father's and/or other horses—for transport to Tuxtla for sale. He is also planting many peach trees on his hillside land near the chicken coop—with plans to graft them with plums once they are established.

The story of his peach trees is particularly interesting because of all the types of labor employed: children to collect fallen fruit and make pits (paid by the bucketful), an adult worker to split the pits and dry the seed, other adults to dig holes for trees, and finally, skilled workers he planned to hire when the time came to have the plums grafted into the trees (for he does not know how to do it). He planned to put more peach trees in Pig in May 1985, and hoped to have about 450 trees in all.

4.11. Chronology of work and other major life events: *1969 to 1976* Was in school in Nachig. Repeated one year, finished in June 1976. Summer vacations and occasional other weeks worked at Chicoasén. *1976* June–Oct.: traded in the Tuxtla market. Nov.–Dec.: worked in the reforestation program in Navenchauc. *1977* Jan.–Feb.: worked in the reforestation program in Nachig. Jan.–April: married for the first time. April–Dec.: worked at times as an agricultural or construction laborer. (May: seeded corn in lowland near sister's husband.) *1978* Jan.: married present wife. At times did agricultural or construction labor. Farmed corn in the lowlands. *1979* At times did agricultural or construction labor. Farmed corn in the lowlands. Sept.: became SARH agricultural *promotor* (extension agent): he sent others to harvest his corn. *1980* Jan.–Oct.: continued at SARH. Nov.: began course for IMSS-COPLAMAR medical assistants. *1981* Feb.: became IMSS-COPLAMAR rural medical worker. *1982* Jan.–Dec.: served as Mayordomo Virgen de Fátima, Nachig (see Chapter 7). April: had to leave his IMSS-COPLAMAR job. *1983* No work done for others. April: took CONASUPO-COPLAMAR course on grocery-store management and accounting. Oct.: opened own private store in Nachig.

4.12. José's wife, a woman from Paste, works as an extension agent (Promotora de Hogar Rural) for SARH. She teaches cooking and sewing out of a "clubhouse" built in her neighborhood of origin. She cleared roughly $11,000 for the semimonthly pay period preceding the interview (similar to Antonio JJ, the reforester). Shortly afterwards, SARH workers struck, demanding an 80-percent wage increase, among other things.

4.13. José's store carries general merchandise (soap, cookies, cigarettes, soft drinks, beer, and some medicines), and features *estambre* (colored thread used in weaving Zinacanteco clothes). José buys the *estambre* in large quantities from a Mexico City mail-order house and breaks it down to

$50 balls with a manual winding machine. He says the store has about $100,000 in stock, $60,000 of which is *estambre*. He reports that sales are normally $3,000 to $4,000 per day (they range down to $2,000 and up to $10,000 on fiesta days). Markups tend to be about 25 percent or a bit more.

4.14. This Antonio López is one of three farmers described in Cancian (1972: 177–82), and the political leader in Chapter 11.

4.15. Antonio was interviewed on May 2, 1984, while on vacation. He described pay, vacations, and benefits of his job as follows. Those who have worked for reforestation for more than five years get $9,000 twice each month. The total pay is $11,000 or $12,000, depending on how many days are worked, but there are about $2,000 of deductions, for ISSSTE (the government employees' family health program), union dues, and insurance. So you get $18,000 per month.

There are two annual vacations of ten working days each, one in May and one in December, plus the following official holidays (unless they fall on a Saturday or a Sunday and are "lost"): February 5, March 21, Thursday and Friday of Holy Week, May 1, May 5, September 16, October 12, November 1, and December 12.

He also has five *días económicas* (essentially, personal days) every six months, if needed. The first month of sick leave is with full pay, the second month with half pay, and subsequently there is no pay, but the job is held open for you. To take sick leave you have to go to ISSSTE and get a doctor's note. When Zinacantecos are cured by native curers, the union representative fixes things so that it will count as sick leave. Leave without pay is available for three months, and for a second contiguous three-month period if needed. When José Hernández died, the life insurance was $100,000, and the union provided $70,000 for funeral expenses. Now the life insurance is $300,000.

4.16. During March, April, and May 1984, Juan, his laborer, and a mason from another lowland city shared a $2,000-per-month room in Tuxtla. On the job the laborer normally provides Juan with plenty of materials and quits early to cook his own food at the site. Juan usually works a bit later and then eats at the nearby restaurant. Besides the cost of his room, Juan listed the following expenses: $200 for the ride to Tuxtla on Monday morning and $200 or $220 for return on Saturday; $18 each way daily from his room to the work site; $150 for each of two restaurant meals daily; $25 daily for *posole* (corn gruel) about noon, and rarely a bit for a soda pop on the job; $150 per week union dues ($100 for laborers); and a little for fare to the monthly union meeting (those absent are fined $600).

4.17. As far as I know, marijuana production was almost non-existent in the 1970's. During the mid-1970's, Nachig men helped government officials destroy the plants of one local man, and no other cases were reported. In the 1980's (especially after the economic crisis, as far as I can tell) government officials reported that production was substantial, especially in more remote places in the highlands. Opium poppies were also produced. It was rumored that in some densely populated, remote hamlets of Chamula, almost half the population was engaged in some marijuana production. In Zinacantán marijuana production and trade took on the role of treasure tales (Foster 1964); i.e., though details were never confirmed, some people speculated that it explained new wealth that exceeded community expectations. In the mid-1980's I occasionally turned away circumspect inquiries about the drug trade. In summer 1988 there were about six Zinacantecos in the Tuxtla prison for drug offenders. Had this study begun five years later and in a more remote location, I might well have been unable to give a full, honest accounting of local economic activity.

Notes to Chapter 5

5.1. I am concerned about both income and wealth, and sometimes say either to mean both—since they are difficult to distinguish in my data. In thinking about income and wealth in Zinacantán it is useful to see government jobs that provide a secure income stream as a form of wealth.

5.2. In the 1980's, wages in corn were always at least six almudes per week. In summer 1981, at the peak of prosperity, some workers demanded and got eight almudes per week; in 1984 and 1985, after the economic crisis, wages were never less than six almudes per week, when paid in kind. During the peak work period in July 1988, Yermo reported that wages in kind were again eight almudes per week.

The cash wage for agricultural work was usually close to the in-kind equivalent. It went from $6 or $7 per day in the early 1960's to $100 in summer 1981, $200 in summer 1982, $500 to $600 in summer 1985, and $4,000 during July 1988.

In December 1982, after the August crisis, wages in kind shot up to as much as 12 almudes per week; in summer 1983, wages of 8 almudes per week were still reported. As far as I can tell this happened because wage inflation outside agriculture was rapid during this period, the government did not raise the official buying price for corn in the same proportion, and the local market reflected the imbalance. Thus, during the December harvest, cash-short farmers who used their harvested corn to match prevailing cash wages paid extraordinary wages in kind.

The statements on wage rates in agriculture and construction after 1980 are based on reports made by Zinacantecos (and some Ladino employers) during each of my field trips.

5.3. Summer 1988 was something of an exception, for agricultural workers during the peak weeding period earned $4,000 and rarely $5,000 per day, while construction laborers in Tuxtla earned $5,000 to $7,000.

5.4. After the economic crisis of 1982, when construction labor was harder to find, many Zinacantecos who had worked in construction increased their farming activity, especially in the highlands (G. A. Collier and Mountjoy 1988). Conditions in 1983 required many innovative adjustments by Zinacantecos. By 1984, government construction was under way again and many Zinacantecos reported that construction work was readily available.

5.5. A few Zinacantecos held government jobs in the 1960's—most of them as INI school teachers or health promoters. Their numbers grew in the decades that followed, and the reforestation programs (Mariano DD, Antonio JJ) provided the security of government employment for many more. In the early 1960's, when only one or two trucks were owned by Zinacantecos, and few owned many pack animals (mules and horses), people often referred to the great wealth of those who had owned as many as 20 pack animals (see Mariano EE) in earlier times. The 1960's was a period of transition from animal to truck transport in the region, and Zinacantecos were losing work as muleteers. Thus, it may have been a period of unusually equal distribution of income and wealth in Zinacantán (see G. A. Collier 1989).

5.6. Prosperous families that owned forested land hired men with chain saws to cut down their trees and make firewood. In 1988 many Nachig families acquired a source of firewood by participating in the purchase of a large nearby private property.

Overall, women's contributions to family production decreased significantly before the crisis. By 1988, many Nachig women, including some in a group sponsored by SARH, were weaving elaborate traditional clothes for sale to passing tourists. Diane Rus (1988) describes women's responses to the crisis.

5.7. Of course, people disagree about whether these changes are improvements. Most Zinacantecos would agree with my statements.

5.8. As is usual when cross-sectional statistical data confront historical problems, it is impossible to untangle precisely the various influences that led to the occupations of Nachig men in summer 1983, when the census was taken. I base my assumption that the 1983 cross-sectional data reflect enduring individual work patterns on information in the case studies (Chapter 4), and on common sense. The latter is not always reliable.

5.9. As noted in Chapter 2, the relative homogeneity of the 1960's also has historical roots in government action. George Collier (1989) has pointed out that the status of senior men in the 1960's reflects the opportunities and limitations presented their generation by the land-reform movement during the years when they came of age.

5.10. As far as I can tell on the basis of comparing an incomplete census taken in 1981 to the complete 1983 census, the crisis of 1982 is not importantly reflected in my 1983 census data—in part because people adjusted slowly, and no doubt in part because my consultants had limited knowledge of the most recent adjustments people made.

Notes to Chapter 6

6.1. The two sentences left out of the quotation at this point confuse me, because they suggest that opposition candidates for Presidente Municipal were listed on ballots in the 1960's. I now find no evidence for this. In the 1980's, Zinacantecos said opposition candidates were not listed until the late 1970's.

6.2. The precise degree of participation is discussed at length in Chapter 11 of Cancian (1965).

6.3. Navenchauc's local officials had legal status under the state constitution.

> There are two other civil officials who do not serve at the town hall [in Hteklum]. These are the *Agente Municipal* of Navenchauc and his alternate. The Agentes have an office in the miniature town hall, with attached jail, near the chapel of the Virgen de Guadalupe in the Navenchauc plaza. Although the Agentes are representatives of the civil government, they function as minor hamlet elders. They handle the routine disputes that occur in their hamlet—marital problems and drunken fights—and carry out the orders of local political leaders in more complex cases. The fact that they maintain an official jail allows them to act as minor Presidentes, but they have considerably less power. (J. F. Collier 1973:33–34)

Navenchauc's special status came out of long-standing competition of the hamlet and its leaders with the political power concentrated in Hteklum. The formal arrangements were begun after a Fiesta of Guadalupe in the early 1960's, when a man accused of bothering a young woman almost died after the informal elders ordered that he be tied to a post to restrain him.

6.4. Jane Collier (1973) and Vogt's (1969) work add substantially to this brief description. Wasserstrom's (1983) work adds much on both recent and earlier politics.

6.5. Jan Rus and Robert Wasserstrom (1980) document the existence in the nineteenth century of some Mayordomos (including a Mayordomo from Salinas), Mayordomos Reyes, Mesoneros, Alférezes, Regidores, and Alcaldes. The latter two originated as civil officials. Their research interprets the role of the cargo system and the antecedent *cofradía* system in the political economy of the colonial period and the nineteenth century (see also Vogt 1969: 26). They (1980: 476, note 3) say new civil officials took over the civil functions of the Alcaldes and Regidores after 1916.

6.6. Various sources from the Tax group (Tax et al. 1947) through José Sánchez, who was Presidente Municipal in 1965, said that six was the official number of Mayores. In the early part of the century, service as Mayor did not count for progress in the religious hierarchy; men who passed Mayor were expected to follow it with a Mayordomo cargo (Cancian 1965: 162). By the early 1940's (Tax et al. 1947: 35) some men went directly from Mayor to Alférez, and others did not.

I believe that this account is more accurate than my statement that eight existed since the turn of the century (1965: 17). Sánchez said that there were six Mayores by tradition (three named by the Presidente and three named by the Elders) and that more sometimes volunteered or were appointed. During his term of three years (1965–1967) Sánchez had 12, ten, and then eight men serve the post. As I understand it, the number of Mayores was, or became, much less rigidly fixed than the number serving in other cargos. Little was lost or gained by controlling their numbers carefully. Not infrequently they entered late or did not finish the term of office.

6.7. The origin of the Navenchauc and Apaz cargos, and a rumor that Paste would also add cargos, are described in Cancian (1965: 164–65).

6.8. At some points in the process, the hamlets had asked for separate ejidos, but in the end people from different hamlets were allocated plots on the same ranch, and the ejido had a single central administration. As part of the process, Zinacantecos purchased the remaining small properties left to the Ladino owners of Pig, Yalentay, and Shucun, and the people who had lived on the ranches as peons were given land and made part of the Zinacanteco community (Edel 1966; Vogt 1969: 27–29). Few Zinacantecos actually moved their residence to their ejido plots. Edel's study, especially the unpublished version (1962), is an excellent source of detail on political life in the 1930's and 1940's, and on the process through which Mariano Hernández Zárate emerged as cacique of Zinacantán. Table B.2, in columns 3, 4, 5, and 6, shows the changing census status of places.

6.9. The Elders collected small additional taxes to support their part of fiestas.

6.10. Government censuses provide useful population counts, and use slightly different definitions of places within Zinacantán. Both tax lists and censuses are described in Appendix B. Here I want to describe the features of tax lists that make them the appropriate basis for the description of hamlets in the following section.

John Haviland (1977: 19) notes that in some cases hamlet boundaries cut across other social groupings. This involved a very small part of the population. Most Zinacantecos were born and lived out their lives in a single hamlet—though most of them at some point took up temporary residence in Hteklum while serving in a civil or religious office (Cancian 1965: 161ff.). Thus, hamlet membership was usually an important part of a person's identity. The cases of Antonio AA, Manuel BB, and Mariano EE in Chapter 4, and the discussion of Nachig hamlet membership in Appendix C, illustrate the reasons some moved.

6.11. The special status of Navenchauc was marked by the Agencia Municipal and by the church and the cargos located there. Although outsiders saw the church and the cargos as responses to the work of Protestant missionaries in the community (Cancian 1965: 164), both were also deeply embedded in other political controversies.

6.12. Economic change connected with the ejido movement was relatively fast during this period.

Notes to Chapter 7

7.1. Yermo remembers that the first Agentes entered in 1974, when Mariano Pérez became Presidente, but the first Agentes may have served a partial term when Marcos Pérez was Presidente (1971–73); see Table 7.2, especially the notes on column E. Yermo was Agente with the second group, who served from 1977 to 1979, while Domingo Pérez was Presidente.

During the 1985–88 term, the arrangements were formalized further: one Agente Municipal, one Juez Rural (the hamlet version of Alcalde Juez), and one alternate for each were appointed. The two pairs, one Agente and one Juez, alternated two-week periods of service (Antonio AA).

7.2. Land-tenure arrangements are discussed in more detail below in the section "Hamlet Organization and Civil Offices." These Communal Land Committees and the Ejido Committees were organized for units that were less than the entire municipio. Domingo Pérez, who was head of the Navenchauc-Apaz Communal Land Committee in 1986–88, said the hamlets closer to the Center had a separate master plan and committee. Pig and Yalentay, formerly private properties, fell into another category. The Cornfields was organized as an ejido and had no Communal Land Committee (see the discussion later in this chapter). Nachig did not have fixed numbers of members on the committees relevant to its lands. I have data for 1981, when there were three Nachig men on the Communal Land Committee and three on the Ejido Committee. As far as I can tell, these men functioned as a local committee for problems confined to the hamlet.

7.3. I have figures for 1982: the number paying fiesta taxes in Nachig proper (246) was five-eighths of the number (392) contributing for church expenses, for which exemptions were not given. Population growth lessened the burden, but the rate of population growth was much slower than the rate of office expansion.

7.4. This was another aspect of decentralization, for the Elders had traditionally named men from the Center as their Scribes (see Table 6.3, note *a*; Cancian 1965: 45). Before schools spread, literate people were concentrated in the Center, and men from the Center could live at home during the period of service, thus lowering expenses to the Elders. For the 12 years from 1968 through 1979, the 24 annual slots for Scribes were filled 19 times by Hteklum people (including seven times by one man), three times by one Vochojvo man, and twice by one Patosil man. In the late 1970's, the dominance of Hteklum was challenged and it was decided that Scribes would be named by the hamlets following a fixed rotation, with each appointee entering as the Junior Scribe and then serving a second year in the Senior position. This decentralizing move proved to be short-lived (see Part III), but in 1981 when Nachig's turn came, it produced this situation.

7.5. In Nachig a one-year office gave two years of tax exemption (the year of service and the year after service) and a three-year term six years of tax exemption. Hamlets differed. Hteklum, for example, gave one year of rest for both one-year and three-year offices. Vochojvo used Nachig's system.

7.6. This is according to Yermo, who was still an Agente in Nachig at the time. Domingo Pérez reported that formal recognition as a hamlet came in December 1981, while Manuel Conde was Presidente.

7.7. The political split between Jechchentic and Nachig has some personal lines of continuity that go back many decades. In the late 1930's, Mariano Hernández Zárate was the leader of the ejido movement, and his rise to power apparently eclipsed the power of Lorenzo Pérez Hil (Tax et al. 1947; Edel 1966), father of Marcos Pérez's father (Manuel Pérez Hil). When Yermo was named candidate for Presidente (to serve for 1960–61), he was Zárate's alternative to Manuel Pérez Hil, who had been named but was cooperating with Fafian Chainatic, the opposition to Zárate.

Yermo said that in the 1940's he was a Nachig member of the Ejido Committee and organized (at Zárate's suggestion) the capture of a Nachig wife killer whom the Presidente had freed. The Presidente was Mariano Pérez Ocotz (father of Antonio Ocotz, who led Jechchentic in the late 1970's). Mariano Pérez Ocotz named Yermo as Mayor to punish him, and Yermo was released by the Elders with Zárate's help, only to be named again by Mariano Pérez Ocotz. Though Zárate said he would help again, Yermo got out of the appointment by asking, in July 1948, for Mayordomo Rey, which he served in 1950. Mariano Pérez Ocotz was also involved when Yermo was named Cobrador for 1951.

7.8. Chiapas law recognizes two kinds of Agentes. One type includes official recognition of the political subunit by the state government. The second type of Agente is created and appointed directly under the legal authority of the Presidente. In Zinacantán in the 1970's, only Navenchauc was of the first type.

Some of the buildings that housed the Agentes were not constructed until the early 1980's, when the CODECOM program brought new infusions of funds to Zinacantán (Table 7.2, column F). In the early part of the period it was common for Agentes to work out of local schools or houses "borrowed" from individuals.

7.9. In 1987 when data on schools were collected, the federal school system administered the Hteklum school, and the other "early" schools were administered by the State of Chiapas. In about 1960 the National Indian Institute (INI) turned over administration of its schools in Zinacantán to the federal system.

7.10. In 1970 communal land tenure was confined to 1,231 legally organized *comunidades* in all of Mexico. Most of them were in Indian areas. At the same time there were more than 21,000 ejidos (Sheridan 1988: 160; Yates 1981). In some places (including the one described by Sheridan) substantial parts of the land were exploited communally, e.g., as grazing or wood-gathering land.

In both Zinacantán and Cucurpe (Sheridan 1988), members missed meetings, despite heavy fines, and complained about their frequency (up to once per month).

7.11. In 1987 Yermo was head of a society of 117 members who had purchased land at Pig some years before.

7.12. According to one man with experience in land-tenure issues, the move combined the communal land area where many ejido members lived (the hamlets of Zequentic and Jocchenom, on Map 3) and the ejido lands into the same unit—thereby meeting the legal requirement that members live on their ejido lands. For most other purposes the switch from hamlet to ejido organization made little practical difference.

7.13. The hamlet of Tierra Blanca had a church before this period; it was rebuilt about 1974. It established a single Mayordomo cargo about 1968, and was otherwise organized like Salinas in Table 7.3. A large proportion of the population was Ladino. There was only one Tierra Blanca man on the cargo waiting lists in 1987, and none in all previous years for which I have lists (Chapter 8, Appendix D). I do not know much about the Tierra Blanca cargo, but guess it was not fully parallel to the other new cargos. I do not count the cargo in my calculations, but have not dropped the small Tierra Blanca population.

7.14. Robert Wasserstrom, writing from data gathered in the early and middle 1970's, characterized the arrangements then current in Nachig, Paste, and Elanvo, as well as Zequentic, as a sign of egalitarian sentiments among hamlets declaring their independence from the hierarchical patterns dominant in Hteklum.

> Since 1940, many hamlets have grown so rapidly that cargo service and year-renewal ceremonies no longer provide a common ground on which rich and poor might meet as equals. Under these circumstances, hamlet elders have encouraged local residents to build new chapels and to organize cooperative, not hierarchical, festivals. By creating such institutions, it seems, they hope to restrain and reconcile in some measure, those inequalities that modernization has created. (Wasserstrom 1983: 239)

Whatever the intentions of the elders, events in Nachig, Paste, and Elanvo soon moved the organization in a hierarchical direction. In making his interpretation of the new rituals in the early 1970's, Wasserstrom abandoned his focus on the long-term historical trends, and fell in with the functionalists that he (successfully) aimed to correct in the remainder of his study.

7.15. Padre José Luis Argüelles, who helped organize and train the Catechists, said all the positions were established between 1976 and 1979. Chajtoj had Catechists in 1974 because the idea came directly from the neighboring settlement of San José Bocemtenelte, which was not part of the Zinacanteco ritual system.

7.16. Table 7.2: SOURCES: Column B—1973 Fiesta San Sebastián band tax list; see Appendix A. Column C—1980 Fiesta Rosario tax list from Manuel Hernández. Column D—1983 Fiesta Rosario tax list; see Appendix A. Material for columns E, F, G, and H are principally from three men: Manuel Hernández (MH), who was Secretary to the Municipio Development Foundation (see Chapter 3) in 1980 and the first half of 1981; Domingo Pérez (DP), who was First Regidor Civil (1971–73) and Presidente (1977–79); and José Sánchez (JS), who was Presidente (1965–67) and a *promotor* (extension agent) and educational administrator for INI for 30 years (1953 to 1986, except when he was Presidente). Column E—interview with DP in August 1982. Column F—Interview with MH in July 1981. Columns G and H—interview with JS in September 1987.

Column A: Not all these places are hamlets (*parajes*). Criteria for assigning hamlet status differed among consultants. MH, working from memory, named all those listed here except Jechtoch, Jechchentic, Pig, and the last five in the table. He divided Vochojvo into Tsahalnab and Vochojvo Alto—yielding 24 places, of which he said 22 were hamlets. He (like most anthropologists who have worked in Zinacantán) said that all places with Principales were hamlets, and that Joigel shared a Principal with Chainatic, and Chiquinibalvo shared one with Jocchenom. DP and JS both said there was no single criterion for identifying a hamlet. Starting from the 1980 tax list (column C) DP added Tierra Blanca; of those 26 places all but the last three had Principales. He also said that Salinas, Petztoj, and Tierra Blanca shared a Principal until the 1974–76 period, Shulvo separated from Paste in the late 1960's, Chajtoj separated from Elanvo about 1975, Shucun and San Antonio were "ranchos" (not hamlets), Ocotal was populated by Chamulas who paid taxes in both Zinacantán and Chamula and took cargos in Chamula if at all, La Selva was formerly part of the San Nicolás ranch and had been sold to Chamulas who changed clothes and became Zinacantecos, Jechchentic was part of Nachig and had no separate Principal, and that Jechtoch was formally separated from Nachig by the Presidente in December 1981, and had its own Principal.

Column B: Hteklum and Vochojvo did not contribute for the band at this time. San Nicolás was listed separately on the same page, and Chajtoj was listed on a different page. Joigelito was not listed, but there was a regular entry for "Seguentic Segundo."

Column C: Because of the political division then current (see Chapter 8) the 1980 tax list included only some of the taxpayers. I think it included all hamlets, but cannot be absolutely sure of that.

Column D: Chiquinibalvo does not appear on this tax list, but does appear on the list for the Fiesta of Cuarto Viernes in 1983.

Column E: DP listed no Agente for Chajtoj. MH did. DP said that hamlets that thought the Agente's work would be very demanding (Nachig, Paste, and Elanvo) named three Agentes so each could have two periods off for each period of service. Chainatic and Joigelito each named a single Agente, and the other hamlets named two. In a brief interview Marcos Pérez stated that there were 22 hamlets during his administration and that he named Agentes for all of them. If this was the actual legal situation during that period, few Zinacantecos recognized it. Other informants support Domingo Pérez's picture displayed in the table. Yermo said that the Agente was first appointed in Nachig in 1974 (with the Presidente following Marcos Pérez). The earlier date given by Domingo Pérez suggests that there may have been an earlier arrangement that was informal or not fully recognized by hamlet leaders.

Column F: MH did not know the origin of the buildings in Nachig and Navenchauc. Those in Apaz and Zequentic were built by the hamlets themselves, he said. Those built in 1980 and 1981 were built with funds from CODECOM. He said that Shulvo had a building but no Agente, and that the Joigelito Agente worked out of the school. The Paste building was reconstructed in 1981. Some of the buildings are called "Casa del Pueblo," some "Agencia Municipal." All the hamlets with public buildings (and Salinas) had jails.

Column G: The 1965 Vochojvo school was in Vochojvo Alto. In 1981 a school was built in the Tsahalnab area of Vochojvo, and in 1986 another was built in Vochojvo Bajo. In 1958 a second school was added in Navenchauc.

Most of the schools provided three years of instruction (years 1 to 3) when they were first established. By 1987 (when JS was interviewed) most schools had all six primary grades (see José II and Antonio JJ); by the middle 1980's, Hteklum, Nachig, and Navenchauc had secondary schools (years 7 to 9) that met in late afternoon and evening. In many locations, schools were rebuilt and expanded as their enrollments and programs increased. In 1960 few girls attended schools, but in the 1970's they made up a large part of the classes.

7.17. Table 7.3: SOURCES: Unless otherwise indicated, data in this table come from Padre José Luis Argüelles (JL), who served Zinacantán and its hamlets beginning in 1975. In 1984, on the basis of his knowledge and interviews done with hamlet residents during his visits, and with the help of Padre Rafael Mendívil (who began his work in Zinacantán before Padre José Luis's arrival), Padre José Luis filled in a form with questions about each of the hamlets with a church. In many cases I have interview information that confirms what he provided. For columns B and C, I have also used data from Wasserstrom (1983) (RW) and my own recent interviews (FC).

Column B: Salinas: RW (p. 229). Nachig: RW (p. 228) says it was constructed "since 1970." Paste: from RW (p. 234); JL says 1973. Navenchauc: rebuilt 1975. Apaz: from Cancian (1965: 164); JL says 1964. Zequentic: from RW (p. 235); JL says 1972.

Column C: Salinas: Jan Rus and RW (1980: 476). Paste: FC. Navenchauc: RW (p. 231); Cancian (1965: 64) says circa 1954; my recent information is that the new cargos formally began 1983. Apaz: see Table 6.1, note *d*).

Notes to Chapter 8

8.1. It is hard to calibrate violence and the threat of physical force, especially because, when the threat of force is effectively delivered, the use of force may be rare. Murders have been infrequent in Zinacantán, as compared with the Oaxaca community studied by Greenberg (1981a), or even some nearby Chiapas communities (J. Nash 1970). Economic domination backed by force has been less in Zinacantán than in neighboring Chamula in recent decades, it seems to me and to some other anthropologists who have worked in the area for many years.

8.2. The hamlets of origin of the ten Presidentes Municipales listed in Table 3.2 were Nachig, Paste, Hteklum, Hteklum (?), Vochojvo, Nachig, Navenchauc, Chainatic (?, definitely the Cornfields), Hteklum (moved there from Navenchauc in the early 1970's), and Vochojvo (or Hteklum). Some observers thought the campaign to give Navenchauc and the Cornfields independence or power within the township was important at the time of the troubles described in the text above, but most felt it was not a central issue. The tension between the Center and the outer hamlets was not an explicit part of the retrospective interpretations Zinacantecos made of the events of 1976.

8.3. From the perspective of the 1980's, participants and observers of the 1960's saw the period as lacking political conflict. In the 1980's, Zinacantecos routinely asserted that the "politics" started in 1976, and those who were asked uniformly declared that there was no comparable trouble during earlier periods.

8.4. I am fortunate to have recorded Yermo's descriptions of and comments on the nomination and election on five occasions (once each in 1981, 1982, and 1983, and twice in 1984). His accounts are ordered, consistent with each other and with the written record, and include emphasis on the issues he thought most important. Padre José Luis Argüelles provided me with a three-page list entitled "Political Happenings in Zinacantán 1976–1979" and the church newsletter quoted below in the text, as well as his personal recollections. I also have accounts of various lengths from Pablo Ramírez, who was the outside PRI official responsible for coordinating nominations in Indian municipios, Domingo Pérez and Marcos Pérez, the two most important principals, Robert Laughlin, an anthropologist who attended one crucial meeting, and seven other Zinacantecos whose accounts I can use more freely if I do not identify them.

Some fairly important details remain obscure. It is not surprising that most accounts clearly reflect the speaker's position in the events, and that not all observers found the same aspects of the activity significant. What participants carried from the events into the political activity that followed varied greatly. My purpose here is to represent some of the positions that had substantial support, and to highlight some themes that remained important for many years and through various changes of administration inside and outside Zinacantán. Given the contradictory realities that came out of the turmoil that began in 1976, it would be fruitless to seek a single linear account of the events of the August meeting and the weeks that followed.

8.5. PAN, the major opposition party in Mexico at that time, got a foothold in Chamula after the Indian Congress of 1974 discussed in Note 8.8. I know that some of the Zinacantecos who fled after the November 7 meeting took refuge in Chamula, and that Marcos Pérez had *compadres* among state PRI officials, direct access to the governor, and a relationship with one official who had connections to both PRI and PAN, but I do not know the details or the exact date of PAN's formation in Zinacantán. I see no consistent relation of the national party's ideological position and the concerns of the opposition in Zinacantán.

8.6. The open split between Pérez and religious officials continued during his first year in office. The incumbent religious officials became part of the opposition. Pérez did not participate in the installation of Alféreces (Cancian 1965: 57–61). According to one Alférez who was installed during the year, the religious authorities simply did not invite Pérez to the ceremonies. This was done, he said, because they felt he wanted to destroy tradition and customs. Another former Alférez, a man who was particularly concerned with proper religious celebrations, complained that Pérez had been deficient as a Presidente because he did not attend the ceremonies during his term. According to a third account, Pérez regularly attended during the last two years of his term—after a change in church officials gave control of many church functions back to PRI people.

By April 1977, the split spread further in ceremonial life: the opposing groups sought to have separate Masses during fiestas, and the bishop of San Cristóbal wrote an open letter (in Spanish and Tzotzil) to the people of Zinacantán encouraging them to reunite.

8.7. Public construction provided still another arena for conflict during Pérez's term. The construction of a new town hall, with funds provided by the state and with unpaid labor contributed by Zinacantecos, established a new and lasting split. PAN members refused to give the days (usually three) customarily owed to municipio projects, and the ledgers recording PRI contributions went into the political caldron to simmer until a PAN Presidente was elected in 1982 (see the account of Pedro Vázquez's conference with the governor of Chiapas later in the text).

Another major construction project of the Pérez years, the rerouting, construction, and paving of the road into Zinacantán Center was completely financed and administered by the state. Outside officials hired and paid all labor, and kept all records. This procedure, the usual one for expensive government projects in the 1970's, was soon to be changed radically under the CODECOM program that arrived with the new Presidente Municipal's term.

A major fire that did extensive damage to the church of San Lorenzo also contributed to turmoil during the period.

8.8. The events of Pérez's term fit the activist mood that grew in the Echeverría administration (1970–76). During the period, Indian participation in politics increased, especially through the large and maturing group of Indian employees of INI, who had been recruited as young men in the 1950's and 1960's. Government agencies competed to influence (control) these Indian leaders and their communities.

A major mobilization of Indian leaders occurred in October 1974 at a four-day congress commemorating the five-hundredth anniversary of Fray Bartolomé de las Casas, the sixteenth-century Bishop of San Cristóbal de las Casas, who was famous for his defense of the interests of Chiapas Indians. The Congress was opened by Pablo Ramírez in the name of the governor (Velasco Suárez, who later spoke) and Angel Robles, then director of PRODESCH (and the state Department of Indian Affairs); the congress had been organized under the direction of Bishop Samuel Ruiz of San Cristóbal, at the request of Angel Robles. As far as I can tell, it represented a rather tense standoff of state and PRI interests, which sought to incorporate all effectively mobilized populations, and church programs, which sought to promote activism in support of social justice.

More than 1,000 Indian delegates attended. They produced resolutions on land, commerce, education, and health that clarified Indian "demands" of rights and resources, and received extensive coverage in the national press. Though lasting changes are hard to isolate and identify, the congress clearly reflected and reenforced the Indian political activism on the state-wide scene that made the events in Zinacantán possible. Conflict during the Pérez administration in Zinacantán reflected many events in the region.

All my information on the congress comes from documents provided to me by Robert Wasserstrom, who also gave me his recollections of the period.

8.9. The boxes were in Hteklum, Patosil, Nachig, Navenchauc, and Zequentic. The Center constituted one district, and Patosil and Salinas another. Otherwise, the districts corresponded to the superhamlets (Chapter 6, especially Table 6.3). One consultant lumped Hteklum with Patosil and Salinas, and said the Nachig district actually voted in Paste.

8.10. As I understand it, CODECOM was unique to Chiapas, and served as a model for other state-level programs that began later. The national program was López Portillo's Convenio Unico de Coordinación (CUC).

8.11. According to Patricia Armendáriz, Acting Director of PRODESCH during part of 1981, state law allowed more than one Foundation, though all had to report through the Presidente Municipal.

8.12. For example, from CODECOM funds a park was built in Hteklum, gravel was spread in a low, wet spot near the church of San Sebastián in the Center (Vogt 1969: 376–77), and the Municipio Secretary (Chapter 6) was paid his monthly salary. The park cost $347,600, exactly half of which was value attributed to labor contributed by Zinacantecos who provided unpaid, unskilled labor as part of their obligation to the municipio. According to Manuel Hernández, the CODECOM secretary from January 1980 until mid-1981, $165,000 of the $173,800 in CODECOM money in the project went directly to an Apaz man who contracted for the job. The gravel-spreading project involved $125,000 paid directly to a man from the Center who owned dump trucks, and $25,000 as value attributed to contributed labor; and the Municipio Secretary's salary ($20,000 per month) was an expense without matching labor contributions.

8.13. A list of more than 150 projects was in the books kept by Manuel Hernández (see note 8.12). They included, for example, stairs built in a public area of Chainatic. That project was administered directly by the Agente Municipal, who came to Hteklum each Sunday to get the money he needed, and, according to Manuel Hernández, it used $54,300 in CODECOM funds, and showed $50,000 in labor contributed by the men of Chainatic. Many hamlets built public open spaces including basketball courts and buildings to house their Agente, and improved streets, added to schools, and acquired public property (including marimbas). As noted in Chapter 3, more than $10 million were spent over the three years.

8.14. De la Cruz had headed the group that controlled the first Zinacanteco-owned truck in the early 1960's, and Marcos Pérez had run buses from the Center to San Cristóbal in the 1970's. The microbuses (at roughly $290,000 each, without finance charges) were financed by a commercial bank with the help of a high PRODESCH official, who was de la Cruz's *compadre*, according to one knowledgeable man.

8.15. Each group had legal status with state agencies and regulated competition among its vehicles. In 1984, the Altos de Chiapas group, a union of owners, included 41 vehicles owned by Zinacantecos and six by people from other municipios (of the 41, 17 were from Nachig and 12 from Navenchauc). The other three groups were organized as cooperatives: the two that made an agreement with the Altos de Chiapas group had a total of 16 vehicles and 23 members, and the de la Cruz/Conde group had six vehicles and 36 members. This information is from Hernández (1984).

8.16. Benjamin (1989: 236) reports that PAN victories were recognized in 1982 municipio elections in Acala, Arriaga, and Zinacantán. My sources may have missed Arriaga.

8.17. I was in the field from June 19 to 29, again from July 17 to August 11, and again from December 10 to 15, 1982. Thus I was not present for most of the events described below. They are reconstructed from interviews given in December, by Yermo and a number of others, and from notes and texts made at the time by Juan Vázquez and others. Yermo attended an August 15 meeting of PRI leaders and the August 22 public meetings. Most of the important points in his account of the August 22 meeting are confirmed by other accounts, and none are contradicted.

8.18. Yermo's report makes sense. A Martínez supporter said that he had lost by more, 3,209 to 2,318, but said that it was because the Camioneros loaded people up on trucks after they voted and took them by the outside officials to vote again.

8.19. I find no earlier references to "Campesinos" in field notes and texts, but the usage may have begun earlier. For more on the use of group names see notes 8.29 and 11.10.

8.20. This event, like many others in the years that followed, involved blows that drew blood. Usually they involved much smaller groups, and may have been personal as well as political in nature. In 1985 there was one killing that was apparently the direct result of an argument about political differences. I know of no others.

8.21. Prices rose in many sectors, but the government kept food prices and corn prices down by avoiding increases in prices paid to farmers. Corn was cheap ($1,200 per 100-kg bag) and, in order to compete with prevailing cash wages of $400 to $500 per day for laborers in Tuxtla and up to $200 per day (with meals and transport) for fieldwork, many farmers paying in kind had to give more than twice the wage that prevailed in the 1960's (Cancian 1972: 51). For more see note 5.2.

8.22. Two consultants said that Pedro Vázquez was in the town hall for a few days at the beginning of his term. Then he was forced out by Manuel Garcia and the Truckers. Most others apparently forgot this detail.

8.23. I have only one report of totals for this election (compared to many for the November election). The numbers are reasonable.

8.24. Only one other issue was discussed at any length. The Official spoke about the importance of registering women to vote, and about the program for women that the party was going to sponsor. For the most part his remarks were met by smiles, smirks, and bits of laughter. I observed many women voting in Nachig in the 1988 national elections.

8.25. When this arrangement was made, the special status of Hteklum and Vochojvo was eliminated. Expenses for decoration that they tradition-ally paid were added to band expenses, and they were assigned shares as regular hamlets were.

8.26. Salaries for political officials in Indian municipios, where they had formerly served without pay, were introduced during the period of govern-ment decentralization in the 1980's.

8.27. These supporters still included most of PAN in Apaz and most of PRI in the Cornfields. According to various Zinacantecos, the three bands were sponsored by what amounted to four groups, for both PAN and PRI sup-porters of the Presidente were loyal to their party.

8.28. Pedro Vázquez also lost his traditional role as initiator of prepara-tions for major fiestas. For the Fiesta of Sagrado Corazón in June, a new practice was established: the Church Committee Head administered the naming of the Fiesta Committee Head and the calculation of the hamlet shares of expenses. Though Vázquez was now out of the process, troubles continued, and bands continued to represent major political factions. The same three groups sponsored bands at the Fiesta of Sagrado Corazón and again in August at the Fiesta of San Lorenzo.

8.29. I have simplified the names of factions somewhat to make it easier to follow the events. Names varied by period and by party of speaker. For example, after the May 1984 establishment of the committee called the "Foundation," people who supported those who controlled it often referred to themselves as supporters of the Foundation, while the opposition called them "Truckers." At other points they called themselves "PRIistas" and la-beled the opposition Peasants as the "two-faced" party (because of their votes for the PAN candidate in 1982). A Peasant member said: "They're not PRI. We're PRI. They're Truckers." The Truckers rarely called themselves Truckers, but always acknowledged the common use of the name after it emerged. For more see note 11.10.

8.30. Some made an effort to maintain harmony despite the disarray. One Scribe, for example, encouraged the Elders to accompany all the bands during fiestas.

Notes to Chapter 9

9.1. For more on the waiting lists see Cancian (1965: 176). Jan Rus and Robert Wasserstrom (1980) differed with my earlier description of the origin of the waiting lists in Zinacantán (1965), and I responded (1986, 1990). Rus recently discovered documents that show there were waiting lists in Cha-mula in the nineteenth century. Given my purposes, historical origins are less important than the changes in demand analyzed in this chapter. Wait-ing lists of various kinds have been associated with cargo systems for a long time (Thompson 1978).

9.2. The former Alcaldes Viejos whose lists are used include Antonio Pérez Shulumte of Apaz; Pedro Uch, Domingo Sánchez Es, and Mariano Vázquez Shulhol of Navenchauc; Lorenzo López and Mariano Pérez of Paste; Juan Pérez Hacienda (through his sons Domingo and Manuel) and

Andres Ahte of Hteklum; and José Hernández Ko' of Patosil. Without their help, and that of many Scribes and friends, this work would not have been possible.

9.3. In 1981, Nachig had four men waiting (three for the senior position and one for the junior position), and Paste had 17. Navenchauc had three for its new cargo in 1982, and in 1984 Elanvo had two and Tierra Blanca seven. For older cargos, Navenchauc had 15 in 1982 and Salinas had 20. I have no information on Apaz.

9.4. Some noted that the Junior Alcalde Viejo often had served only two previous cargos, but, they said, the Senior Alcalde Viejo had to serve three cargos before taking his position. As far as I can tell, no Senior Alcalde Viejo in at least the previous 20 years had entered after two previous cargos. My records of careers since 1970 show no previous case, and my memory of and questioning about the 1960's make it almost certain that no such compromise happened in that period. Yet, if the data I collected in the early 1960's are accurate, a similar compromise had happened in the distant past. Among 22 careers leading to Senior Alcalde Viejo, two showed only two previous cargos (Cancian 1965: 208). Whatever the history of actual careers, in the mid-1970's Zinacantecos saw the Elders' action as unusual, even unique.

9.5. My sense is that, by the late 1980's, the norm had changed; i.e., Zinacantecos no longer expected a Senior Alcalde Viejo to have three previous cargos.

9.6. In the early 1980's, Marcos Pérez helped PAN men get official papers in San Cristóbal, so that they would not have to serve.

The tension in the religious cargo organization caused by the political factionalism seemed to subside in the middle 1980's, but in summer 1988 it appeared in a new form. The civil authorities led by the Presidente decided to use revenue-sharing funds (Chapter 3) to construct a market in an area above the back part of the church of San Lorenzo—an area traditionally used by the Sacristans for a small cornfield. (The new market was needed because a previous public-works project had paved over the old market site below the church, and vendors could no longer drive in stakes to hold up canopies over their stalls.) The political opposition (including two active Sacristans) soon had an injunction against the project, arguing that the church, like all churches in Mexico, is official federal-government property and that the Presidente sought to convert land that benefited the church into a source of market taxes for himself. Before long, one opposition leader was beat up, and others were jailed. Most important, given our present concern, the Mayordomos as a block supported the Sacristans and threatened to skip a scheduled flower change (Cancian 1965) in the church.

9.7. The hamlet managed to keep them filled for more than 25 years. Occasionally, when a man withdrew just before or during his cargo, the hamlet was served by only three cargo holders. When cargos served in the Center were empty for similar reasons, the Elders rushed to fill them.

I am indebted to George Collier for the news that the two Apaz Mesonero cargos were eliminated in 1987. He also reported (in 1987, and in 1989) that from about 1960 to 1987 the mean age of first cargo for Apaz men dropped from the middle forties to 32 or 33, and that a number of Protestant families had left Apaz.

9.8. When Apaz was a PAN stronghold led by Hernández, politics played a small part in the cargo system. In 1980, PRI men withdrew from the local waiting lists, but in August 1981 (when PRI had 50 of the 220 men in Apaz) Hernández thought they were about to return, and one of them was scheduled to serve a cargo in Apaz beginning in December. In November when Hernández (and Marcos Pérez) signed an agreement that returned them to PRI, some Apaz men were angered by the move (see Chapter 8), and the hamlet became more evenly divided (63 percent PAN to 37 percent PRI in 1983, and 60 percent PAN to 40 percent PRI in 1987).

9.9. Salinas, with Petztoj and Tierra Blanca, had supported the Salinas cargos since the nineteenth century, and the Tierra Blanca cargo in recent years, but no requests for first-level cargos in the Center by men of these hamlets are recorded on any of the waiting lists, while Elanvo had two in 1983, and one in 1980 and 1987. I cannot explain the substantial decrease in tax shares of both Elanvo and the Salinas area in the 1980's (Table B.4). Population figures from government censuses give them both greater shares (Table B.2).

9.10. I have identified the Senior Alcalde Viejo for every year from 1960 to 1988, except for 1964, 1965, and 1967. During the 1960–88 period, the only men from Apaz to serve were the three just mentioned (information on the third man was gathered before he entered and not confirmed after service). Of the 23 men not from Apaz, Nachig had six (1963, 1970, 1976, 1977, 1981, 1987), Navenchauc six (1966, 1971, 1973, 1974, 1978, 1984), Paste five (1968 [from Shulvo], 1972, 1975, 1980, 1986), Jechtoch two (1985, 1988), Vochojvo two (1969, 1983), Hteklum one (1979), and Zequentic one (1982).

9.11. There are more complex frameworks that make our understanding more complex, but they do not permit us to exclude alternative approaches. Of course, events in Zinacantán and elsewhere are not obligated to facilitate the choice between alternative theories.

Notes to Chapter 10

10.1. In this chapter I use both "meaning" and "social implications" to talk about the importance of cargos in Zinacantán's social life. "Social implications" is a good term to use because it emphasizes the distinction between the cargos as institutionalized roles (perduring sets of behaviors) and the social/cultural meaning they were given in context. Since the context changed over the period discussed, the implications of "the same" (in terms of institutionalized roles) behavior changed. "Social implications" is also good because, to some people, "meaning" is given only in human consciousness—while the "meaning" I am pointing to is more often revealed in behavior. On the other hand, "social implications" seems overly abstract for activities so central to everyday life in Zinacantán.

10.2. See Cancian (1965: chapter 8), and J. B. Haviland (1977: chapter 6), for discussion. Haviland suggests (p. 111, and see also p. 105) that my difficulty in getting simple ratings in the abstract reflects the complex ways Zinacantecos use cargo service and other factors to construct an individual's reputation.

10.3. John Haviland is clearly uncomfortable with the use of the Prestige Scale as a complete measure of reputation (1977: especially p. 111). I agreed with him in the 1960's when I said, "Rank on the Prestige Scale is less than a complete measure of an individual's community-wide standing" (1965: 109); and I agreed more in the 1980's. Nevertheless, his discussion entitled "Cargos and Public Identity" (J. B. Haviland 1977: 113–20) was greatly weakened because he decided not to use the difference between cargos in his analysis (p. 113). All cargoholders were lumped and contrasted with all those who had not held cargos, leading him to the conclusion that

> the Who's Who [his extensive interviews on reputation] suggests that cargo service is simply a feature of advancing age in Zinacantán, with other socially important variables equally distributed among participants and nonparticipants. As men get older they are increasingly likely to take cargos; but participation may arguably not affect their social standing except as it allows them to conform to the expectation that a man will perform cargos as befits his age. (p. 116)

As far as I can see, Haviland's conclusion does not follow from his data. The extensive case materials he presents suggest that the differences between cargos do matter, and the display of many cases on which he bases this conclusion (figure 8, p. 115) does not include data that speak to the issue.

10.4. Here, as in 1965 (p. 109), I believe that the consistency with which the Prestige Scale orders data on cargo careers and the cargos served by sons and their fathers (shown later in this chapter) is further evidence of its soundness. While the scale remained valid, the prestige measured by the scale became less important as cargo service became less important.

10.5. As expectations change, what constitutes an exception changes. Given the many innovations and the many negotiations between Elders, individuals, and hamlets cited in Chapter 9 and later in this chapter, expectations probably shifted faster and were less widely shared in the 1970's than in the 1960's. As I see it, new expectations become traditions (and thus become stickier, see the Introduction to Part II) as time passes. The changes in Zinacantán that I am describing remained new (and therefore less traditional) because behavior continually shifted. I have no systematic evidence for this framework in this context.

10.6. The numbers of cargos served at each level by men in the Nachig Census were, for 1967, 99, 36, 20, 4; for 1983, 126, 54, 20, 3; and, for 1987, 134, 55, 24, 4.

The lone exception in 1967 was to a man who served Junior Alcalde Viejo (D2) as a first cargo. His is the case mentioned by Haviland (see the text below). He died before the 1983 census.

The other exceptions (identified by letter and number codes found in

Table D.1) follow. All the cases in the 1983 census were also in the 1987 census. Five cases involved serving Alcalde Viejo as a third cargo (A1, B2, D1; MFN, B5, D1; A1, B1, D2; A2, B1, D2; A8, B11, D2). The second and fifth of these were not in the 1983 census. Four cases involved serving Regidor as a second cargo (A1, C2; A7, C2; A4, C4; A6, C1). The last of these was not in the 1983 census. The A10, MFN case is discussed in the text, as is the career with two exceptions in it (A5, A4, B1, D1).

In searching the 1967 census for exceptions, I used data on cargos available for the total number of married men *(N = 258)*, not the 208 men for whom complete data are available (see Table C.4). For 1983 and 1987, all the relevant men are included in the regular population *(N = 315 for 1983 and N = 305 for 1987)*.

10.7. Once, Mayor did not count as a first-level cargo, so men who passed it had to serve a mayordomo-type cargo also if they wanted to continue a career in the cargo system. Later, when Mayor did count, in rare cases men who passed it stepped back and started again at the first level, usually saying that they wished to have a proper career (see Cancian 1965: 163; J. B. Haviland 1977: 97).

10.8. I heard this explanation often in the 1980's. Many men who offered it were Elders or sympathetic to Elders. I suspect that lower-ranking individuals, who were more likely to be on the other end of the pressure to serve, may have seen it differently.

10.9. In the 1970's and 1980's, the Elders often recruited men to serve C3 and C4, for, as Table D.2 shows, after the mid-1970's they were the least-popular cargos. But those efforts were more routine; the problem was obvious long before the service was to begin. These cargos were probably often served as second cargos as well—as for example the C3, 1981 and the C4, 1984, who were not from Nachig. Most Nachig men who passed Regidor took the position as a third cargo (13 of 17 in the 1967 census).

10.10. In 1965 I knew about the D2 served as a first cargo (note 10.6), but ignored it when making my interpretations. My Total Career Sample (1965: 208–9) included only careers with more than the one cargo (p. 203). Two cases dominated the "unusual careers" category in my field notes from the early 1960's: this D2 case and an Alcalde Shuves who had been removed from a previous Alférez cargo for drinking excessively. Descriptions of the D2 case by three consultants (with names of persons and cargos made consistent with the conventions used here) follow:

By Mariano: Mariano mentioned José, who was to be given A11, but asked for D2 and got it. Mariano seemed to think it funny in some way.

By Juan: It happened this way: the man who was to have the post died shortly before he was to enter. . . . None of the other people on the waiting list wanted the cargo for there was too little time to get ready, so the Elders named José, who was old enough to have the cargo, even though he had passed no other cargos. Juan knows of no other people who have similar records, and didn't seem to expect there should be any.

By Antonio: José didn't pass anything—not even A11 or Principal. Then when he was old, about 68, he went to ask for something like A10 or A4. The Elders contended that this was not a cargo in keeping with his advanced age and they gave him D2. . . . Antonio's explanation of this is that José was away for a long time working in the [plantations].

Otherwise the "unusual careers" category contained only the case of a man who said he wanted ADC as a fourth cargo, and an unconfirmed report of a four-cargo, three-Alférez career that met order of service rules.

10.11. A second difference between John Haviland's conclusions and mine points in the same direction. In 1965 I said, "The Alférez Santo Domingo [ASD] may be served as a second, third, or fourth cargo. In recent years it has seldom been served as a second-level position" (p. 31). My Total Career Sample (pp. 208–9) listed ASD served at the second, third, and fourth levels in one, ten, and six cases, respectively, plus one man who served it as both his second and his third cargos. Haviland says:

Cancian claims that . . . [ASD] can be a second-, third- or fourth-level cargo. I have no case in the entire Who's Who of a man passing this cargo as a second-level position. . . . Judging by the reported careers, the rule seems to be for . . . [ASD] to come as third, more often fourth cargo. . . . At least one man reportedly did . . . [ASD] twice, as both his third and fourth cargos. (1977: 234)

Perhaps ASD was popular as a third cargo before 1960, and became more frequently a fourth cargo in the period of cargo fever around the time of Haviland's fieldwork. An item from my 1961 field notes suggests that the pressure for change in expectations was building even then.

ASD: Mariano stated with confidence and repeatedly that ASD is always a fourth cargo. This is obviously not true from the comments of others and from cases. It seems to be always a terminal cargo, but Mariano insisted that one must always pass three cargos before it. Can it be that this is a new attitude that is forming—for Mariano is still young—not nearly as old as the informants who with confidence and calm give cases of ASD as a second, third, and fourth cargo.

ASD remained a way to end one's career. By the early 1980's, it was possible to have a complete career in three cargos; thus, disagreement about whether ASD was more properly a third or a fourth cargo was moot. The 1967, 1983, and 1987 Nachig censuses show one, one, and two cases of ASD as a third cargo, and two, one, and no cases of ASD as a fourth cargo.

Haviland reported that, counter to what my consultants said in the early 1960's (Cancian 1965: 31), his consultants said that ADC could not be served as a second cargo (J. B. Haviland 1977: 233). All the cases in my Total Career Sample (1965: 208), and all the cases in the Nachig censuses (seven, two, and two cases for 1967, 1983, and 1987) support his consultants.

10.12. Zinacantecos commented on inconsistent careers—especially when a low-ranking second cargo following a high-ranking first cargo was connected to some kind of personal scandal. They also noticed people who took cargos that seemed inconsistent with their economic resources, especially when a rich man tried to get away with an inexpensive cargo. But the norms invoked usually concerned what might be called social propriety, as contrasted with conformity to ritual patterns.

10.13. There are many reviews of the various interpretations of the cargo system. Greenberg (1981b) sees various interpretations as appropriate to different contexts. See also Greenberg (1981a), Cancian (1967), Wolf (1986), Stephen and Dow (1990), and the work they cite.

10.14. The difference in cargo careers between mobile and non-mobile men reported on the basis of the 1967 data from Nachig and Apaz (Cancian 1974a) does not appear clearly in the 1983 data for Nachig. The numbers are too small to support speculation.

10.15. There were 32 first-level cargos in 1960, when the municipio's population was 7,650. Estimated (1965: 162–65) and (actual) cargos in 1970 and 1980 were 36 (36) and 40 (42). Population figures were 9,257 (11,428) and 11,201 (15,000). The 15,000 actual population figure for 1980 is a compromise between the national census (13,006) and the CNEP census (18,798). See Appendix B.

10.16. They took 51 of the 320 mayordomo-type cargos served in the Center that were available during the 16-year period. Because Nachig had 10.4 percent of the municipal population during the period, that was 153 percent of their share. Because they took less than their share of Mayor positions, and less than their share of cargos served outside the Center, overall they filled 114 percent of their share of all cargo service in the municipio. This figure assumes eight Mayor cargos per year (and a varying number of hamlet cargos based on the date of their creation). Counting just the desirable mayordomo-type cargos in the Center and the other hamlets, Nachig men took 127 percent of their share.

10.17. Interpretation of marriage patterns is complicated by the limitations of the census data: data on the bridegrooms are limited because many of them were not old enough to have passed cargos, and data on fathers are limited because many of them were not assigned economic ranks, because they had died before the census was taken. Interpretation is also limited because the economic rank measure represents different points in the life cycle for different bridegrooms. Nevertheless, it seems likely that people and families involved in marriages attended to the economic status of the other parties. The Spearman correlation of fathers' 1967 wealth for the 67 couples who were new in the 1983 census (i.e., were not in the 1967 census) and had both fathers in the 1967 census was .29 ($p<.02$). Further evidence for the tendency is in Table E.1. It uses cargo service as an index of wealth for the older (parental) generation for which I have no direct wealth rating, and wealth rank from the 1983 census for the younger (sons/husbands) generation. It is apparent that young men who are themselves wealthier tend to marry women whose fathers are wealthier. The pattern is clearest if all the middle categories (which usually are based on a small number of cases) are left out; i.e., the pattern shows best in the corners of the three tables. Though it involves a dangerous leap from the cross-sectional data on husband's rank to the factors that led to the marriage, I assume that the husband's rank involves qualities he brought to the marriage. If that is so, then we may conclude that choice of marriage partners in 1983 still reflected social stratification; but that cargos were no longer good markers of social position. The new patterns were tied more directly to wealth.

Notes to Chapter 11

11.1. The two without wealth ranks were added to the census after the 1983 wealth ranking was done.

11.2. Among those attending, the poorer man was not the one who supported the Peasants. By 1987, however, both he and the Peasant supporter had switched parties—such that wealth and party were perfectly aligned. The one Truckers supporter among the men who did not attend was the rich man.

11.3. Because the 1967 and 1983 data in Table 11.1 have roughly similar numbers of cases and marginals, it is possible to see the substantive pattern in the counts, and more easily in the residuals. Clearly there is not much of a relationship (interaction) between wealth and age in the 1983 data.

11.4. "Standardized residuals are obtained by dividing each residual by the square root of the expected count. Adjusted residuals are calculated by dividing each standardized residual by the estimate of its own standard error. If the number of cells in the table is large when compared to the number of estimated parameters for a model, then the adjusted and standardized residuals should be similar" (Norušis 1988: 330). "The value 2 [of the adjusted residual] is a rule of thumb for 'suspiciousness' since, in a standard normal distribution, only 5% of the absolute values exceed 1.96" (ibid.). Adjusted residuals are also called adjusted standardized residuals (SPSS-X 1983: 294).

11.5. Table 11.2 also introduces the new occupational categories that will be used in this chapter. The first five are the most important—the first four because of their size and their relation to traditional Zinacanteco occupations, and the fifth (truck owners) because it is new, fairly large, and very sharply defined in terms of both age and wealth. To create this simplified classification of occupations I (1) placed most men with two occupations in the category that produced the greater income for them; (2) put those who got equal income from corn farming and wage labor into a semiproletarian category; and (3) put ambiguous cases and difficult-to-classify jobs into the "Other" category shown in Table E.2. I then lumped that "Other" category with small categories ($N \leq 15$; see Table E.2) to make the "Other" category shown in Table 11.2.

The classification of occupations created by the first three steps just mentioned is summarized in Table E.2. The 91 corn farmers in the first row include 75 who farmed corn exclusively and 16 who got more from corn farming than from wage labor (N = 12, from row 12, Table 2.4), operating a grinding mill (N = 2), or owning a truck (N = 2). The second row includes those whose incomes from corn farming and wage labor were equal. Five men who are listed in Table 2.4 (row 7) as selling popsicles and/or soda pop in Tuxtla are classified as wage earners in the third row here. They include Antonio AA. The 36 cases in "Other" include 12 with single occupations that do not fit the simplified categories, and 25 with two occupations—15 whose incomes from corn farming and other activities were equal (trade five, mason three, other seven), three where labor and trade produced equal incomes, one that was hard to classify, and five old men who had retired and were not included in Table 2.4.

11.6. "Wealth" is a concept, a label, for continuing control of economic resources. As I use it, wealth implies more than "income," which can be easily lost, and more than control of capital. In Nachig in the 1980's both the income from secure government jobs and the income from secure control of transport routes were components of wealth. My measure for wealth is a rank scale constructed (in octiles) from averaging pile-sort ratings by Yermo and other consultants (Cancian 1972: 166; Appendix C, herein). I believe my description of the wealth concept above is similar to the idea they used in making their rankings.

11.7. Here, in keeping with the emphasis on social position, the variables are relabeled as occupations and public roles. I use the term "social position" where I might have used "individual roles." They are essentially equivalent in an analysis that is neither macro (societal) nor micro (individual), but focuses on people as expressions of social positions (Burt 1980). While many social scientists believe this is an appropriate level of analysis, thinking tends to flow to the macro or the micro pole (see Cancian 1979: 4–6 for a related discussion).

11.8. Tables 11.1 and 11.2 include an anomaly that suggests we cannot fully understand the new inequality by looking at only two variables at a time. Older men tend to be corn farmers and corn farmers tend to be richer (Table 11.2); yet older men are not richer (Table 11.1). The anomaly is dispelled by separating corn farmers (N = 91) from others (N = 224). In each subpopulation the younger men are slightly richer than the older men. This is true despite the fact that when the tables are merged there is no relationship (interaction) between age and wealth (cross-product ratio = 1.0). Because such complex interactions may be hidden by bivariate analysis, I used log-linear analysis to check for higher-order interaction effects. Among the many combinations of age, wealth, occupation, father's cargos, wife's father's cargos, public service, and political affiliation, only one three-way interaction produced a partial chi-square great enough to exceed the .01 probability standard I used. It was age, father's cargos, and occupation. It depended mostly on the fact that older men who were in trade tended to have fathers with high cargos, and younger men in trade tended to have fathers with low cargos.

11.9. The census data show that more than half of the young had served at least one civil position by 1987, while only 38 percent of older men had done any civil service—despite their longer years of eligibility. Civil service done by older men many years ago may have been undercounted in the Nachig Census, but such undercounting would account for only a fraction of the difference shown in the table.

11.10. Labeling for the groups varied with the position of the speaker and over time. PRI/Truckers called themselves "PRI" and called the Peasants "PAN" or used circumlocutions like "two-faced people" for them. PRI/Truckers recognized but rarely used the "Truckers" label for themselves. Peasants routinely used the Peasant/Truckers contrast. Core PAN people used the terms "PAN," "PRI," and sometimes "PAN/Peasants." The "Truckers" and "Peasants" labels were used by more people of all parties towards the end of the period. My use of the term "opposition" for the Peasants is intended to describe their position: they were not in power in Nachig, despite their majority.

11.11. Table 11.3 shows that wage workers are from poor families and that semiproletarians, overall, are from average families. Data on their fathers' cargo careers show both groups to be, on the average, from poor families.

11.12. George Collier is preparing a book that includes discussion of important Mexican Marxist thinkers and rich data on household formation in Apaz over recent decades. Collier (1989) gives a preview of part of his argument.

11.13. At least one approach would lump most Zinacantecos as an undifferentiated mass of peasants or marginalized people. There are, I think, obvious good reasons to reject this approach—especially when focusing on analysis of the local situation.

Notes to Chapter 12

12.1. Generalizing about the political system remains difficult.

12.2. Because local systems, at least in these times, are always embedded in larger systems, some scholars have been tempted to focus almost exclusively on the most inclusive system. Immanuel Wallerstein, the major leader of this expansionist movement (Cancian 1985), made clear statements and is thus a useful point of contrast. His framework oversimplifies in two important ways. First, Wallerstein's ideal type is based on a single, inclusive, self-contained system (1976b: 229). This quest for analytic totality drives out more complex analytic schemes, including ones that use multiple systems of different sizes. Second, since the dynamics of the most inclusive system (popularly the capitalist world-system) are primarily economic, his analysis appropriately emphasizes economic relations—and thereby obscures the dynamics of smaller systems.

Notes to the Epilogue

Ep.1. Among the landmark books are Clifford and Marcus (1986) and Marcus and Fischer (1986). The writers I cited in Chapter 1 (Karp 1986; Myers

1988; Spiro 1986; Watson 1987) and Sangren (1988) contribute to the discussion and cite many other contributions.

Ep.2. Francesca Cancian pointed out the many parallels between my statement and the scholarly statement by Carr and Kemmis (1986: 120–22). I also find much of value in Hull (1988) and Longino (1990).

Ep.3. There are two great Western ways of making the balance: democratic institutions that protect diversity, and Christian institutions that forgive transgressions. The former seems more appropriate to this situation, but both may be useful.

REFERENCES CITED

Aguirre Beltrán, Gonzalo, Alfonso Villa Rojas, et al.
  1975. El Indigenismo en Acción. XXV Aniversario del Centro Coordinador Indigenista Tzeltal-Tzotzil, Chiapas. México: INI y SEP.
Almanaque
  1984. Almanaque de Chiapas de 1984. México: Almanaque de México.
ANDSA
  1964. Esquema Social y Económico de los Estados de la República Mexicana. Almacenes Nacionales de Depósito, S.A. (Vol. II).
Barkin, David, and Blanca Suárez
  1981. El Fin de la Autosuficiencia Alimentaria. México D.F.: Nueva Imagen.
Bender, Thomas
  1978. Community and Social Change in America. New Brunswick: Rutgers University Press.
Benjamin, Thomas
  1989. A Rich Land, A Poor People: Politics and Society in Modern Chiapas. Albuquerque: University of New Mexico Press.
Bricker, Victoria Reifler
  1981. The Indian Christ, the Indian King—The Historical Substrate of Maya Myth and Ritual. Austin: University of Texas Press.
Bricker, Victoria R., and Gary H. Gossen, eds.
  1989. Ethnographic Encounters in Southern Mesoamerica: Essays in Honor of Evon Zartman Vogt. Institute for Mesoamerican Studies, SUNY Albany, Study in Cultures and Society, Vol. 3 (Distributed by University of Texas Press).
Bunnin, Nicolas F.
  1966. La Industria de las Flores en Zinacantán. Pp. 208–32 in E. Z. Vogt, ed., 1966.

Buraway, Michael
  1987. The Limits of Wright's Analytical Marxism and an Alternative. Berkeley Journal of Sociology 32: 51–72.
Burt, Ronald S.
  1980. Models of Network Structure. Annual Review of Sociology 6: 79–141.
Buzaglo, Jorge
  1984. Planning the Mexican Economy: Alternative Development Strategies. New York: St. Martin's Press.
Cancian, Francesca
  1975. What Are Norms? New York: Cambridge University Press.
Cancian, Frank
  1963. Informant Error and Native Prestige Ranking in Zinacantán. American Anthropologist 65: 1068–75.
  1965. Economics and Prestige in a Maya Community: The Religious Cargo System in Zinacantán. Stanford: Stanford University Press.
  1967. Political and Religious Organizations. In the Handbook of Middle American Indians, Vol. 6, Robert Wauchope, ed. Austin: University of Texas Press.
  1972. Change and Uncertainty in a Peasant Economy: The Maya Corn Farmers of Zinacantán. Stanford: Stanford University Press.
  1974a. New Patterns of Social Stratification in the Zinacantán Cargo System. Journal of Anthropological Research 30: 164–73.
  1974b. Another Place: Photographs of a Maya Community. San Francisco: The Scrimshaw Press.
  1976. Economía y Prestigio en una Communidad Maya. México: Instituto Nacional Indigenista.
  1979. The Innovator's Situation: Upper-Middle-Class Conservatism in Agricultural Communities. Stanford: Stanford University Press.
  1985. The Boundaries of Rural Stratification Systems. Pp. 69–82 in Billie R. DeWalt and Pertti J. Pelto, eds., Micro and Macro Levels of Analysis in Anthropology: Issues in Theory and Research. Boulder: Westview Press.
  1986. Las Listas de Espera en el Sistema de Cargos de Zinacantán: Cambios Sociales, Políticos y Económicos (1952–1980). America Indígena 46: 477–94.
  1987. Proletarianization in Zinacantán, 1960–1983. Pp. 131–42 in Morgan D. Maclachlan, ed., Household Economies and Their Transformations. Lanham, Md.: University Press of America.
  1989. Economic Behavior in Peasant Communities. Pp. 127–70 in Stuart Plattner, ed., Economic Anthropology. Stanford: Stanford University Press.
  1990. The Zinacantán Cargo Waiting Lists as a Reflection of Social, Political, and Economic Changes, 1952–1987. Pp. 63–76 in Lynn Ste-

phen and James Dow, eds., Class, Politics and Popular Religion in Mexico and Central America. American Anthropological Association.

Carr, Wilfred, and Stephen Kemmis
1986. Becoming Critical: Education, Knowledge and Action Research. London: The Falmer Press.

Castellanos Domínguez, Absalón
1983. Primer Informe de Gobierno, Chiapas. Tuxtla Gutiérrez.

Censo
1960, 1970, 1980. Censo General de Población. México: Estados Unidos Mexicanos.

Cernea, Michael M.
1983. A Social Methodology for Community Participation in Local Investments: The Experience of Mexico's PIDER Program. Washington: World Bank Staff Working Paper 598.

Chiapas
1980. CODECOM: Instructivo de Operación del Convenio de Confianza Municipal. Tuxtla Gutiérrez: (Gobierno del Estado).
1982a. Chiapas: Plan y Programas de Gobierno 1982–1988. Tuxtla Gutiérrez: (Gobierno del Estado).
1982b. Gobierno del Estado de Chiapas, 1980–1982: CODECOM, Resumen Estatal. Tuxtla Gutiérrez: (Gobierno del Estado).
1982c. Gobierno del Estado de Chiapas, 1980–1982: CODECOM, Resumen Municipal. Tuxtla Gutiérrez: (Gobierno del Estado).
1982d. Gobierno del Estado de Chiapas, 1980–1982: Obras del Gobierno de Juan Sabines Gutiérrez. Tuxtla Gutiérrez: (Gobierno del Estado).
1983. Plan Chiapas. Pub. Gobierno Constitucional de los Estados Unidos Mexicanos. Gobierno Constitucional del Estado de Chiapas.

Clifford, James, and George E. Marcus, eds.
1986. Writing Culture: The Poetics and Politics of Ethnography. Berkeley and Los Angeles: University of California Press.

Collier, George A.
1975. Fields of the Tzotzil: The Ecological Bases of Tradition in Highland Chiapas. Austin: University of Texas Press.
1987. Peasant Politics and the Mexican State: Indigenous Compliance in Highland Chiapas. Mexican Studies/Estudios Mexicanos 3: 71–98.
1989. Changing Inequality in Zinacantán: The Generations of 1918 and 1942. Pp. 111–23 in V. R. Bricker and G. H. Gossen, eds., 1989.

Collier, George A., and Daniel C. Mountjoy
1988. Adaptandose a la Crisis de los Ochenta: Cambios Socio-económicos en Apas, Zinacantán. San Cristobal: INAREMAC.

Collier, Jane F.
1973. Law and Social Change in Zinacantán. Stanford: Stanford University Press.

Columbia
1975. The New Columbia Encyclopedia. New York: Columbia University Press.

Comaroff, John L.
1982. Dialectical Systems, History and Anthropology: Units of Study and Questions of Theory. Journal of Southern African Studies 8: 143–72.

Comaroff, John L., and Simon Roberts
1981. Rules and Processes: The Cultural Logic of Dispute in an African Context. Chicago: University of Chicago Press.

Conrad, Geoffrey W., and Arthur A. Demarest
1984. Religion and Empire: The Dynamics of Aztec and Inca Expansionism. Cambridge: Cambridge University Press.

COPLADE
1983. Informes de Gobierno: Municipios del Estado Libre y Soberano de Chiapas. Tuxtla Gutiérrez: (Estado de Chiapas).

Cornelius, Wayne A.
1985. The Political Economy of México under de la Madrid: Austerity, Routinized Crises, and Nascent Recovery. Mexican Studies/Estudios Mexicanos 1: 83–124.

Coughenour, C. Milton
1984. Farmers and Farm Workers: Perspectives on Occupational Complexity and Change. Research in Rural Sociology and Development 1: 1–35.

Dahrendorf, Ralf
1968. Essays in the Theory of Society. Stanford: Stanford University Press.

Deere, Carmen Diana
1987. The Peasantry in Political Economy: Trends of the 1980's. Program in Latin American Studies, Occasional Papers Series, no. 19. University of Massachusetts at Amherst.

Dennis, Philip A.
1973. The Oaxacan Village President as Political Middleman. Ethnology 12: 419–27.

Edel, Matthew
1962. Zinacantán's Ejido: The Effects of Mexican Land Reform on an Indian Community. Columbia-Cornell-Harvard-Illinois Summer Field Studies Program in Mexico. (Mimeo)
1966. El Ejido de Zinacantán. Pp. 163–82 in E. Z. Vogt, ed., 1966.

Fabrega, Horacio, Jr., and Daniel B. Silver
1973. Illness and Shamanistic Curing in Zinacantán: An Ethnomedical Analysis. Stanford: Stanford University Press.

Fallers, L. A.
1961. Are African Cultivators to Be Called "Peasants"? Current Anthropology 2: 108–10.

FAO
   1983. Statistics on Agricultural Support Price—1972–1981. Rome: Food and Agriculture Organization of the United Nations (ESS/Misc/ 1983/1).

Fienberg, Stephen E.
   1980. The Analysis of Cross-Classified Categorical Data. 2d ed. Cambridge, Mass.: MIT Press.

Foster, George M.
   1964. Treasure Tales, and the Image of a State Economy in a Mexican Peasant Community. Journal of American Folklore 77: 39–44.

Geertz, Clifford
   1962. Studies in Peasant Life: Community and Society. Pp. 1–41 in Bernard J. Siegel, ed., Biennial Review of Anthropology, 1961. Stanford: Stanford University Press.

Greenberg, James B.
   1981a. Santiago's Sword: Chatino Peasant Religion and Economics. Berkeley and Los Angeles: University of California Press.
   1981b. Social Change and the Fiesta System in Mexican Indian Communities. Latin American Digest (University of Arizona) 15:1–5.

Haviland, John B.
   1977. Gossip, Reputation, and Knowledge in Zinacantán. Chicago: University of Chicago Press.
   n.d. Flowers for a Price. In Dennis E. Breedlove and Robert M. Laughlin, The Flowering of Man: A Tzotzil Botany of Zinacantán. Washington: Smithsonian Contributions to Anthropology. (In press)

Haviland, Leslie Knox McCullough
   1978. The Social Relations of Work in a Peasant Community. Ph.D. Dissertation, Department of Sociology, Harvard University.

Hernández, Hector Hugo
   1984. El Transporte en la Actividad Económica Campesina en Zinacantán, Chiapas. (Manuscript)

Hewitt de Alcántara, Cynthia
   1984. Anthropological Perspectives on Rural Mexico. New York: Routledge and Kegan Paul.

Heynig, Klaus
   1982. The Principal Schools of Thought on Peasant Economy. CEPAL Review 16: 113–39.

Hull, David L.
   1988. Science as Process. Chicago: University of Chicago Press.

IMF
   198–. International Financial Statistics Yearbook. Washington: International Monetary Fund. (Various annual volumes)

de Janvry, Alain
   1981. The Agrarian Question and Reformism in Latin America. Baltimore: The Johns Hopkins University Press.

de Janvry, Alain, and Ann Vandeman

1987. Patterns of Proletarianization in Agriculture: An International Comparison. Pp. 28–73 in Morgan D. Maclachlan, ed., Household Economics and Their Transformations. Lanham, Md.: University Press of America.

Karp, Ivan

1986. Agency and Social Theory: A Review of Anthony Giddens. American Ethnologist 13: 131–37.

Laughlin, Robert M.

1975. The Great Tzotzil Dictionary of San Lorenzo Zinacantán. Washington: Smithsonian Contributions to Anthropology 19.

Lenin, V. I.

1899. The Development of Capitalism in Russia. 2d rev. ed. Moscow: Progress Publishers, 1964.

Longino, Helen E.

1990. Science as Social Knowledge: Value and Objectivity in Scientific Inquiry. Princeton: Princeton University Press.

Loyola, Luis J.

1988. Brokerage, Capital Accumulation and Economic Development: Transporters in the Process of Economic and Political Change in Chiapas, Mexico. Ph.D. Dissertation, Ph.D. Program in Anthropology, City University of New York.

Marcus, George E., and Michael M. J. Fischer

1986. Anthropology as Cultural Critique: An Experimental Moment in the Human Sciences. Chicago: University of Chicago Press.

Montanez, Carlos and Horacio Aburto

1979. Maiz: Politica Institucional y Crisis Agricolo. Centro de Investigaciones del Desarrollo Rural (CIDER). México: Editorial Nueva Imagen.

Myers, Fred R.

1988. Locating Ethnographic Practice: Romance, Reality, and Politics in the Outback. American Ethnologist 15: 609–24.

Nash, June

1970. In the Eyes of the Ancestors: Belief and Behavior in a Mayan Community. New Haven: Yale University Press.

Nash, Manning

1958. Political Relations in Guatemala. Social and Economic Studies 7: 65–75.

Norušis, Marija J./SPSS, Inc.

1988. SPSS-X Advanced Statistics Guide. Chicago: SPSS, Inc.

Pearse, Andrew

1978. Technology and Peasant Production: Reflections on a Global Study. Pp. 183–211 in Howard Newby, ed., International Perspectives in Rural Sociology. New York: John Wiley and Sons.

Polanyi, Karl
1957. The Economy as Instituted Process. Pp. 243–79 in Karl Polanyi, Conrad M. Arensberg, and Harry W. Pearson, eds., Trade and Market in the Early Empires. Glencoe, Ill.: The Free Press.

Pozas, Ricardo
1959. Chamula: Un Pueblo Indio de los Altos de Chiapas. Instituto Nacional Indigenista, Memorias, VIII.

Pozas, Ricardo, and Isabel H. de Pozas
1971. Los Indios en las Clases Sociales de México. México: Siglo Veintiuno.

Price, Richard, and Sally Price
1970. Aspects of Social Organization in a Maya Hamlet. Estudios de Cultura Maya 8: 297–318.

PRODESCH
1975. PRODESCH, Plan Quinquenal, 1972–1976.
1977. Sintesis Evaluativa, 1970–1976. (Mimeo)
1979. Experiencias de Programas de Desarrollo Rural Integrado, Los Altos de Chiapas. PRODESCH-UNICEF 1979. (With letter from Lic. Salomón González Blanco)

Riding, Alan
1984. Distant Neighbors: A Portrait of the Mexicans. New York: Random House.

Rivapalacio, Ricardo
1979. Geología y Geotecnia del Proyecto Hidroeléctrico de Chicoasén, Chiapas. México, D.F.: CFE.

Rodriguez, Victoria Elizabeth
1987. The Politics of Decentralization in Mexico: Divergent Outcomes of Policy Implementation. Ph.D. Dissertation, Department of Political Science, University of California, Berkeley.

Roseberry, William
1988. Political Economy. Annual Review of Anthropology 17: 161–85.
1989. Peasants and the World. Pp. 108–26 in Stuart Plattner, ed., Economic Anthropology. Stanford: Stanford University Press.

Rus, Diane
1988. Responding to the "The Crisis": Changing Economic Roles of Indigenous Women in the Chiapas Highlands. San Cristobal: INAREMAC.

Rus, Jan, and Robert Wasserstrom
1980. Civil-Religious Hierarchies in Central Chiapas: A Critical Perspective. American Ethnologist 7: 466–78.

Sanderson, Susan R. Walsh
1984. Land Reform in Mexico: 1919–1980. New York: Academic Press.

Sangren, P. Steven
1988. Rhetoric and the Authority of Ethnography: "Postmodernism" and the Social Reproduction of Texts. Current Anthropology 29: 405–35.

Scheer, Sara J.
   1983. Resolving the Agriculture-Petroleum Conflict: The Experience of Cacao Smallholders in Mexico. Ithaca: Cornell/International Agricultural Economics Study.

Sheridan, Thomas E.
   1988. Where the Dove Calls: The Political Ecology of a Corporate Peasant Community in Northwestern Mexico. Tucson: University of Arizona Press.

SIC
   1963. VIII Censo General de Población. México: Secretaría de Industria y Comercio.
   1972. IX Censo General de Población. México: Secretaría de Industria y Comercio.

Silverman, Sydel
   1979. The Peasant Concept in Anthropology. Journal of Peasant Studies 7: 49–69.

Skinner, G. William
   1971. Chinese Peasants and the Closed Community: An Open and Shut Case. Comparative Studies in Society and History 13: 270–81.

Smith, Carol A.
   1984. Local History in Global Context: Social and Economic Transitions in Western Guatemala. Comparative Studies in Society and History 26: 193–228.

Solís, Leopoldo
   1981. Economic Policy Reform in Mexico: A Case Study for Developing Countries. New York: Pergamon Press.

SP
   1975. Monografía del Estado de Chiapas. Secretaría de la Presidencia.
   n.d. Chiapas, Datos Básicos. Secretaría de la Presidencia.

Spiro, Melford E.
   1986. Cultural Relativism and the Future of Anthropology. Cultural Anthropology 1: 259–86.

SPP
   1981. México: Estadística Económica y Social por Entidad Federativa. México: SPP.
   1982. El Sector Eléctrico en México. México: SPP.
   1983. X Censo General de Población y Vivienda. México: SPP.

SPSS-X
   1983. SPSS-X User's Guide. New York: McGraw Hill.

Stephen, Lynn, and James Dow, eds.
   1990. Class, Politics, and Popular Religion in Mexico and Central America. American Anthropological Association.

Stuart, James W.
   1990. Maize Use by Rural Mesoamerican Households. Human Organization 49: 135–39.

Tax, Sol, et al.
1947. Notas sobre Zinacantán, Chiapas por Miembros de la Expedición a Zinacantán—1942–3, Bajo la Direccion de Sol Tax. Microfilm Collection of Manuscripts on Middle American Cultural Anthropology, no. 20. Chicago: University of Chicago Library.

Thompson, Phillip Covington
1978. Tekanto in the Eighteenth Century. Ph.D. Dissertation, Department of Anthropology, Tulane University. Ann Arbor: University Microfilms (7910255).

Velasco S., Jesús, and Javier Matus Pacheco
1976. Chiapas en Cifras 1970–1976. Tuxtla Gutiérrez: Gobierno del Estado de Chiapas.

Velasco Suárez, Manuel
1971. Primer Informe de Gobierno, Chiapas. Tuxtla Gutiérrez.
1973. Tercer Informe de Gobierno, Chiapas. Tuxtla Gutiérrez.
1975. Quinto Informe de Gobierno, Chiapas. Tuxtla Gutiérrez.
1976. Sexto Informe de Gobierno, Chiapas. Tuxtla Gutiérrez.

Vogt, Evon Z., ed.
1966. Los Zinacantecos: Un Pueblo Tzotzil de los Altos de Chiapas. México: Instituto Nacional Indigenista, Colección de Antropología Social, 7.

Vogt, Evon Z.
1969. Zinacantán: A Maya Community in the Highlands of Chiapas. Cambridge, Mass.: Harvard University Press.
1970. The Zinacantecos of Mexico: A Modern Maya Life Way. New York: Holt Rinehart and Winston.
1978. Bibliography of the Harvard Chiapas Project: The First Twenty Years, 1957–1977. Cambridge, Mass.: The Peabody Museum of Archaeology and Ethnology, Harvard University.

Wallerstein, Immanuel
1976a. A World-System Perspective on the Social Sciences. British Journal of Sociology 27: 343–52.
1976b. The Modern World-System. New York: Academic Press.

Wasserstrom, Robert
1978. The Exchange of Saints in Zinacantán: The Socioeconomic Bases of Religious Change in Southern Mexico. Ethnology 17: 197–210.
1980. Ingreso y Trabajo Rural en los Altos de Chiapas. Final Report of Project "Minifundismo y Trabajo Asalariado: Estudio de Caso II: San Juan Chamula, 1975–1977." San Cristóbal: Centro de Investigaciones Ecológicas del Sureste.
1983. Class and Society in Central Chiapas. Berkeley and Los Angeles: University of California Press.
1985. Interview with Frank Cancian, Washington, D.C., December 5.

Watson, Graham
1987. Make Me Reflexive—But Not Yet: Strategies for Managing Essen-

tial Reflexivity in Ethnographic Discourse. Journal of Anthropological Research 43: 29–41.

Weber, Max
    1948. Class, Status, Party. Pp. 180–95 in From Max Weber: Essays in Sociology. Translated, edited, and with an introduction by H. H. Gerth and C. Wright Mills. London: Routledge and Kegan Paul.

Wolf, Eric R.
    1955. Types of Latin American Peasantry. American Anthropologist 57: 452–71.
    1957. Closed Corporate Peasant Communities in Mesoamerica and Central Java. Southwestern Journal of Anthropology 13: 1–18.
    1960. The Indian in Mexican Society. Alpha Kappa Deltan 30: 3–6.
    1981. The Mills of Inequality: A Marxian Perspective. Pp. 41–57 in Gerald D. Berreman, ed., Social Inequality: Comparative and Developmental Approaches. New York: Academic Press.
    1982. Europe and the People Without History. Berkeley and Los Angeles: University of California Press.
    1986. The Vicissitudes of the Closed Corporate Peasant Community. American Ethnologist 13: 325–29.

World Bank
    1983. World Tables. 3d ed., Vol. 1. Baltimore: Johns Hopkins University Press.

Wright, Erik Olin
    1987. Reflections on Classes. Berkeley Journal of Sociology 32: 19–49, 73–78.

Wyman, Donald L.
    1983a. The Mexican Economy: Problems and Prospects. Pp. 1–28 in Donald L. Wyman, ed., 1983b.

Wyman, Donald L., ed.
    1983b. Mexico's Economic Crisis: Challenges and Opportunities. Center for U.S.-Mexican Studies, University of California, San Diego, Monograph Series, 12.

Yates, P. Lamartine
    1981. Mexico's Agricultural Dilemma. Tucson: University of Arizona Press.

INDEX

In this index "f" after a number indicates a separate reference on the next page, and "ff" indicates separate references on the next two pages. A continuous discussion over two or more pages is indicated by a span of numbers. *Passim* is used for a cluster of references in close but not consecutive sequence.